6/24

Published by Straight Talk Books
P.O. Box 301, Milwaukee, WI 53201
800.661.3311 · timeofgrace.org

Printed in the United States of America
ISBN: 978-1-949488-67-8

IN GOD'S PRESENCE EVERY DAY

365 Daily Devotions

JANUARY

I will give them an undivided heart and put a new spirit in them; I will remove from them their heart of stone and give them a heart of flesh.

Ezekiel 11:19

New year, new YOU?
Katrina Harrmann

Do you ever make New Year's resolutions? Better yet, have you ever kept one?

Why do we do this every year? Is it because we look back at the old year and think we can do better? or *be* better? No matter how hard we try, it's never quite "good" enough, is it?

That's because only Christ can fill that void of longing within us. **"If anyone is in Christ, the new creation has come. The old has gone, the new is here!"** (2 Corinthians 5:17).

Sometimes I think all this striving toward a "better" version of ourselves gets rather exhausting. We are constantly trying to get skinnier, earn more money, have more than the neighbors, or just be more—reaching toward perfection.

But we won't get perfection on this side of heaven because the truth is: it's not possible!

Of course, that doesn't mean it's wrong to try new things—to try to be healthier or set goals for ourselves—especially spiritually.

The new year is a great time to sit and reflect on how we can get closer to God this year.

"Not that I have already obtained all this, or have already arrived at my goal, but I press on to take hold of that for which Christ Jesus took hold of me" (Philippians 3:12).

Thank God for the kingdom of God!
Pastor Mike Novotny

Around 701 B.C., Sennacherib, the king of Assyria, marched from modern-day Iraq to Jerusalem. His army was not known for being nice. Sennacherib's palace walls had art of Assyrian soldiers carrying decapitated heads, skinning enemies alive, and setting up spikes for gravity to impale their foes. During the days of the prophet Isaiah, those same soldiers marched to Jerusalem to repeat such atrocities. Imagine if you live in a little village outside of Jerusalem and, one day, see the glimmer of 185,000 shields held by savage warriors who have skinned, impaled, and beheaded entire nations. What do you do? You run! You run into the kingdom.

King Hezekiah has built a wall, rerouted the water, and opened the gates of his kingdom to you. Archaeologists have discovered both the "broad wall" and "Hezekiah's tunnel," the former a 23-foot thick wall of stone to keep people safe, the latter an ingenious way to get water inside the city to keep the people alive (you really should Google both discoveries right now). Hezekiah provided safety when there was danger. That's what good kings do.

God is a good king too. When the spiritual forces of evil threatened your eternity, when the devil was close to capturing you forever, God built a wall of love that stretches higher, deeper, and wider than any architect could measure. He then channeled waters of forgiveness, bubbling up from springs of grace, inside those walls. And through Jesus, he opened the gates wide to helpless souls like us.

Thank God for the kingdom of God!

Un-deck the halls
Katrina Harrmann

I don't know if "undecorate" is a word, but it's easily my least favorite part of the Christmas season. It usually happens in early January, and the cozy, twinkling lights that have made my 100-year-old home so snug and welcoming for the past several weeks are all packed back into boxes and put in the basement.

It makes me so sad! The guests have gone home; the cookies have all been eaten; the tree has been tossed to the curb (I can never bear to watch the dump truck haul it away); and all the Christmas radio stations have gone silent.

I start to feel blue. Do you? I think it's normal to feel sad when the thing you've looked forward to for so long is over.

The GOOD news is—this is a human complaint.

The INCREDIBLE news is—we still get to look forward to the perfection of heaven.

The ASTONISHING news is—that once we're there with our Lord and Savior, there will be no post-holiday blues because the celebration will never end!

But in the meantime—here on earth—share a smile with a neighbor who might be having trouble getting through this time of year. **"Anxiety weighs down the heart, but a kind word cheers it up"** (Proverbs 12:25).

And of course . . . take comfort in this: **"May the God of hope fill you with all joy and peace as you trust in him, so that you may overflow with hope by the power of the Holy Spirit"** (Romans 15:13).

Want more faith?

Pastor Mike Novotny

There is something tricky about church. Many of the things that we love about our favorite church have zero ability to strengthen our faith.

For example, I love pastors who are organized thinkers, worship leaders who are skilled singers, and church buildings that are visually beautiful. You might love a fun children's ministry that your kids beg to go back to. Or a culture of hospitality that welcomes Sunday guests with open arms. Those are all wonderful blessings! Personally, I prefer them to disorganized pastors, unskilled worship leaders, ugly buildings, boring kids' programs, and chilly congregational cultures.

But here's the tricky part. Nothing I just listed has the ability to strengthen our faith. The apostle Paul taught, **"Faith comes from hearing the message, and the message is heard through the word about Christ"** (Romans 10:17). If you want faith, more faith, and stronger faith, fill your church with the message. Turn your ears to the words about the works of Jesus Christ.

Perhaps today you could pray for the best of both worlds. Take a few minutes to pray for pastors who, in an organized way, preach the message of Jesus' mercy. Pray for singers who, after much practice, lift up their voices to declare the saving name of Jesus. Pray for buildings where the Word is opened in the church sanctuary, in the kids' classrooms, in the counseling offices, everywhere.

The Word. That's where faith comes from.

Hurt people hurt people
Pastor Jon Enter

The Big Book of Revenge: Dozens of Wicked Ways to Have the Last Laugh. That was the title of a book donated to our church garage sale. And its pages were highlighted! Revenge isn't just a problem in the world; it's a problem in the church.

We love stories of sweet justice and swift revenge. We know we shouldn't, but when the bad boss, the cheating spouse, or the unethical coworker gets what he or she deserves, our sinful nature smiles. And we aren't afraid to bring our own revenge. From the condescending comment to that bozo driver, to bad-mouthing the boss in the break room to the passive-aggressive way we treat our siblings or in-laws, we fight fire with fire.

What actual firefighter battles a house blaze by throwing gasoline into the flames? It would make a bigger fire. Hurting someone who hurt you doesn't even the score. It adds pain. It makes the fiery feud bigger.

Why do it? Well, hurt people hurt people. We want them to experience the pain we're enduring. Jesus knew this broken logic was coursing inside us, so he gave this specific word order of the Lord's Prayer: **"Forgive us our sins, for we also forgive everyone who sins against us"** (Luke 11:4). Plead to the Lord to forgive your anger, resentment, and want for revenge. Release the hurt. Hurt people hurt people, but forgiven people forgive people. The way to finally end the hurt isn't with more hurt; it's with forgiveness. That forgiveness starts in you.

Worship with the wise men
Pastor David Scharf

Everyone celebrates Christmas. We give and get gifts. Everyone celebrates Easter. We hide Easter baskets around the house. How many of us celebrate Epiphany? I think we should! Epiphany is important, especially for those of us who are not Jewish. The Epiphany account says, **"After Jesus was born in Bethlehem . . . Magi from the east came to Jerusalem and asked, 'Where is the one who has been born king of the Jews? We saw his star when it rose and have come to worship him'"** (Matthew 2:1,2). Do you see the significance? The wise men were not Jews. They were Gentiles, like many of us. And yet they made the long trek from the East to worship the baby Jesus. God shows that Jesus is the Savior for all people—including us! That's why this festival is known as the "Gentile Christmas."

In the cathedral of Cologne, Germany, you can see the Shrine of the Three Kings. Visitors are told that their number was three and that their names were Caspar of Tarsus, Balthazar of Ethiopia, and Melchior of Arabia. But the Bible doesn't mention any of that—no number, no names, no place of origin. Why? I think it's because none of that really matters. Instead, Scripture records what really matters. These Gentiles came to worship Jesus as their Savior—Jesus is for all people! So what Epiphany traditions could you start to help you worship with the wise men this Epiphany?

Give God all glory
Andrea Delwiche

In the Lord's Prayer, we begin by saying, "Father, may your name be regarded as holy. May your kingdom come and your will be done on the earth in the same way that your will is done in heaven."

Can you hear some of these same desires in Psalm 57:11: **"Be exalted, O God, above the heavens; let your glory be over all the earth"**?

Have you noticed any ways in which God's glory shines here on earth? Romans 1:20 tells us that ever **"since the creation of the world God's invisible qualities—his eternal power and divine nature—have been clearly seen, being understood from what has been made."** Through the world of God's creation, we can see God's glory displayed.

In addition, we ourselves help make God's glory known to others: **"We are therefore Christ's ambassadors, as though God were making his appeal through us"** (2 Corinthians 5:20).

Why do we *want* to give glory to God? Well, he deserves praise for all that he has made and sustained. In addition, we *are meant* to praise God. We will never find lasting satisfaction in this life unless we give God credit for all that is good and praise his name.

How do we, as human beings, participate in making God's glory radiate over all the earth? By loving God, loving our neighbors, and loving ourselves as unique children of our heavenly Father. When we marinate in God's love, we are equipped to shine like the stars in the night sky.

It's not fair . . . or is it?
Pastor Clark Schultz

My firstborn son learned very quickly to say these three words (not necessarily in this order): *Mom, Dad,* and *MINE!* Those born after the first child learned these: *Mom, Dad,* and *It's not fair!*

Growing up, I remember my second-oldest brother, Faron, complaining that it wasn't fair that my oldest brother, Kyle, got to do everything first, from using the chain saw to driving a car. And I was the baby of the family, so I really thought it wasn't fair. But that's the way life works sometimes.

"Christ Jesus: Who, being in very nature God, did not consider equality with God something to be used to his own advantage; rather, he made himself nothing by taking the very nature of a servant" (Philippians 2:5-7). It is not fair that the God of the universe should become one of his own creatures. It is not fair that he should suffer in any way, let alone undeservedly. It is not the way life works! God's amazing love, grace, and mercy fly in the face of everything we know about the way life works. And you know what? THANK GOD! Our God and his amazing grace do not treat us as we deserve.

Marvel in what Jesus did and still does for you, and share that joy with others. By God's grace alone, say it with me people: "That's fair!"

This little light of mine
Pastor David Scharf

A little boy forgot his lines in a Christmas program. His mother was in the front row to prompt him. She gestured and formed the words silently with her lips, but it did not help. Her son's memory was blank. Finally, she leaned forward and whispered the cue, "I am the light of the world." The child beamed and with great emotion, he belted out with a loud, clear voice, "My mother is the light of the world!"

We give thanks to God for the "light" that our mothers have been in our lives. Abraham Lincoln once said that "no man is poor who has had a godly mother." Mothers who reflect the love of Jesus in their lives to their children are priceless. They shine to everyone around that Jesus is the priceless treasure they cherish.

If you had such a mother, thank God (and thank her while you're at it!). If you did not, thank God that he has led you to see the true light of Jesus in your life. Thank God that he has made you light in this dark world by removing the darkness of sin from you by his death on a cross. Then, whether you are a mother or a father or a sister or a brother or a child, shine so brightly that others might be led to say, "You are the light of the world!" After all, your Savior does: **"You are the light of the world"** (Matthew 5:14).

The good news about weak faith
Pastor Mike Novotny

My childhood pastor was a football guy. Not only did he play football during his formative years; he also was a pastor in Green Bay, Wisconsin, a city famous for its green-and-gold football addiction.

Perhaps that's why he brought a football to the youth group when he wanted to teach us about faith. He said, "When a running back crosses the goal line, what does he need in his hands to score a touchdown?" (We mumbled the obvious answer.) "A football. And how tightly does that running back have to hold on to it to count as a touchdown? Does this count?" (He wrapped the football tightly in his arms.) "Would this count?" (He held the football away from his body, holding on to its ends with only the tips of his fingers.) Obviously, both grips get you six points.

"That's like getting to heaven," my pastor explained. "Jesus is like this football. Faith is like holding on to Jesus. Sometimes our faith is strong. Sometimes our faith is weak. But we get to heaven, not by the strength of our faith but by the fact that our faith is in Jesus."

He went on to encourage us to seek strong faith, and his words have brought me great comfort over the years. When my faith is weak, I am still saved. You are too. Because Jesus is what counts. **"Truly I tell you, if you have faith as small as a mustard seed . . . nothing will be impossible for you"** (Matthew 17:20). Even the eternal victory of seeing God's face in heaven.

Living hope
Pastor Matt Ewart

I listened to a story that broke my heart. A relatively young woman was recounting when her husband received a terminal diagnosis and only had a short amount of time to live. As she told the story, it was evident that she had learned many difficult lessons before her husband passed away. One lesson caught my attention.

She mentioned how her husband was not accepting what was happening. He continued to live with hope for survival rather than facing the reality of his situation.

It hit me in that moment that she was on to something. Life in this world requires a continual balancing act. We can live in hope, but only up to a certain point. Eventually we must come to terms with the reality of our mortality.

Jesus turned that upside down. He offers a hope that doesn't get tempered by reality. His hope transcends reality. He provides a hope that is living.

Living hope is like a light that illuminates the darkness of death and takes away its power. And if it can do that to death, what about the many other fears that might be waiting for you today?

Don't settle for a hope that is tempered by this life. Embrace the transcendent, living hope that Jesus won for you.

"Praise be to the God and Father of our Lord Jesus Christ! In his great mercy he has given us new birth into a living hope through the resurrection of Jesus Christ from the dead" (1 Peter 1:3).

Live at peace
Andrea Delwiche

Here are some words to hold in tension. In Psalm 58, David proclaims, **"The righteous will be glad when they are avenged, when they dip their feet in the blood of the wicked"** (verse 10).

Contrast David's words with the words of Jesus: **"I tell you, love your enemies and pray for those who persecute you, that you may be children of your Father in heaven. He causes his sun to rise on the evil and the good, and sends rain on the righteous and the unrighteous"** (Matthew 5:44,45).

What are we to make of David's words? This psalm is honest. Doesn't this cry of anguish resonate? Haven't you and I felt something similar in the face of intentional brutality? When terrible things happen, we cry out! We *can* ask for God's kingdom to come and his will to be done to stop evil and bring just consequences to the perpetrators. But sometimes we are bitterly angry, caught in something that can end up destroying us.

Our loving and gracious God knows us so well. He knows that when we enact vengeance upon one another, it harms our souls. Far better for us to live the words of Jesus, echoed by the apostle Paul: **"If it is possible, so far as it depends on you, live at peace with everyone"** (Romans 12:18). Paul's counsel on this subject continues for several verses. Perhaps spending some time meditating on Paul's words could help us figure out how to cope with our anger and grief. God's peace be with you.

Homework for a year
Pastor Mike Novotny

Your school days might be a part of the distant past, but I want to give you a year's worth of homework. Up for it? (Before you answer, let me explain what it is and why it is.)

What is the homework? To pray the Lord's Prayer every day for the next year. Here's one version of Jesus' classic conversation with the Father: **"Our Father in heaven, hallowed be your name, your kingdom come, your will be done, on earth as in heaven. Give us today our daily bread. Forgive us our sins, as we also forgive those who sin against us. Lead us not into temptation, but deliver us from evil. For the kingdom, the power, and the glory are yours now and forever. Amen"** (based off Matthew 6:9-13 and Luke 11:2-4).

Why this homework? Because happiness is bundled up in that brief prayer. Knowing that you have a perfect Father in heaven, marveling at his holy name, believing that he is the protecting King of your soul, being part of his will to bring more love to more lives, trusting you are forgiven of all your sins, escaping bitterness by forgiving others, denying self and every evil temptation, and fixing your eyes on his glory are the best ways to find happiness that lasts.

So, student of the Word, are you ready for your homework? You won't regret following Jesus as you talk to our Father.

A natural resistance
Jan Gompper

People who are approaching death sometimes have a surge of energy a day or two before they pass. They may be able to do things physically they had been incapable of doing or become alert and verbal when they were previously uncommunicative.

I witnessed this with my own father. The afternoon before he was admitted into hospice (where he died a day later), he could no longer stand on his own. I slept on my parent's sofa that night, and at 3:00 A.M., he walked into the kitchen, desiring a bowl of cereal.

Perhaps the "surge" some experience suggests that our earthly bodies have an innate resistance to death. After all, God initially created a world where death was never to be part of the picture. Sadly, sin changed that. **"When Adam** [and Eve] **sinned, sin entered the world.** [Their] **sin brought death, so death spread to everyone, for everyone sinned"** (Romans 5:12 NLT).

Death is now inevitable. Still, it wouldn't surprise me that moments before dying we may innately try to resist what was never intended for us.

Thankfully, believers in Christ can rest peacefully, knowing that death, though inevitable, is not permanent. Christ has given us this assurance: **"I am the resurrection and the life. Anyone who believes in me will live, even after dying"** (John 11:25 NLT).

I can only imagine the surge we will experience when we awaken on the other side of death into eternal life!

Today's devotion is made possible by God's Word

Pastor Clark Schultz

Sesame Street is dedicated to helping children learn. The Muppets or cast involved help teach them how to read and write. Every episode is dedicated to a specific word or number. They drill that word into the audience through songs, repetition, or through various skits. Their goal is that by the end of the show, a child will know the word of the day so well that he or she will be able to use it in everyday life.

The apostle Paul reminds us, **"The word is near you; it is in your mouth and in your heart"** (Romans 10:8). Paul drills home to us a different type of word—God's Holy Word. This Word has implications for our daily lives because it is much more than just a noun or a verb word. It's an action Word! A Word that leads to our salvation. A Word that calls for a response, and a Word that is intended for all.

Sesame Street ends with something like this: "Today's show was made possible by the letter or word _____." They thank and give credit where credit is due. We come together today and give credit where credit is due—to our heavenly Father. Our salvation, our home in heaven, our peace, our joy, and our forgiveness have been brought to us this day and for the rest of our lives by the blood of Jesus Christ. That motivates us to keep this Word near and share this Word far.

How to deal with anxiety (Part 1)
Pastor Mike Novotny

About 18 months ago, I had an illogical but emotional experience with anxiety. I was standing in the living room of a vocal coach who was helping me fix some of my bad habits while public speaking, and suddenly I could feel my brain and my body starting to unravel. At one point, I noticed my toes were curled up, standing vertical in my shoes. "You okay," the guy asked me, but I didn't know what to say besides, "I'm sorry; I have to go." Looking back, there was nothing logical about it, but there was something powerful.

Have you been there? Twenty percent of American adults say they have, and I have a hunch that number is just as high within the church. Even though Christians know we shouldn't worry, we still do. Even though Christians know we should trust, we still don't.

He worries about dying young, even though he's not actually sick and Jesus conquered death. She worries about being good enough for God, even though she's perfect through Christ. He worries that his struggle with worry is proof that he isn't really that sorry and maybe he's not that worthy and maybe God is that angry.

Given how many of us have dealt with anxiety, I want to take some time to figure out how to deal with it from a biblical perspective, truths that fit wonderfully with good medication and professional counseling. After all, Peter encouraged us, **"Cast all your anxiety on him because he cares for you"** (1 Peter 5:7).

How to deal with anxiety (Part 2)
Pastor Mike Novotny

This might sound like heresy, but if you're super anxious, it might be better to start with breathing than with your Bible. I say that because of your amygdala. That almond-shaped thing in your brain appears to be God's way of keeping you safe from danger. If a roaring lion prowled into your home, your amygdala would trigger your body to fight it or take flight from it. It would reallocate blood from your brain and other organs and send it into your muscles so you could sprint out the door or grab a chair and start swinging. You don't need to do complex thinking when your life is in danger, right?

However, your amygdala is famous for false alarms. It goes off even when there's not a lion within 100 miles. A random thought can trigger the same physical responses, which is why worry makes your stomach ache or prevents you from thinking logically. So if your brain is freaking out, I could grab my Bible and try to reason with you, but you're not ready to reason. That is why the first way to deal with anxiety is to breathe. Deep breathing literally uses your nervous system to tell your amygdala—*It's okay. You're okay. You're not running from a lion. You can stop and slow down and think again.*

"I am fearfully and wonderfully made" (Psalm 139:14). Remember those famous words. They will help you take a physical step that can lead to spiritual blessings. Breathe. It will help you meditate on the truth that will calm your anxious heart.

How to deal with anxiety (Part 3)
Pastor Mike Novotny

There are 30 Bible passages where words like *anxious* or *worry* show up, and two of them specifically encourage us to pray. Paul wrote, **"Do not be anxious about anything, but in every situation, by prayer and petition, with thanksgiving, present your requests to God"** (Philippians 4:6). Peter added, **"Cast all your anxiety on him because he cares for you"** (1 Peter 5:7). Your Father doesn't want you to be anxious about anything. He wants you to cast off all your anxiety and put it on his solid shoulders, because he cares that much for you. Your constant worries might wear down your friends or your mom or your husband, but not God. What a thought!

There's a woman from our church whose faith I really respect who recently told me that anxiety has been part of her story for a long time. She said her anxiety was a survival mechanism during her dangerous childhood but that it stuck around even after the danger was gone. How does she learn to deal with it? She told me, "I don't. I don't handle it, because I cannot. It is only through Christ that victory is found."

I love that. When you're one-on-one with the father of lies, it's hard to win the mental fight. So bring God into the room. Or, more accurately, close your eyes and remember that your Father is already there. Pray. That's another powerful way to deal with anxiety.

How to deal with anxiety (Part 4)
Pastor Mike Novotny

Out of the 30 times that words like *worry* and *anxiety* show up in the Bible, 8 of them are in Jesus' classic teaching on the subject. **"Do not worry about your life. . . . But seek first [God's] kingdom and his righteousness"** (Matthew 6:25,33). When you get stuck in some looping, negative thought, Jesus encourages you to seek first God's kingdom and righteousness.

God's kingdom is where God is the King, where he uses his authority to offer you safety. As a child of the King, your Father will keep you safe from all the stuff outside the walls of the kingdom. The lion might be prowling out there, roaring lies, telling you you're not worthy, that God is angry, but he can't take you away from the kingdom. Jesus died on a cross so that you would be safe from that, so that you would be with God, right with God, always right with God. That's what his righteousness is, the gift of being right with our Father through the blood of his Son. That gift is yours, not because you are such a trusting, perfect Christian but because Jesus was perfect in your place. Let me repeat that—you are right with God, not because you're perfect or your faith is perfect but because Jesus was perfect.

Fix your thoughts on thoughts like that, writing them on note cards if you need to, and you'll be one step closer to God's way of dealing with anxiety. **"When anxiety was great within me, your consolation brought me joy"** (Psalm 94:19).

How to deal with anxiety (Part 5)
Pastor Mike Novotny

I loved the email I received from a fellow Christian who is doing better than ever in dealing with her anxiety. Her secret? She wrote, "Group, group, group, group, group." (I think she was trying to make a point.) When you're stuck in your own head, it's easy to forget to breathe, to cast your anxiety on God in prayer, and to seek God's kingdom and righteousness mentally. That's why doing life together with other Christians in humble and honest confession is so essential. Because you can snap me out of it. You can bring me back to Jesus.

Proverbs 12 says, **"Anxiety weighs down the heart, but a kind word cheers it up"** (verse 25). A kind word from a friend, a pastor, or your small group is God's way of helping you deal. A friend who says, "Okay, let's breathe for a second." A father who says, "Can I pray that God would take this away?" A group who guarantees, "King Jesus isn't going to let you go." Having a "group" is the way that God helps us deal with everything, anxiety included.

If you were my anxious friend, I would encourage you to breathe, pray, seek, and group. That's the best way I know to deal with anxiety.

Snow prowl
Katrina Harrmann

There's usually one night (somewhere near the middle of winter) when my family—tired of being stuck inside—decides to go out for a snow prowl. This requires two things:

1. A big, bright moon
2. Several inches of snow

It's always decided on the fly, and we bundle up in thick layers of coats, hats, and gloves and troop out late—usually around 8 or 9 P.M. What follows is an hour or so of exploring our local woodsy trail by the light of the moon and our headlamps.

We slip and slide on the ice and snow; step cautiously through dark, deep drifts; smack snow off tree branches with our mittens; and listen for owls. An outing that would have been cold, lonely, and dark all alone becomes something to enjoy and remember because we're all together.

Togetherness is a wonderful thing.

Our lamps help us see better. When one person falls down, there is another mittened hand to pull him back up again. There are multiple sets of eyes to point out unseen obstacles or deer tracks . . . more ears to listen for owl calls.

"How good and pleasing it is when God's people live together in unity!" (Psalm 133:1). We aren't meant to walk alone. The journey is much easier—and enjoyable—with folks around us to ease the way and share our burdens. **"So in Christ we, though many, form one body, and each member belongs to all the others"** (Romans 12:5).

God so healed you
Pastor Matt Ewart

When Mark recorded his account of the life of Jesus, he included a brief mention of a miracle that is easy to let go unnoticed. Here's how it went: **"Simon's mother-in-law was in bed with a fever, and they immediately told Jesus about her. So he went to her, took her hand and helped her up. The fever left her and she began to wait on them"** (Mark 1:30,31).

At first glance it seems natural to focus on the last six words. Did Jesus heal Simon's mother-in-law because he needed someone to wait on him? No. Something else was happening here—something beautiful, and I don't want you to miss it.

The only reason she could wait on her guests was because she was completely healed. In other words, her service was a testimony to her wholeness.

Jesus did not just calm her fever. He took it away. He didn't just take the edge off her aches and pains. He healed them. Jesus so thoroughly healed her that she was able to serve. What a miracle in so many ways!

He healed you too, you know. Maybe the aches and pains haven't gone away from your body, but your sin has been forgiven. Your guilt has been addressed. Your shame has been taken away. God so healed you that you are whole.

Now go and serve. Let your service be a testimony to the wholeness that God won for you.

Pray for God's justice
Andrea Delwiche

One of the beautiful things about biblical writing is that it does not whitewash human thought processes. Even amongst those who wrote under God's inspiration, such as King David, we still see honestly into their hearts: **"Arise to help me; look on my plight! . . . Rouse yourself to punish all the nations; show no mercy to wicked traitors"** (Psalm 59:4,5). David is called "a man after God's own heart," and he dreams of his enemies being destroyed by God's mighty hand.

Yet we know from David's life that despite his calls for vengeance against Saul, he did not personally act against him. David waited for God's own timing in Saul's life. David protected Saul's life and showed kindness to his descendant.

Don't be afraid to look honestly at your own desire for justice. It comes from the depths of the soul. According to the example of the psalms, beg God to hand out justice where you need it. Sometimes, even as you pray, you must remove yourself and those you love from violent situations. You must also ask others for help. These options can be God's gift to you, his good way of delivering you.

With David, you can say, **"O my strength, I will sing praises to you, for you, O God, are my fortress, the God who shows me steadfast love"** (Psalm 59:17).

That doesn't seem right!

Pastor Jon Enter

When Jesus taught the disciples about forgiveness, he said, **"Even if they sin against you seven times in a day and seven times come back to you saying 'I repent,' you must forgive them"** (Luke 17:4). Imagine a coworker slaps you and says, "I'm sorry." Then he does it again, again, and again. Are you really going to let it happen seven times? This is a TOUGH command. The disciples' instantaneous reaction was, **"Increase our faith!"** (Luke 17:5). They knew it would take a sizeable faith to forgive like that.

Jesus doesn't ask you to do anything he hasn't already done for you.

How many times have you repeated the same sin even though you promised to never do it again? Lovingly, mercifully, continually, God forgives you.

God asks you to reveal what mercy is by treating others the same. Whom do you have a difficult time forgiving? Got that person on your heart? Good. Now, forgive them. "But that's not fair! If I forgive them, they get away with it, and that doesn't seem right."

You're misunderstanding forgiveness and responsibility. When you forgive someone, that doesn't wipe away the responsibility of their sin before God. All sin is held accountable before God. When you forgive someone, you release yourself from the pain. You're not a fake or a phony when you forgive someone when they don't seem to deserve it; you're being Christian, Christlike and compassionate. It'll change your heart and, Lord willing, their heart when they experience grace!

What a relief!
Pastor David Scharf

I remember being lost once when I was young. I was at a department store with my mother. I walked along very contentedly behind a flowing dress until I realized that it was not the flowing dress of my mother. I remember the feeling of panic to this day. I also remember, with tears in my eyes, the warm embrace of my mother after she found me. What a relief!

I don't remember being lost spiritually. I was baptized as an infant and have only known the warm embrace of my heavenly Father. And yet, sin separates you and me from God's embrace. Every day we stray in sin and feel that separation. It is why, every day, we need to find our Father's arms of forgiveness in the cross of his Son, Jesus. What a relief!

In the parable of the lost coin in the Bible, Jesus talks about the joy he has when he finds us: **"'Rejoice with me; I have found my lost coin.' In the same way, I tell you, there is rejoicing in the presence of the angels of God over one sinner who repents"** (Luke 15:9,10). This is what happens every time someone repents and receives forgiveness.

Do you know someone who could make the angels rejoice? It may be someone you have a grudge against or who's carrying guilt. Bring that person back to the arms of their Father in heaven by announcing his forgiveness. Then one day, with tears in their eyes, they too will feel the relief of heaven!

A patient teacher
Pastor Clark Schultz

One of my favorite teachers was my freshmen Algebra teacher. Math and I have a love-hate relationship. You may love it; I do not. What made this teacher awesome was his love, patience, and willingness to get down on his students' level to make sure everyone in the class understood the concept before moving on. The other 18 freshmen could figure out what X equals, but yours truly would be lost in space. This teacher would stop the lesson and work with just me. Then when it finally clicked, he would move on. Other teachers were more like: "Tough cookies, Clark, we're moving on without you."

When Jesus taught, he showed a similar love and patience. One of Jesus' enemies, a Pharisee named Nicodemus, came to Jesus with some questions. Jesus showed him love and patience, even when key concepts went right over Nicodemus' head. Jesus found common ground—the Bible. He said this to Nicodemus: **"Just as Moses lifted up the snake in the wilderness, so the Son of Man must be lifted up"** (John 3:14). As someone well versed in the Old Testament, Nicodemus knew about the bronze snake recorded in Numbers 21. Just as folks who looked to that snake were saved from the deadly bite, so too all who look to Jesus as their Savior are eternally saved from the venom of sin. Nicodemus left the Teacher a changed man.

Perhaps there is someone you know who could use some love and patience. Whom could you teach today?

Whom he walked toward
Pastor Matt Ewart

The miracle of Peter walking on water always amazed me. I wondered what it must have been like for him to take that first step out of the boat and experience the weird feeling of water supporting his weight. Out of the 12 disciples, Peter was the only one who had the courage to step out onto that water.

It was not until recently that a different part of this event caught my attention. The miracle isn't just about what Peter walked on. It is about whom he walked toward. Look carefully at how Matthew recorded it:

"'Lord, if it's you,' Peter replied, 'tell me to come to you on the water.' 'Come,' he said. Then Peter got down out of the boat, walked on the water and came toward Jesus" (Matthew 14:28,29).

Peter did not ask for the supernatural ability to walk on water. His request was to come to Jesus, even though water was in the way. The point of the story isn't to amaze us by what Peter was able to walk on. The point is all on the One whom Peter walked toward.

Right now there might be something in your life that's getting in the way of growing closer to Jesus. It could be a busy schedule, a distracted mind, or a cloud of worries. Whatever is getting in your way, Jesus tells you the same thing he said to Peter: "Come." He will give you the ability to walk toward him.

A light on a hill
Katrina Harrmann

When the snow falls thick and fast on a Michigan winter's night, my family has been known to troop through the neighborhood to an old, reliable sledding hill tucked in a ravine behind some houses.

It's a classic hill . . . steep, with a creek running along the eastern end, which causes a thrill of fear for the wayward sledder who veers off course.

When it's dark, it's hard to see because the hill runs down into a deep forest. But the folks who live in the house at the top of the hill have a large floodlight. And if they notice sledders, they will turn it on, lighting up the whole hill.

Such a simple, kind gesture.

I've seen them light up the hill for 20 sledders. But more often than not, they'll light it up for just our family. And the kindness of the gesture is like when you're cold and someone hands you a cup of something warm.

"As we have opportunity, let us do good to all people," the apostle Paul advises in Galatians 6:10.

Turning on a lamp is such a simple gesture. These folks don't do it for acclaim or to look good. They do it out of pure kindness.

This makes me wonder about the little chances we get every day, opportunities to show love to others when no one else is looking: hold a door for someone, check on a neighbor, help someone with a heavy load. The opportunities are endless.

Who can you "turn on a lamp" for today?

Don't be a stumbling block to the Great Commission
Jan Gompper

Years ago, I sang for a wedding of a former student from the Christian high school where I had taught. Her fiancé grew up in another church denomination, and both had been questioning where they wanted to continue going to church.

They had selected "Wedding Song (There is Love)," by Peter, Paul and Mary for me to sing. The music director at the church would not approve the song until I offered to rewrite some of the lyrics. (Apparently, he was fine with copyright infringement.) The couple also wanted the song to be accompanied on guitar, but evidently guitar was not on the church's "approved musical instrument list." I have no doubt that after they were married, this couple never again stepped foot in that church (or maybe any other).

Statistics show that many people stop attending church because of a bad experience they had in the church. While most churches would claim that their focus is on showing people the love of Jesus, enforcing religious traditions can sometimes be the tail that wags the dog. Adhering to sound biblical teaching is, of course, important, but bombarding new or lapsed Christians with every biblical doctrine or practice of the church right away can be a sure way to get them to never return.

Jesus commanded us to **"go and make disciples [followers]"** of *him* (Matthew 28:19), not of a particular church denomination or way of doing things. Neither we nor our churches want to be stumbling blocks to this.

Good cuts from an expert
Pastor David Scharf

A diamond needs to be cut in order to achieve its greatest beauty. That kind of seems counterintuitive, doesn't it? How can cutting a diamond smaller make it better? Those cuts make the diamond shine so much brighter.

Did you know you have something in common with diamonds? First Peter 4:12,13 says, **"Dear friends, do not be surprised at the fiery ordeal that has come on you to test you, as though something strange were happening to you. But rejoice inasmuch as you participate in the sufferings of Christ, so that you may be overjoyed when his glory is revealed."** You know what it is to experience cuts from others for simply living as a Christian. Your neighbor thinks you are unintelligent for trusting God's Word instead of science. Your co-worker thinks you're old-fashioned and bigoted for believing what God tells us about living for him. Friend, do not think this is strange. Your Savior experienced it too. Your Savior is readying you for the joy of heaven that he won for you by his life and death on a cross.

Jesus tells us we need to be cut and refined as Christians so he can make us shine so much brighter. Take comfort in that today. When you suffer persecution or embarrassment or judgment for being a Christian, know that those cuts are far from a mistake. Instead, God, the most skilled lapidary in the universe, is using them to make you shine even brighter for him.

The unvarnished cross
Pastor Mike Novotny

The Romans used the cross to scare people into submission. They wanted the thought of crucifixion to be so excruciating that potential rebels would put down their swords and pay their taxes. So they tinkered with their torture, finding a way for gravity to suffocate a man slowly over the course of hours, if not days. Sometimes a small seat was placed under the buttocks, preventing the body from slumping too far down. The Roman poet Seneca and the Christian author Justin Martyr suggest that the seat was spiked like a horn, which would impale your private parts. Most victims were crucified naked, a degrading and shameful detail, especially since crosses were put up at major intersections to scare as many people as possible. You would bleed, cry, beg, urinate, defecate, vomit, and beg some more. There is no word that captures the horror of the cross.

I wonder what expression was on the face of the apostle Paul, a Roman citizen, when he wrote, **"[Jesus] humbled himself by becoming obedient to death— even death on a cross!"** (Philippians 2:8). I shudder to think of someone as gentle and holy as Jesus on something as gruesome and cruel as a cross.

Yet a crucified Savior says much to our hearts. It says that Jesus will do anything to save us, that his love for us is extreme, that his desire to reunite us to God is relentless. You might not be able to trust a king on a comfortable throne, but a King on a rugged cross is worthy of every ounce of your faith.

FEBRUARY

God demonstrates his own love for us in this:
While we were still sinners, Christ died for us.

Romans 5:8

Your six hundred people

Pastor Mike Novotny

According to a 2013 *New York Times* study, you know about six hundred people. Put together your neighbors, family, friends, coworkers, church community, etc., and the average American ends up with just around six hundred people in their lives.

That number both excites and scares me because people have potential. One of those people could become your new best friend, your sponsor, your mentor, your boyfriend, or your wife. Or one of those people could be the person who takes you down the road of addiction, breaks your heart, or ends up as the "bad influence" your mother feared. People matter. And there are about six hundred of them waiting for you in the year to come.

So how do you deal with all those people? Here's what the world's wisest man once said: **"The righteous choose their friends carefully"** (Proverbs 12:26). Righteous people—those who are right with God and want to do the right thing—choose their friends carefully.

What does that mean? I will explain more in the devotions to come, but here's the big picture: Stay away from fools (those who assume they will get away with sin consequence free). Look for wisdom among your acquaintances (people who inspire you with the way they worship, handle money, date, raise kids, etc.). Walk with the wise as often as you can (intentionalize time with the truly wise people God has placed in your life).

That's what righteous people do. What will you do?

Stay away from fools
Pastor Mike Novotny

This might seem unchristian to say, but sometimes God wants you to stay away. There are people you know whom God wants you to unknow in the same way that there are kids whom a loving mother wants her son to stay away from. If that feels unbiblical, read this: **"Stay away from a fool"** (Proverbs 14:7). You can love and you can pray, but, for God's sake, stay away.

Hmm . . . who qualifies as a fool? Recently, I read the entire book of Proverbs, that Old Testament book about how wise people live, and saw a repeated thread that tied fools together. The thread was an attitude of "whatever." We all sin. We all struggle mightily with certain sins. But foolish people shrug their shoulders and assume that it's fine even when God says it isn't. When you run into such people, our Father begs his children, "Stay away from a fool."

As a dad, I get that. I long for my daughters to be loving, selfless, in-but-not-of-the-world missionaries who share Jesus with those who don't know him just yet. But I also know that I don't want my kids to trust everyone and get too close with just anyone. Their relationships will require wisdom.

Yours do too. Take a moment to consider the people you choose to spend time with on a regular basis. Is there anyone your Father is asking you to stay away from?

Hanging with coal?

Pastor Mike Novotny

When I was a kid, my pastor showed the kids at our church how friendships work. He took a giant ziplock bag and dropped a few pieces of dusty coal inside of it. "These are your friends," he said. Then he picked up a marshmallow and held it up for all of us to see. "And this is you," he continued. "So what do you think will happen if I put you in here with them?" Even before he dropped the marshmallow inside, zipped up the bag, and shook it all together, we knew what would happen.

God taught the same lesson through the proverbs three thousand years ago. King Solomon wisely stated, **"A companion of fools suffers harm"** (Proverbs 13:20). Notice how Solomon doesn't insist that a companion of fools becomes a fool himself. Rather, the friend of fools "suffers harm," much like the buddy of a hotheaded guy finds himself in the middle of too many arguments and altercations.

Is this warning God's personal word to you today? Are there any foolish people—angry, drunken, gossipy people who don't seem to care about changing their ways—whom our Father wants you to avoid?

He's a good dad and would hate to see you suffer harm. So before it's too late, stay away from fools and spend your time walking with the wise.

Drug court wisdom
Pastor Mike Novotny

The other day I was in a courtroom to offer encouragement to a friend facing serious legal charges for her drug-related decisions. The judge, who oversaw the county's drug court program, listened to the details of my friend's transgressions and offered this advice: "Young lady, if you really want to change, you are going to need new people, new places, and new things."

I found that wisdom to be profound (it inspired a sermon series with that title!). Change is hard. Worrying less, drinking less, or being selfless in a relationship are some of the biggest personal challenges we face, and the status quo rarely produces different results.

But what if you found some new people, perhaps some friendly and godly people from your church? And what if you found some new places, like a nonprofit to volunteer at where your light could shine? And what if you embraced some new things, a fresh habit like starting your day with the Word and prayer? I can't guarantee results, but I do know that **"faith comes from hearing the message"** and those who **"walk with the wise . . . become wise"** (Romans 10:17; Proverbs 13:20).

Through the blood of Jesus, we are already righteous and blameless in the sight of God, an identity that frees us from needing the approval of toxic people and the short-term pleasure of destructive habits. Remember who you are through Jesus, and you'll be empowered to embrace all the "new" that God wants you to do.

What the dying would have done differently

Pastor Mike Novotny

A few years ago, Bronnie Ware, an Australian author, wrote a book about her experiences in listening to dying people. As she dialogued with those in palliative care, Bronnie asked them if they had regrets, anything they would do differently if they could start life over. One of their top five answers would have made King Solomon smile: "I wish I would have stayed in touch with my friends." In the desire for more money/status/power, work filled people's waking hours, taking them away from those whom they loved most.

The gospel of Jesus possesses the incredible potential to free us from such busyness and backward priorities. Through our Savior's life, death, and resurrection, we are already loved, cherished, included, and affirmed by someone infinitely greater than a boss or board of directors. We are adored by God himself!

This status frees us to say no to 60-hour workweeks and the allure of club tournament trophies so that we have time for the wonderful people God has placed in our lives, the wise friends and godly family who are a text or phone call away. You can schedule that weekly cup of coffee or that monthly dinner with a small group of friends, prioritizing time for one of life's greatest blessings—people.

Embrace your identity in Jesus, and you'll be free to **"walk with the wise and become wise"** (Proverbs 13:20).

Certain hope

Jan Gompper

"I *hope* the weather will be nice tomorrow." "I *hope* that cute guy asks me out." "I *hope* this new medical treatment will work." I'm sure we've all expressed sentiments like these at one time or another. Often our use of the word *hope* conveys a sense of doubt as to whether the things we hope for will come to fruition. And sometimes in this life they don't. Our plans get rained out. Our phones never ring. Our loved ones don't get better.

Sadly, when asked if they will be in heaven after they die, some people answer, "I *hope* so," with the same type of uncertainty. This apprehension comes from thinking that somehow their place in heaven is linked to their good deeds or behavior on earth.

Thankfully, the hope we have of eternal life is not dependent on us or anything we did in this life. It was signed, sealed, and delivered when Christ lived perfectly, died on a cross, rose from the dead, and ascended into heaven. Listen to Jesus' promise: **"My Father's house has many rooms; if that were not so, would I have told you that I am going there to prepare a place for you? And if I go and prepare a place for you, I will come back and take you to be with me that you also may be where I am"** (John 14:2,3).

So cast aside any doubt about your eternal destiny and **"hold unswervingly to the hope we profess, for he who promised is faithful"** (Hebrews 10:23).

Jesus is with you
Andrea Delwiche

Times are hard. These words of Psalm 60 may just roll off your tongue: **"You have rejected us, God, and burst upon us; you have been angry—now restore us! You have shaken the land and torn it open; mend its fractures, for it is quaking. You have shown your people desperate times; you have given us wine that makes us stagger"** (verses 1-3). You might feel personally shaken and torn open. Your suffering may seem pointless and endless. You may feel completely cut off.

First, not one of your experiences in this broken world is wasted. Consider these words from the New Testament book of James: **"Consider it pure joy, my brothers and sisters, whenever you face trials of many kinds, because you know that the testing of your faith produces perseverance. Let perseverance finish its work so that you may be mature and complete, not lacking anything"** (1:2-4).

Second, you are *never* cut off. Let these words of Jesus speak to you: **"Peace I leave with you; my peace I give you. I do not give to you as the world gives. Do not let your hearts be troubled and do not be afraid"** (John 14:27).

Take time to let these words sink in. Then read them again, and let them sink in even deeper. Christ Jesus knows your struggles. He is with you, and he knows.

White as snow
Katrina Harrmann

Living in a northern state, I really enjoy snow. There are few cozier feelings in this world than snuggling up with a good book—across from a crackling fireplace—while the snow falls so hard you can't see across the street.

In English, snow is simply called *snow*. We don't have many other words for it. But the Inuit have around 50. And the Scots? According to the University of Glasglow, the Scots have 421 words for *snow*. Words like *skelf*, which is a large snowflake, or *spitters* for small, driving snow.

When I think of snow, I think of the blue glowing color it turns at dusk. But I also think of how blindingly bright snow can be in the sunshine.

Isaiah 1:18 says, **"Though your sins are like scarlet, they shall be as white as snow."**

When I ski in the winter, the snow is so bright that I have to wear sunglasses. But do you want to know something interesting? Snow isn't white. Sure, it looks white. But in reality, it's translucent. What makes it appear white is the way it reflects the light.

This makes me look at the verse in Isaiah with new eyes. Isaiah doesn't say we're whiter than snow because of anything WE'VE done. On our own, we can only become muddier and filthier till we are hopelessly stained in our sins.

Instead, we appear as white as snow because we reflect the LIGHT—the light of our Savior, who died to make us clean!

3 essential verses
if you feel ashamed
Pastor Mike Novotny

If you frequently feel shame, that humiliation over your sins that makes you feel like you don't belong and that you need to hide, there are three Bible passages you need to read, hand copy on a note card, and place right next to your bed.

Here's the first: **"Therefore God is not ashamed to be called their God"** (Hebrews 11:16). These words are written about Abraham, Noah, Isaac, Jacob, and you, people who have both faith and flaws. Despite Abraham's fear, Noah's drunkenness, and Jacob's issues with honesty, God was not embarrassed to be known as their God and Father. He isn't embarrassed by you either.

Here's the second: **"Jesus is not ashamed to call them brothers and sisters"** (Hebrews 2:11). You might be on parole, facing charges, or in prison, but Jesus is not ashamed of you. You might need a meeting every day to stay sober, but Jesus is not ashamed of you. Your family might be a mess of separation, divorce, and complicated relationships, but Jesus is not ashamed of you.

Here's the third: **"Anyone who believes in [Jesus] will never be put to shame"** (Romans 10:11). Anyone. Jesus. Never. Let each word sink into your soul, and you'll know how to deal with your shame.

Through the love of God and the blood of Christ, shame is a temporary visitor and not a full-time resident of the Christian heart. Yes, we feel shame because of our sins, but we don't live in it because our God is not ashamed to call us his own.

Plug in to the power source
Pastor Clark Schultz

A young man was studying to be a pastor when he learned that his brother had been killed. He felt he should be able to ride it out. But what followed was a downward spiral to the point where counseling was needed.

The counselor asked him to journal the details of his week. The young man proudly turned in his journal, and the counselor identified the problem immediately. "How much time did you spend working out today?"

The young man answered, "At least an hour or more."

"Why?" the counselor asked.

"So I don't become stressed."

"Okay, and how much time did you spend in God's Word?" And there it was. "An hour on the treadmill and nine minutes in prayer? Why did you spend so much time working out and only giving God the table scraps?"

The tears flowed from the young man's face. That young man was me. I knew I was not following what Paul had encouraged Timothy to do: **"Continue in what you have learned"** (2 Timothy 3:14).

Many of us have similar stories of the "stuff" we have to do, but we forget why we do it or what the most important thing is. Like a cell phone that goes dead unless it is charged, God encourages us to stay plugged in to our power source, which is his Word, to bask in the love and forgiveness that God gives. And yes, if counseling is needed, do not be afraid to ask for help.

God alone
Andrea Delwiche

"For God alone my soul waits in silence; from him comes my salvation. He alone is my rock and my salvation, my fortress; I shall not be greatly shaken" (Psalm 62:1,2 ESV).

God alone—some version of this phrase is used at least ten times in Psalm 62. *God alone* is capable of truly defending us. *God alone* works true change in us and for us. How does this change our daily lives?

For one thing, the pressure is off us to make things happen. There's no such thing as "the ends justify the means." God wants us alongside him to accomplish good things, operating under his principles. We can, and should, work to bring God's goodness to pass on earth, but we don't need to worry or use ungodly means that fall outside of God's goodness and justice.

Second, because God is in control, we can rest quietly, whether we are working with him or must wait on his timing.

By nature, we are skeptical of relying on God. As we intentionally spend time with the Lord each day, opening our hearts to him, we will make a good beginning. We can *pay attention* to the many ways God does protect us and bring good to pass.

Have you ever asked friends and family for their stories of waiting for God or working with God to accomplish God's goodness? Their stories will amaze you and reinforce God's protection in your own life. Retell these stories so that God's protection becomes rooted concretely in your everyday experience.

Hope for the future
Katrina Harrmann

I just love it when my seed catalogs arrive in the mail this time of year! I like to take a day—in the deepest, darkest part of winter—to page through the glossy pages, dreaming and planning my spring garden. It feels rebellious—as though a small part of me refuses to acknowledge the snow and bitter temperatures and hopes for something *more*.

And as I glance through the photos of beets and turnips and flowers of every color imaginable, it reminds me how important it is to have a hope for the future and to nurture my faith in God daily so that I can grow *spiritually* strong.

"May the God of hope fill you with all joy and peace as you trust in him, so that you may overflow with hope by the power of the Holy Spirit" (Romans 15:13).

The dark winter will come. It always does. It happens in the seasons of our own lives as well . . . times when we'll need to have those seeds of faith ready to germinate into something really amazing that's ready to break forth in its time.

"But now, Lord, what do I look for? My hope is in you" (Psalm 39:7).

How do we nurture our faith during hard times? Not with a seed catalog! But through prayer, Scripture, and meeting with other Christians.

"For our light and momentary troubles are achieving for us an eternal glory that far outweighs them all" (2 Corinthians 4:17).

A victor's crown
Pastor David Scharf

Would you sacrifice your life for your spouse? Of course! But would you sacrifice your pride or your preferences? Sometimes not. Are you willing to *live* for those you claim to be willing to *die* for? Jesus said, **"Be faithful, even to the point of death, and I will give you life as your victor's crown"** (Revelation 2:10). Are you willing to die for Jesus? Remember, it is more difficult to *live* a martyr than to *die* one.

You and I can think mistakenly that being faithful is like taking a $100 bill and laying it on a table: "Here's my life, Lord. I'm giving it all!" However, for most of us, being faithful means sacrificing 25 cents here and 25 cents there.

Doing the right thing at work or at school, as unpopular as it may be, instead of taking the easy way out . . . 25 cents. Saying the right thing to a friend living in sin and really loving them instead of trying to avoid the ridicule of your "narrow" way of thinking . . . 25 cents. Holding to God's promises even when everything in life seems to be falling apart . . . 25 cents. Admitting that Jesus is more important than sleeping in, time with friends, popularity, sports, weekends away, family relationships . . . 25 cents. Usually remaining faithful is done by all those little acts of standing with Jesus, 25 cents at a time. Thank Jesus that he was perfectly faithful in our place. Now you and I want to be faithful to him. Now the victor's crown of life awaits!

The real Valentine's love
Pastor David Scharf

Today is Valentine's Day. For many, Valentine's Day has become a Hallmark holiday filled with sappy sentiment and red hearts . . . everywhere. But the original St. Valentine fought for godly love and faithfulness.

The exact details are a little unclear, but apparently St. Valentine ignored a Roman Emperor's edict to discourage young people from marrying. You see, the emperor believed that single soldiers fought better. This edict, which prohibited soldiers to marry, resulted in rampant promiscuity. Valentine performed marriages in violation of the edict and apparently lost his life for it. He died for love. Real love.

There is a love story that trumps even that of St. Valentine: **"God so loved the world that he gave his one and only Son, that whoever believes in him shall not perish but have eternal life"** (John 3:16). What love! This love story involves a bride who is unfaithful, constantly losing in her fight against temptation. God calls us the bride of Christ. This love story involves a Bridegroom who credited his perfect record to her and then gave his life in a most horrific way for her. He died for love. Real love. Now that is a love story St. Valentine could get behind!

As you seek to thank God for the love of your life today and show that love to your significant other, remember to thank God for the true love of your life, Jesus. His love will never fail you!

Treasure time
Pastor Matt Ewart

It is interesting how many of the verbs that apply to money also apply to time. You can *spend* time. You can *waste* time. You can *lose* time. You can *save* time. In many ways, time and money are similar.

But they are different in one important way. If you end up wasting money or losing some money, you can always get more of it. That is not true of time, however.

Time is the stuff that, once you spend it, you never get it back. Time is the most valuable thing you have. Are you intentional with how you use it?

The biggest miracle in the Bible is how Jesus used his time. He invested his entire life—every moment of it—for you. He spent it all being perfect so he could earn God's favor and give it to you as a gift. Then he gave his final moments suffering a sinner's death so he could take that punishment away from you.

Aware of how God loved you, be intentional with your time today.

Invest some time in your health. Invest some time in rest. Invest some time with God. Invest some time in other people.

The biggest impact God made in your life was based on the way he used his time. Consider the impact you can make with yours.

"But store up for yourselves treasures in heaven, where moths and vermin do not destroy, and where thieves do not break in and steal" (Matthew 6:20).

The Lord's Prayer 101
Pastor Mike Novotny

You may or may not know that Jesus' favorite thing to talk about was the kingdom of God. My simple definition of God's kingdom is "a place of authority and safety." God gets the authority, and God provides the safety. You submit to Jesus. Jesus saved you. If you believe that, the kingdom is within you.

Recently, I realized how much of the Lord's Prayer is about that very thing. Jesus taught us to pray, **"Our Father in heaven, hallowed be your name, your kingdom come, your will be done, on earth as it is in heaven. Give us today our daily bread. And forgive us our debts, as we also have forgiven our debtors. And lead us not into temptation, but deliver us from the evil one"** (Matthew 6:9-13).

Did you notice all the authority? We are praying for God's name, God's kingdom, and God's will (not our name, our kingdom, and our will). Some people add a conclusion that declares that the "kingdom, power, and glory" are God's too! And did you notice all the safety? Our loving Father saves us from starvation with daily bread, saves us from damnation with forgiveness of sins, and saves us from temptation by delivering us from the evil one's lies.

Authority + Safety. That's the kingdom of God. What a glorious kingdom for our hearts to live in!

Temporary shame
Pastor Mike Novotny

While shame is a good thing (Jeremiah 6:15), God doesn't want it to last too long. Just ask Eve. A few summers ago, I snapped a picture in the Metropolitan Museum of Art of a famous sculpture of Eve by Rodin, the guy who also created *The Thinker*. Rodin captured Eve just having eaten the forbidden fruit, burying her head in her bronze arms. Which from God's perspective was good.

Can you imagine if Eve felt no shame? If she brought disease and death, COVID and cancer, anger and abuse into God's perfect world and yet was proud of it? Shame was essential in softening her heart and opening her ears for a message that could deal with her shame.

Which is what God gave her. The first promise of Jesus from Genesis 3:15 would later be explained by the author of Hebrews: **"For the joy set before him** [Jesus] **endured the cross, scorning its shame"** (12:2). By enduring the shame of crucifixion, Jesus made shame a temporary experience for every Christian.

Through the cross, sin no longer defines us. We don't have to consider ourselves an embarrassment to God or live in the humiliation of the sins of our past. Instead, through Jesus, we realize that our shame has been taken away and our new identity is secure—we are children of God, sons and daughters whom the Father is not ashamed to call his own.

Jesus passed the test for us
Jan Gompper

Do you remember the standardized tests you took in school where you had to color in tiny circles with your #2 yellow lead pencil? I hated those tests. I was always afraid either I wouldn't get the circle fully filled in or that I would color outside the lines of the circle. In both cases, the answer could be marked wrong.

I bet Old Testament Christians sometimes felt as if they were taking a standardized test. They had so many rules and regulations to follow; it had to be extremely difficult to adhere to them completely or perfectly. And there were often harsh penalties for "coloring outside the lines" God had established for them.

I am so grateful that I'm a New Testament believer, aren't you? This doesn't mean that God's law (test) no longer applies to us, but we no longer have to worry about passing it perfectly because Christ passed it for us. **"Do not think that I have come to abolish the Law or the Prophets; I have not come to abolish them but to fulfill them"** (Matthew 5:17).

Christ perfectly "filled in" the circles (requirements) of the Old Testament law with his indelible blood. Furthermore, he has erased every mark we have ever made outside the lines. And his eraser is still working on our behalf.

Old Testament believers had to trust in God's *promise* of a Savior to free them from the boundary lines of the law. We are blessed to live in the *fulfillment* of that promise.

The rock that is higher
Andrea Delwiche

In northeastern Wyoming, a monolithic rock formation called Devil's Tower rises 867 feet out of the dry and flat land. You can see it from miles away, solid and unshakeable. It is flat topped, with very little vegetation, but at its base is a sort of oasis. Rugged pines abound, providing respite on hot summer days.

This picture comes to mind in the opening verses of Psalm 61: **"Hear my cry, O God; listen to my prayer. From the ends of the earth I call to you, I call as my heart grows faint; lead me to the rock that is higher than I. For you have been my refuge, a strong tower against the foe"** (verses 1–3).

In times of anxiety and despair, we may feel as if we are in a flat expanse of nothingness. No shade, no higher ground, no water to quench our thirst. No hope, no help, no change.

But there is *a rock that is higher*. That rock is God. No one and nothing can move the tower of the all-sufficient love and power of God. But our heavenly Father is not stone-cold. He yearns for us and draws us into his warm embrace. He is both rock and oasis.

"For I am convinced that neither death nor life, neither angels nor demons, neither the present nor the future, nor any powers, neither height nor depth, nor anything else in all creation, will be able to separate us from the love of God that is in Christ Jesus our Lord" (Romans 8:38,39).

You want me to believe what?!

Pastor David Scharf

Reason is a gift of God. Reason aids us in understanding, if only partially, the beauty of God's creation. However, if reason is misused by subjecting everything God says to our reason, it becomes an enemy of faith.

The Trinity. The virgin birth of Jesus. Jesus' resurrection from the dead. You could fill a book with the things God says that seem so unreasonable. It's no wonder much of the world looks at their everyday experience and rejects the miracles of the Bible as impossible. "You want me to believe what?!"

The misuse of human reason has hidden Jesus' glory from their eyes. However, rejecting God and his Word because we cannot understand God's reason is foolish. Proverbs 14:12 says, **"There is a way that appears to be right, but in the end it leads to death."**

Instead, the Bible says, **"The fear of the Lord is the beginning of wisdom"** (Proverbs 9:10). And it says, **"No one can say, 'Jesus is Lord,' except by the Holy Spirit"** (1 Corinthians 12:3). Only when God works faith in our hearts through his Word can we truly "understand" God's reasoning as higher than our own.

If you're a believer, do not miss this miracle for you: you believe *all* these things. The Holy Spirit has spoken to your "reasonable challenges" with the power of his Word and his love. The Trinity, the virgin birth, the resurrection—you receive these things by faith because God says them, not because you can explain them. It is evidence that the Holy Spirit is with you!

Chill out
Pastor Clark Schultz

About eight years ago at a local Barnes & Noble, while looking at the overpriced DVDs, I found something amusing. Those who say God doesn't have a sense of humor will appreciate this. Tucked back under the restroom sign was the book section entitled "SELF-HELP." How true of life!

Too often we get ourselves into messes and think that *we* can help ourselves out of them. Sadly, we realize the more we try to fix things, the worse they get. But we have a God who is *always* with us, 24-7, a God who can walk on water, a God who can raise the dead, a God who can feed thousands with a boy's boxed lunch. The God who can defeat armies is the same God who is your *refuge and strength*, and not just when you feel it, but an *ever-present help* (Psalm 46:1). Trust him. You are safe in his arms!

When things are spinning out of control, look to Psalm 37:7: **"Be still before the Lᴏʀᴅ and wait patiently for him."** A modern translation would be, "Chill out and know that God has your situation under control."

We want to drive the car, but Jesus is in the driver's seat. We need to put our mistakes and struggles in the rearview mirror and enjoy the ride. We miss too much of what we call life because we want to play God or we want to drive.

So, friends, chill out. Let God be God and do what he does so well.

.1% happy
Pastor Mike Novotny

If you don't think being happy is hard, listen to the words of tenth-century ruler Abd al-Rahman III: "I have now reigned above fifty years in victory and peace; beloved by my subjects, dreaded by my enemies, and respected by my allies. Riches and honors, power and pleasure, have waited on my call, nor does any earthly blessing appear to have been wanting to my felicity. In this situation, I have diligently numbered the days of pure and genuine happiness which have fallen to my lot: they amount fourteen."

Fourteen?! I'm not sure how Abd did his math, but my calculations say that this man was only happy for .1% of his life. Despite all his earthly success, he missed the genuine happiness that all of us desire.

But you don't have to make the same mistake. The simple words of an imprisoned Christian can offer you more: **"Rejoice in the Lord"** (Philippians 4:4). Notice where the apostle Paul found his joy—in the Lord. Not in his money, power, or reputation but in the Lord.

In the Lord Jesus, you are loved, forgiven, accepted, included, invited, chosen, known, safe, and destined for eternal glory. Meditate on the gospel of your salvation and all the blessings that come along with it, and you will end up happy much more than 14 days of your life. The Spirit will produce an increasing amount of joy in your soul.

Take a census
Pastor Matt Ewart

King David got in trouble when he took a census of his people. The census itself was not wrong, but David's motivations were. The number of his people made him feel more important, more powerful, and more wealthy.

This is something for us to be careful with too. It can go to our heads when a lot of people like us or follow us or listen to us. Be careful when you take a census to measure the influence you have.

What strikes me is how Jesus never took a census. He preached, but he never took attendance numbers. He gathered great crowds, but he never pointed to the numbers as a measure of success. There were only two times when Jesus counted his crowds, and those two times have something in common. One of those times is recorded here:

"The number of those who ate was about five thousand men, besides women and children" (Matthew 14:21).

When Jesus took a census, it had nothing to do with measuring his importance or his success. It had everything to do with how many people he could serve.

Have you been counting people as a way of proving your own success or measuring your importance? Jesus has given you something so much better. You are counted among God's children because of what Jesus did as your Savior.

As you consider the influence you have, start counting the number of people you get to serve.

Why do we always confess our sins?
Pastor David Scharf

Most people like to think positive thoughts and be surrounded by positive people. If you've been to a church recently, perhaps you've wondered why we often confess our sins in worship. Doesn't it seem too negative to start a service off on a downer?

Luke 7:37,38 speaks of a worship service that began this way: **"A woman . . . who lived a sinful life learned that Jesus was eating at the Pharisee's house. . . . She began to wet his feet with her tears. Then she wiped them with her hair, kissed them and poured perfume on them."**

This was not a downer! These were good tears. These were cleansing tears. The woman realized deeper than most just how awful her life had been when lined up with what God requires. She also realized the only One who could wash away her sin and dry her tears was Jesus. Jesus said in response, **"Therefore, I tell you, her many sins have been forgiven—as her great love has shown. But whoever has been forgiven little loves little"** (Luke 7:47).

Why confess your sins? Because these are good tears that help you understand the depth of the forgiveness Jesus won for you on the cross. When you understand the depth of where you were, you can truly appreciate the height to which Jesus' forgiveness has taken you. You and I are his children, citizens of heaven, priceless in his eyes. We can love much now because we understand how much we have been loved!

February 25

Power up
Katrina Harrmann

Last winter we had a lot of snow, so much snow that we had an unexpected power outage. This isn't normally a big deal, but when it happens in the depths of a Michigan winter, with 6-8 inches of snow on the ground, you get a little nervous.

As evening closed in and my family and I ate dinner by candlelight, we got even *more* anxious. And as the hour grew later still, I started to feel even more isolated and fearful. We brought in a large pile of logs to feed the fireplace through the night, and everyone got their sleeping bags and had a campout on the living room floor. The power was on again by morning, but it made me realize how much we take power for granted.

Do you ever do that with God's power? I know I do! It's always there—humming along in the background— so easy to underestimate or even forget. There are many times in life when we face difficulties. Life would be so much easier if we relied on God's power, which is always there to nourish and protect us—a FREE gift from heaven.

"Now to him who is able to do immeasurably more than all we ask or imagine, according to his power that is at work within us . . ." (Ephesians 3:20). Not only does God have the power to help us but "immeasurably more" than we can imagine!

The next time you need help, don't forget about your main power source—God himself!

The prodigal God (Lesson 1)
Pastor Jon Enter

Luke 15 is famous for the story of the prodigal son. Do you know what *prodigal* means? *Prodigal* is "pouring out more than is necessary" or "lavish spending." That's exactly what the son did. He demanded his inheritance and then spent it in lavish, sinful living. *Prodigal* in this sense is a negative.

God is also prodigal. He lavishly pours out more grace on us than we deserve. *Prodigal* in this sense is a positive. We see a beautiful reflection of God's love for us in how the father treated his wayward son. There are three truths to learn in back-to-back-to-back devotions.

The first: God loves you so much he lets you leave.

God does not chain you to his laws. He understands you have the freedom to make choices (though spiritually they are always sinful ones if he isn't involved) just as the father in Luke 15 realized his son made his own sinful choices. Out of love, the father let his son go because forcing him to stay wouldn't have solved anything. It would've made it worse when he left because he may have never come back.

God loves you so much he lets you leave. Imagine if every time you walked away from God's law, he broke your leg. You'd never heal; you'd be furious at God. God lets you go so you realize how bad it is away from him.

Careful. Our tendency is to blame God for *our* sinful choices, *our* prodigal problems. It's our responsibility, not his. What decision are you blaming God for that you made?

February 27

The prodigal God (Lesson 2)
Pastor Jon Enter

We blame God for *our* sinful choices. After an affair, the adulterous husband asked his pastor, "If it was so wrong, why didn't God stop it?" God doesn't send lightning bolts to keep us from every sin we commit. He didn't stop Adam and Eve from eating the fruit; though, he warned them. The father in Luke 15 didn't stop his son from running off into wild living.

When God the Father says, "I love you, so you are free to go," that doesn't mean God turns his back on you. Here's our second lesson. When we leave for sin, God immediately says, "I love you, so I want you back." This is clearly seen in the father's reaction to his son's leaving in Luke 15. He longed for his son. When the son repented and returned to his father, we read this: **"While he was still a long way off, his father saw him"** (verse 20). Not a lookout. Not a servant. The father saw him. The prodigal love of this father caused his heart to yearn for his son's return.

The prodigal love of your Father in heaven causes his heart to yearn for your return. Too often we see God as barely holding back his fiery judgment, almost as if he wants to destroy us. That's not your Father's love for you. God is not out to get back at you; God is out to get you back to him. He longs for your repentant return.

What's holding you back?

The prodigal God (Lesson 3)
Pastor Jon Enter

No sin is too big or done too often. No sin is too damaging to destroy God the Father's love for you. What sin have you committed that you fear God still holds against you?

The sinful son in Luke 15 basically told his dad he wished his dad was dead and then disrespected his father's lifelong work by wildly spending his inheritance. But the son knew his father, so he returned and repented. The father didn't make his son grovel in sorrow to earn back his favor. **"His father was filled with compassion for him; he ran to his son, threw his arms around him, and kissed him"** (Luke 15:20).

In Jewish culture, men wore long robes and didn't run. It was considered highly undignified. But the prodigal love of the father caused him to sprint to his son.

God treats you the same: "I love you, so I will run to you." When God the Father runs to you, he finds you a mess. The son in the parable was a mess, yet the father embraced him. That son reeked! He lived with pigs!

Your heavenly Father runs to you and embraces you just as you are with his presence. He lovingly washes away your sins and adorns you with his perfection. He welcomes you, not as a slave trying to earn back his favor. God gives you his prodigal, lavishly spent grace. He counts you as his and calls you his son or daughter! He treats you as if you never left. Oh, what amazing love!

MARCH

He who testifies to these things says,
"Yes, I am coming soon."
Amen. Come, Lord Jesus.

Revelation 22:20

You know
Pastor Matt Ewart

The prophet Jonah was sent to tell the people in the ancient city of Nineveh that God had taken notice of their wickedness. His warning of pending judgment got the attention of this godless city, and they became hopelessly desperate to avoid what Jonah was predicting. Here's how Nineveh's king summarized their situation:

"Who knows? God may yet relent and with compassion turn from his fierce anger so that we will not perish" (Jonah 3:9).

Just maybe God would pull back his anger if they repented. They had no guarantee of how God would react to their repentance, but it was their only option at that point.

Perhaps there is something going on in your life that is putting you in a similar situation. You feel convicted of a sin and wonder if God could possibly forgive it. Perhaps like the Ninevites, you have acknowledged your guilt to God but afterward you thought to yourself, "Who knows?"

I can give you some good news that the Ninevites wished to have. We do know. We have a guarantee of how God reacts to those who repent. He immediately and fully forgives. How he can do that is through the cross of Jesus. The guarantee is the empty tomb of Jesus.

Take heart today that God has revealed the fullness of his grace to you. There is no doubt how he reacts to your repentance, and that is a good thing to know.

Can God love me?

Pastor Mike Novotny

Did you ever hear about the day John Lennon, one of the Beatles, wrote a desperate note to a televangelist? In 1972 Lennon reached out to Oral Roberts, a famous television minister, and confessed his drug addiction and hopelessness. In that letter, Lennon expressed that he wanted happiness. He also wondered if God could even love him.

There are moments in all our lives when that same question crosses our minds. Maybe it's in the sobering moments during an addiction when we realize how many times we've messed up and how many lives we've messed up. Or perhaps it's the realization that most of our youth was spent pursuing our own glory, building our own kingdom, and seeking our own will with barely a thought of God's will or God's Word. In a million different ways, the devil accuses us with the question, "Can God really love a person like you?"

The Christmas history has the answer. **"But the angel said to them, 'Do not be afraid. I bring you good news that will cause great joy for all the people. Today in the town of David a Savior has been born to you; he is the Messiah, the Lord'"** (Luke 2:10,11). Notice the glorious word *all*.

All includes John Lennon. *All* includes me. *All* includes you. Meditate on these classic words as the Spirit answers the most important question of all. Can God love me? In Jesus, he has, does, and always will.

Jesus' friends
Pastor Clark Schultz

Who is your best friend? Friends are people you can trust through thick and thin. A highlight from my childhood, and maybe yours too, was being allowed to go over to a friend's house for the weekend. We'd have the time of our lives playing in the pool or chasing away bad guys from our secret hideout fort. What fun I had with my friends! You too? As we got older, forts may have been traded in for game night, cards, or watching sports.

My friends, Jesus is our Friend, and he has much more to offer than a tree fort or a swimming pool or game night. We truly are Jesus' friends! **"I no longer call you servants, because a servant does not know his master's business. Instead, I have called you friends"** (John 15:15). When you went over to your friend's house as a kid, you were treated like a guest. You were given the best first. You were able to take the first piece of pizza. You were able to play with the best toy first. As Jesus' friend, he has given you and me many gifts. By his death on a cross, we receive forgiveness of sins and the assurance of eternal life. Every time we go to his house, we are given the best. We are given the news of how much he loves us and how much he has done for us. Truly we have been given the best from our Friend.

Do you know someone who could use a Friend like that?

The morning hymn
Andrea Delwiche

Would you like to join ancient Christians in one of their faith practices? Psalm 63 was called "the morning hymn." John Chrysostom, a Christian who lived from A.D. 347 to 407, wrote, "It was decreed and ordained by the primitive [church] fathers, that no day should pass without the public singing of this Psalm." Maybe you don't want to sing, but give it a read. It's only 11 verses.

Repetition helps us memorize and internalize. When we memorize a section of Scripture, we carry it with us wherever we go. It becomes a resource, a thirst quencher, as we go through life.

Psalm 63 can also give us the words when our own thoughts are muddled. In this case, we have a conversation starter with the Lord for a wide variety of situations: when we long to feel God's presence, when we rejoice in his goodness, when we are awake at night and can't sleep, when we are confronted by evil, when we desire to feel connected to Christians all over the world and throughout the history of the church, when we desire to spend time meditating on God and increasing our faith in him. Day or night, this psalm gives words to our heart's desire.

"On my bed I remember you; I think of you through the watches of the night. Because you are my help, I sing in the shadow of your wings. I cling to you; your right hand upholds me" (verses 6-8).

Encourage others
Pastor Clark Schultz

I love getting mail, even if it's a bill (at least until I open it), but to see my name in print, to see something addressed to me, talk about one of the highlights of my day! My name. I matter, if even to the cable company.

On a larger scale, you and I matter to God. Even if you look in the mirror and don't like what you see, God loves you! I'm not just talking about a mushy butterfly in the tummy love but a love that says you are worth dying for.

Hebrews 10:25 says, "[Encourage] **one another.**" Friend, your past sins do not define you. What defines you is whose you are in Christ. When I taught high school, I would ask my teens to list people who encouraged them on their faith walk. Answers ranged from teachers and pastors to parents and coaches and so on. If I knew the person who encouraged a particular teen, I would share that teen's essay with them. The overwhelming response was joy to see that someone thought they mattered. They were encouraged to hear a teen found their words or actions uplifting.

It's easy to spew venom and talk negative about a group or about ourselves. Be encouraged by knowing you matter to God, and look for someone today to give some encouragement back too. Go old school and write them a letter of thanks. Who knows, maybe they love seeing their name in print, and your words will be more joyful than the cable bill.

Give, not give up
Katrina Harrmann

I always think it's interesting that people like to give up something for Lent. Often it's something like a mini New Year's resolution, with people giving up things they feel are bad for them like chocolate or swear words.

The idea is that by giving up something, we are "suffering" in a way that honors Christ's suffering on the cross. But many of the things we "suffer without" . . . well, if we're being honest . . . how much does it *really* cause us to suffer?

What if we *gave* something instead of *giving up* something? After all—Christ gave an incalculable amount for us on the cross—*everything* really—just for us!

How do we give instead of give up at Lent? One idea is to collect a canned food item every day of Lent to donate to a food shelter. Or donate your time at a local charity, pick up trash at a park with your kids, or visit someone who is lonely. **"Walk in the way of love, just as Christ loved us and gave himself up for us"** (Ephesians 5:2). Be the hands and feet of Jesus!

There are also ways to give of yourself to those in your own home. Spend time with a family member, even if you're tired. Help someone with a chore, or take the time to listen to someone who needs to talk. There are countless ways we can love one another during the season of Lent!

Love at any cost
Pastor Jon Enter

What are you not doing that you know you should? Who are you not helping but know you could? Love at any cost. When God places you into a position to serve, to help, to do, or to give, he expects you to show love without counting the cost. Why does God expect that? Because he can give you even more than you give others.

Esther discovered this truth.

Esther was a Jewish girl whose people had been conquered by the Persian Empire, and yet she amazingly became queen, though she kept her heritage a secret. One day an edict was given for all Jews to be killed. Her uncle alerted Esther to the evil plan and basically said, "Help us, Esther; you're our only hope!" Esther heard the plea to beg the king for mercy, but she hadn't seen him for a month. And to approach him without permission was punishable by death.

Esther knew doing what was right could cost her. **"I will go to the king, even though it is against the law. And if I perish, I perish"** (Esther 4:16). She survived and saved the entire Jewish nation. One person stepping out in trust can make a huge impact on others.

What has God pressed on your heart to do to help someone else? Who knows? What if you are the one God designed for such a time as this to be the bearer of his love and mercy? Don't count the cost. Be the blessing God intends you to be.

Jesus isn't a Gnostic
Pastor Mike Novotny

Have you ever heard of the Gnostics? Gnosticism was a very popular religion that exploded with growth in the early second century, making it a fierce contender with Christianity. The Gnostics claimed that what really mattered spiritually was not what you did but what you knew. If you could tap into the secret knowledge of their religion, you could essentially treat people like trash and still feel good about yourself (like a PhD professor who is kind of a jerk to his students).

The apostle John wanted nothing to do with that kind of religion. **"Whoever does not love does not know God, because God is love. This is how God showed his love among us: He sent his one and only Son into the world that we might live through him"** (1 John 4:8,9).

John slapped every Gnostic in the face with these words. You want to know what love is? It's not that God knows everything. It's that God did something, sending the Son who would imitate his Father and do something too—giving his life as a sacrifice for our sins. You want to know what real religion is? The kind that loves others with our hands, our actions, and our choices, motivated by the God who loved us first.

Thank God that Jesus wasn't a Gnostic! May you or I never become one either.

Looking for the good life?
Pastor Mike Novotny

If you're looking for a good life, listen to what Jesus said. John's gospel is full of Jesus explaining what makes a person's life truly worth living.

Jesus promised, **"I have come that they may have life, and have it to the full"** (John 10:10). We sometimes think of church and God and Jesus as places and people who restrict life, that have dos and don'ts and commandments that take time and energy out of our lives. But Jesus said his biggest goal is for you to have the fullest, best kind of life.

Was he promising you a functional family or your dream job? No, something better: **"Now this is eternal life: that they know you, the only true God, and Jesus Christ, whom you have sent"** (John 17:3). Knowing God is the secret to lasting life, as long as you are thinking of the true God, the God who is glorious, interesting, powerful, faithful, compassionate, loving, there for you always—that's life.

How do you get a life like that, a God like that? **"Jesus answered, 'I am the way and the truth and the life. No one comes to the Father except through me'"** (John 14:6). While Jesus doesn't promise health and wealth (yet), he is promising you a way to come to God, despite all your past sins and current struggles.

We all want a good life. Thankfully, Jesus is offering us just that, a life lived every day in the presence of a perfect Father. Think about that and you will find life to the full.

Don't give up without a fight!
Jan Gompper

"**Thy will be done**" (Luke 11:2 KJV). This can be hard to pray when we or those we love are facing dire circumstances. Perhaps, like me, you have sometimes approached God's throne with an attitude of resignation, thinking you better just get ready to accept that God's will might not be your will.

Yet Scripture tells us that "**the earnest prayer of a righteous person has great power and produces wonderful results**" (James 5:16 NLT). And there are instances in the Bible where, it appears, God's mind was changed.

When God wanted to destroy the children of Israel after they turned their backs on him and built a golden calf to worship instead, Moses pleaded with the Lord on their behalf and reminded God of his promises to them. "**So the Lord changed his mind about the terrible disaster he had threatened to bring on his people**" (Exodus 32:14 NLT).

When the people of Nineveh learned that God was ready to destroy them because of their sinfulness, they repented, and "**when God saw what they had done and how they had put a stop to their evil ways, he changed his mind and did not carry out the destruction he had threatened**" (Jonah 3:10 NLT).

This doesn't mean God will *always* answer our prayers the way we want, but it does teach us not to give up without a fight—to boldly remind God of his great power, mercy, and love.

"**With God, *everything* is possible**" (Matthew 19:26 NLT).

Alive with Christ
Pastor Mike Novotny

Back in 2010, a mine collapsed in Copiapó, Chile. Thirty-three men were trapped a half mile underground, and 68 days later they were still there. Their strength as professional miners and their combined experience were no match against a half mile of solid earth. They needed to be saved. And, on day 69, they were. First, their saviors drilled down to a strategic location. Then they sent a capsule called El Fenix (the Phoenix) down into the darkness. Finally, one by one, all 33 men were brought up into the light, where they were embraced by family, friends, and a celebrating world.

If you came to Jesus later in your life, perhaps you have felt a little of what those men felt on day 69. You were "dead" in sins, unable to fix a half mile worth of sins that separated you from God. But then Jesus saved you. **"But because of his great love for us, God, who is rich in mercy, made us alive with Christ even when we were dead in transgressions—it is by grace you have been saved. And God raised us up with Christ"** (Ephesians 2:4-6).

Through Jesus, you have been saved. You are not dead and distant from God but living today in his presence. You are not hopeless and helpless as you face the challenges of this week but alive, loved, and raised up to new hopes, new expectations, and a new connection with your Father who lives in the light.

Don't be afraid, friend. You are not dead. You are alive with Christ!

Do you have a good memory?
Pastor David Scharf

Perhaps you've heard the phrase, "I was blessed with a bad memory." The person who says this recognizes that it is a blessing not to be able to remember failings, shortcomings, and sins so readily. Indeed, because of Jesus' death on a cross and resurrection from the grave, God gave himself a bad memory by saying, **"For I will forgive their wickedness and will remember their sins no more"** (Hebrews 8:12).

However, as Christians, we do not rejoice in bad memories. We rejoice that we have been blessed with great memories! No, not a recounting of our sins but a remembrance of what our God has done for us. This is the work of the Holy Spirit: **"But the Advocate, the Holy Spirit, whom the Father will send in my name, will teach you all things and will remind you of everything I have said to you"** (John 14:26).

The Father sent Jesus at Christmas. The Son gave his life on Good Friday and rose on Easter. The Holy Spirit *reminds* us of all of it. Without the work of the Holy Spirit, you and I would be doomed to remember our sins forever in hell. But Jesus kept his promise to send the Holy Spirit. And the Holy Spirit keeps his promise to remind us that our sins are forgiven! Isn't it such a blessing to have a good memory?

A full recovery
Pastor Clark Schultz

In an NFL football game, Kansas City Chiefs tight end Tony Gonzalez (now a *FOX Sports* analyst) made a remarkable catch. The momentum of this catch carried his rather large frame forward, and he came crashing down on one of the cameramen on the sidelines. The cameraman was knocked unconscious and taken immediately to a hospital. Tony felt terrible and after the game phoned the hospital to check on the cameraman. The doctors at the hospital ran some CAT scans to see if there was any damage to the man's head. Fortunately, there was not, but as they performed the tests, they found two small tumors growing in the man's head. They were able to catch the cancer in time, and the man received the proper treatment and made a full recovery. Tony was quoted as saying, "I'm a firm believer in God and that he has his hand in this."

Had Tony not hit this man, the man would not have realized just how sick he was. The man certainly had a reason to be thankful to Tony and to God.

First Thessalonians 5:16-18 says, **"Rejoice always, pray continually, give thanks in all circumstances."** We too have a reason to be thankful. We were dead in our sins and deserved eternal death. The cancer of sin infested our bodies and would have claimed all our lives. But God, in his mercy, sent his Son to share our humanity, to take our place, and in turn gives us the full recovery treatment of forgiveness, peace, joy, and the hope of eternal life.

Give thanks in *ALL* circumstances
Pastor Clark Schultz

Please reread yesterday's devotion. There are often two ways of looking at a situation. Yes, that cameraman was fortunate. Yes, we have a reason to be thankful. But what about when life stinks? When you are alone or when you've tasted death or when you're facing divorce or feeling left out? Pain and misery seem to hit you every day that ends in a Y. And who is God to tell you to **"give thanks in all circumstances"** (1 Thessalonians 5:18)? Really God? I'm supposed to thank you for the miserable patch of life I'm in currently?

Dear reader, when the world doesn't seem to give us a break, we have a God who does and understands. It looked bleak for that cameraman as he was being carted off the field on a stretcher. However, good came from that disaster. God has something good planned. How do I know? **"He who did not spare his own Son, but gave him up for us all—how will he not also, along with him, graciously give us all things?** (Romans 8:32).

My assurance is that Jesus died for you and me, a full divorce from his Father. He was left alone on a cross with all the pain and misery we deserved. God's love for you and me means we do not need to suffer being left out of heaven. Whatever the situation you are in, God has NOT left you. This is not some Pollyanna, feel-good, kitten-poster slogan. It is from a real God who really and truly loves you!

Love God . . . that's all
Pastor Mike Novotny

When I take couples through my premarriage counseling course, part of their homework is to invite an older couple out to dinner. The older couple has to be (1) married, (2) Christian, and (3) an inspiration to the young couple. After the homework is done, I get to ask what wisdom and insights they gained from their time together.

Recently, my latest spouses-to-be asked an elderly couple who had been together for over 50 years, loving each other faithfully and seeking Jesus together hand in hand. I couldn't wait to hear the highlights of their conversation, imagining all the PhD-level insights from a happy couple in their 80s.

When we met, post-dinner, this young couple pulled out their notes from the evening. "What did you learn?" I asked.

"Well," the groom answered, "the husband told us, 'Love God.'"

I paused with my pen, waiting for the rest of the quote, but there wasn't any. Love God . . . that's all. The more I thought about it, however, the more I loved it. Love the God who loved you first. Soak in the love of God at the cross, and let it shape and form you. Love God . . . that's all.

I bet another elderly Christian, the apostle John, would have loved that thought. **"God is love. Whoever lives in love lives in God, and God in them"** (1 John 4:16).

I am Jesus' witness
Pastor David Scharf

"I just want my life to mean something! I want to make a difference!" Have you felt that way? God also wants your life to mean something, to make a difference. And he has given you the greatest purpose of all. That purpose is to reflect his love to others so they can learn to know that Jesus is their Savior. As a result, more people will go to heaven.

Talk about making a difference! Could there be anything more meaningful than that? In the end, we will all die because we are all sinners who deserve hell. Only Jesus can rescue us from that fate. Jesus did so by dying on a cross and rising from the dead. Jesus wants people to know about it!

Jesus told the disciples, **"But you will receive power when the Holy Spirit comes on you; and you will be my witnesses in Jerusalem, and in all Judea and Samaria, and to the ends of the earth"** (Acts 1:8). Not only does Jesus give us the honor of being his witnesses, but he empowers us to share Jesus with the world through his Holy Spirit.

Do you see the point? Your life has amazing meaning and purpose! You get the honor of sharing Jesus with others, through your attitudes, through your actions, through your words. God bless you as you witness.

How low can you go?
Pastor Matt Ewart

It must be nice to be an important person. People praise you. Servants serve you. All in all, life is good when you are important.

The Bible records more than one time when Jesus' disciples were arguing over which of them was most important. One day Jesus gave them a very simple way to become important. But what he told them shocked them: **"Therefore, whoever takes the lowly position of this child is the greatest in the kingdom of heaven"** (Matthew 18:4).

In those days, children were taught to lay low and keep humble. They didn't think they were anyone. They saw themselves as small because . . . they were small. That's how all of us enter the world. Small.

Sometime in the process of becoming an adult, we start believing we are bigger than we really are. Maybe it starts by seeing success glamorized in the news. Or maybe it starts when we compare ourselves to others and envy kicks in. It doesn't take very long until we all reach our own idea of what it'll take to reach great heights of importance.

It's good to let Jesus reset that idea regularly. He is important, but his importance does not stem from his awe-inspiring divine powers. It stems from his love that led him to become like a child, making himself nothing, and humbling himself for us.

He invites you to do the same. The way his kingdom works, importance is measured by whom you serve and how low you can go.

Do not fear the kingdom of God
Pastor Mike Novotny

One of the hardest/scariest things about Christianity is that it declares Jesus to be King. That means you don't get to make the rules, call the shots, or get the last word about which words you use, which sexual desires you embrace, or how you use the money God puts into your hands. Your job is to change your mind, bend your knee, and submit to every single word that King Jesus declares. That can be a scary thought.

If you're struggling with submission, I encourage you to think about the cross. A little sign that Pontius Pilate had written in Latin, Greek, and Aramaic hung above Jesus' head: "JESUS OF NAZARETH, THE KING OF THE JEWS" (John 19:19). Our King hung on a cross.

That simple image takes our fear of authority away because it proves Jesus is a humble, sacrificial, for-us kind of King. To keep us eternally alive, our King was willing to die physically. To save us from ourselves, our King was willing to give up himself. To prove he is not a tyrant, not an abusive husband or a self-serving boss, our King hung on a cross. To prove that you could trust him, obey him, submit to him, Jesus endured the shame. There is only one word to describe a King like that—*love*.

So don't be afraid. Yes, Jesus commands you to obey God's Word, to submit "your truth," your feelings, and your way of thinking to his unchanging Truth, but don't be afraid. Your King wants what is best for you. The cross is the proof.

Do you believe in prayer?
Pastor Mike Novotny

Do you believe that prayer works? Do you trust that the words we speak in Jesus' name reach the ears of God and move the hands of God to increase the blessing of God? I do. While I can't fathom the details of the process, I do believe that Jesus was telling the truth when he taught us about the power of prayer.

If you share my confidence in prayer, then confess your deepest spiritual struggles to other people. That's what Jesus' younger brother James said when he wrote, **"Therefore confess your sins to each other and pray for each other so that you may be healed. The prayer of a righteous person is powerful and effective"** (James 5:16).

Note the domino effect—First, you confess your sins to other people. Next, those people can pray for you regarding those sins. Finally, God responds to the words of his righteous people and sends a healing blessing down from heaven.

Pride tempts us to keep our prayers shallow, only asking others to pray for Grandma's cancer or safe travels during spring break. But James urges us to pray for the deep things, the potentially embarrassing things, the sinful habits that we can't seem to shake by ourselves. Why? Because when righteous people pray, God listens. Even better, when righteous people pray, God heals.

So swallow your pride, confess your sins to others, and trust that the resulting prayers are not pointless. By God's grace, they are powerful ways through which God might change your habits and heal your heart.

When the fever breaks

Jan Gompper

Having the flu is no fun, especially when it's accompanied by aches, fever, and chills that make you toss and turn all night, shivering beneath a pile of blankets that offer no respite. But what a relief when the fever breaks and your clammy body necessitates that you toss aside the quilted layers. You know then that the worst of the bug is behind you.

Sometimes life can feel like a prolonged flu bug, filled with physical, emotional, and spiritual chills and aches. Perhaps the death of a loved one or a divorce has filled you with the deep chill of loneliness. Maybe you have a terminal illness or are experiencing the ache of watching someone you love suffer. Or you toss and turn all night, worrying about your wayward child or how you're going to pay next month's rent.

Do you feel like your fever of earthly ills may never break? You're not alone. **"We know that the whole creation has been groaning as in the pains of childbirth right up to the present time"** (Romans 8:22). But we have a promise that **"the God of all grace, who called you to his eternal glory in Christ, after you have suffered a little while, will himself restore you and make you strong, firm and steadfast"** (1 Peter 5:10).

Whatever present or future ills we Christ followers experience in this life, we can rest assured that one day the fever will break. We will shed our earthly coverings and arise, more than merely relieved. We will dance for joy!

God is working
Andrea Delwiche

People, even people within our Christian circles, do destructive, harmful, secretive things. David expresses it well in Psalm 64:6: **"They plot injustice and say, 'We have devised a perfect plan!' Surely the human mind and heart are cunning."**

When we run into those who are deceitful, we can feel angry, helpless, and tired out. What do we do? We can always bring these situations before the Lord and ask him to help us discern the next steps. Sometimes this includes acting decisively. Sometimes we must wait for the Lord.

One thing we know: God sees, he cares, and he will act in his time. In the language of Psalm 64, **"God will shoot them with his arrows; they will suddenly be struck down"** (verse 7).

So, even in the time of waiting, we can have confidence that God is working because he promises to do so. Here is one of those promises: **"Be strong and courageous. Do not be afraid or terrified because of them, for the Lord your God goes with you; he will never leave you nor forsake you"** (Deuteronomy 31:6).

So resting in God's promises, we know that the words of Psalm 64:10 are true: **"The righteous will rejoice in the Lord and take refuge in him; all the upright in heart will glory in him!"**

Imprint your promises on our hearts, Lord!

Cut the engine
Katrina Harrmann

When I was 20 years old, I was writing for the local newspaper and found myself doing an interview in a three-seater Cessna airplane with a student pilot and his instructor. At one point, as we were puttering across the sky—the world spilled out below us like a toy map—the instructor said, "Let's see how you deal with this . . ."

And he killed the engine.

The silence was staggering. The only sound was the wind whistling around the metal shell of the dead aircraft. The only reason I knew we were falling—and falling *fast*—was because my stomach had swooped upward into my throat.

Giving up control is hard, isn't it?

Some people refuse to let go of their grip on the wheel . . . all the way to the grave. We like to be in charge. We don't like leaving it up to others to do what needs to be done.

Recently, I handed my 15-year-old son the car keys and had him drive me to the store for the first time. Wow! Talk about giving up control! But as Christians, we don't need to worry because God has it all under control. **"In his hand is the life of every creature and the breath of all mankind"** (Job 12:10).

God isn't like humankind. He'll never let us down. His plans are perfect, and we don't lose ourselves by trusting in him.

Let's give God the wheel!

Big or small
Pastor Matt Ewart

How big does a problem have to be before God is interested in it?

I wonder about that sometimes when I hear children bring their prayer requests to God. They can offer the most genuine prayers about the smallest things. As a dad, I remember deliberating at one point if I needed to teach my kids how to pray for bigger things that were on more of a God level.

But then I realized something. What seems small to one person can seem big to another person.

Maybe you have a "small" thing going on in your life. You think it's so small that you haven't even prayed about it. After all, why would an all-powerful God who is upholding the universe take time to hear about one of your little worries?

But he does care. It isn't the size of a problem that gets God's attention. It's what a problem—big or small—does to your heart.

Are you really struggling over something that most people would consider small? Then God considers it big. What's most important to God is guarding your heart: **"Above all else, guard your heart, for everything you do flows from it"** (Proverbs 4:23).

What's a small problem or a small worry that you can bring to God today? He will not judge you for coming to him with such a small thing. He is very interested in the little things that bother or shape your heart.

A sense of gratitude
Andrea Delwiche

Have you ever spent time in God's creation and made a list of the signs of God's provision that you encountered? What if you turned your list into a thanksgiving song to God? Enjoy this list composed by King David:

"You care for the land and water it; you enrich it abundantly. The streams of God are filled with water to provide the people with grain, for so you have ordained it. You drench its furrows and level its ridges; you soften it with showers and bless its crops. You crown the year with your bounty, and your carts overflow with abundance. The grasslands of the wilderness overflow; the hills are clothed with gladness. The meadows are covered with flocks and the valleys are mantled with grain; they shout for joy and sing" (Psalm 65:9–13).

We might be quite distanced from countryside and farm fields. We might not pay attention to whether or not we've had too little rain for crops to grow well or enough rain and cool weather to help prevent fires from devouring forests and keep waters coursing in the stream beds.

Because we are distant from the natural processes that feed and clothe us, purify our air, and lift our spirits, we may lose our sense of gratitude—gratitude for creation itself, people who grow our food, and our Creator-God. God crafted and cares for his creation. He crafted and cares for us.

Ask God for eyes to see his goodness, and then exclaim with the psalmist, **"Praise awaits you, our God"** (Psalm 65:1).

You will see him
Pastor Matt Ewart

Have you ever prepared to teach a Bible lesson or a Sunday school class? Or have you put serious thought into how to talk to someone about Jesus? It can be a stressful thing to do because you want to make sure you get it right. Showing Jesus to others is a joy, but there can be a lot of details to figure out on the way.

I'm sure that's what Mary Magdalene and the other Mary were feeling as they walked away from Jesus' empty tomb. An angel had assigned them to tell the disciples to travel to Galilee, where they would see Jesus.

The one they thought was dead was now alive, and there was a very specific place they could go to see him. I'm sure the women were rehearsing how to share this news with the disciples. But before they could do that, something amazing happened.

They saw Jesus while they were on their way to tell others where to find him!

"Suddenly Jesus met them. 'Greetings,' he said. They came to him, clasped his feet and worshiped him. Then Jesus said to them, 'Do not be afraid. Go and tell my brothers to go to Galilee; there they will see me'" (Matthew 28:9,10).

When you tell others where they can find Jesus, watch for the ways that Jesus shows himself to you. He will fill you with joy as you share his good news.

The most powerful antidepressant
Pastor Mike Novotny

Dr. Dale Archer, an American psychiatrist, once claimed that if he could package hope and hand it out, it would be better than any other type of antidepressant. Hope is what keeps us going during the hard times. It's the belief that life won't be this bad forever, that things are going to get better, that soon we are going to turn the corner. If you are dealing with something difficult right now—back pain, a strained relationship with your sister, a stressful project at work, etc.—hope is what assures you that you don't have to bear those burdens for much longer. Things will change.

The problem with most of our hope, however, is that it is not true hope at all. We squeeze the hope out of hope when we say things like, "I hope I feel better tomorrow," a sentence that is a personal wish and nothing more.

But biblical hope is better. Here's my go-to definition: Hope is a for-sure future. Paul wrote, **"But if we hope for what we do not yet have, we wait for it patiently"** (Romans 8:25). We can wait patiently for our future because it is for sure.

Your back pain? It will end. Your relationship with your sister? There will be no drama in heaven. Your stress? Rest will reign on the new earth. I guarantee such a future by the promises of a faithful God.

Be patient, child of God, you have a for-sure future in Jesus.

God is love
Pastor Mike Novotny

Want to hear three words that would have sounded wild to the religious crowd of the first century? Here goes—God is love. Read the myths and legends about Zeus and Apollo and Aphrodite, and you'll realize that a God of love was crazier than a Hallmark movie with a zombie-infested ending!

But this was the claim that swept through the ancient Greek world when Christians like John preached: **"God is love"** (1 John 4:8). Can you imagine hearing that for the first time? I bet that news sounded so strange and so good.

It did for Pop. Pinyaluck, a friend of mine who goes by Pop, grew up in Thailand, where 99.9% of people are religious. The Thai people, in general, have a conception of a higher power that they are accountable to, but one day Pop heard something new—God is love. That thought rocked her world and led her to Jesus, the Bible, and the moment I baptized her in the name of the God who is love.

If that idea seems new to you too, I encourage you to seek answers from a Christian you know and respect (or email us at Time of Grace!). But if God's loving nature is something you've heard since you were a kid, pause today and consider how different life would be if God was not love. Then with all the praise you can muster, give glory to the God who loves to define himself with a short, simple, stunning sentence—God is love.

The storms of life
Katrina Harrmann

My family and I were having a picnic, and it started to rain. As we watched the downpour, we started gathering up our picnic frantically, realizing the rain would reach us within moments. But it never did!

Weirdly enough, as we watched, the rain continued to fall in a deluge right across the street from us . . . but not a single drop fell where we were sitting! In a few minutes, the storm moved on, skirting our little picnic area as if there were a protective force field around it.

How often do we have good, sunny days while those who are walking around us (maybe even right in front of us!) are walking through a storm?

It's so hard to know what people are going through. But that makes it even more important to be kind, understanding, and patient with one another.

"My command is this: Love each other as I have loved you" (John 15:12).

We pray for one another because some people are walking through storms of unimaginable magnitude, something that's hard to realize when our "side of the street" is sunny!

"Then they cried out to the Lord in their trouble, and he brought them out of their distress. He stilled the storm to a whisper; the waves of the sea were hushed. They were glad when it grew calm, and he guided them to their desired haven" (Psalm 107:28-30).

Planning to live
Pastor Matt Ewart

When you read the accounts that describe Jesus on the cross, it might seem like there are a bunch of unrelated details mentioned. The Scriptures explain what happened to Jesus' garments after they put him on the cross. That doesn't seem all that important. The Scriptures also take time to show us how Jesus made sure that John would watch over his mother, Mary. That hardly seems pertinent to our salvation.

When you look at these details and all the other ones, they all point to one stunning reality: Jesus knew he was going to die. More than that, he was planning on it.

It is no fun to make arrangements for what happens after you die. That's why most people neglect to write a will before it is too late. Planning on dying is no way to live.

Here's where Jesus changes everything: **"Or don't you know that all of us who were baptized into Christ Jesus were baptized into his death? We were therefore buried with him through baptism into death"** (Romans 6:3,4).

What this means for you is that you don't need to dread earthly death. You can make arrangements for your death without being overwhelmed by the thought of it. Jesus took away death's sting by conquering it for you.

Jesus planned to die so that you can plan to live forever. Open your eyes to see the life that's before you.

Already but not yet
Pastor Mike Novotny

Do you struggle to believe the glorious things the Bible says about Christian people, like the part where God claims we are "holy" in his sight?

How can that be logically? If you have a long history of embarrassing sins, how could holy be true for you?

The author of Hebrews knows. He writes, **"For by one sacrifice [Jesus] has made perfect forever those who are being made holy"** (10:14). You should adore the grammar in that verse. It admits that Christians "are being made holy," implying a process that is not yet finished. This is why you still are tempted, why you still stumble, why you still are drawn back to the poison of habitual sins.

Yet please don't miss what the author said first. Jesus "has made perfect forever" those very people who are still works in progress. You already are as clean and pure as you could possibly be in the eyes of our Father. You don't have to fear his judgment or anger or disappointment because your Savior endured all that on a cross.

Theologians call this the "already/not yet" of the Christian life. So, child of God, keep fighting. You are not yet holy in your habits. And, child of God, keep resting. You are already holy in your blood-bought identity.

Love to the end
Pastor David Scharf

To what extent have you been loved?

For a family devotion one evening, the reformer Martin Luther read the account of Abraham offering Isaac on an altar (Genesis 22). His wife, Katie, said, "I don't believe it. God would not have treated his son like that!"

"But, Katie," Luther replied, "he did."

It was the night before Jesus' death. He was in an upper room with his disciples. **"Jesus knew that the hour had come for him to leave this world and go to the Father. Having loved his own who were in the world, he loved them to the end"** (John 13:1). Where does Jesus' love end? That night he stooped low, and his hands washed feet with water. But his love did not end there. The next day he washed souls with his blood on Calvary's cross. That night the Savior in love handled his disciples' feet. But his love did not end there. The next day, in a far greater display of love, Jesus handled the world's sin—every last one. That night he poured wine, gave it to them, and said, *"This is my blood."* But his love did not end there. The next day, he poured that blood out on a cross to show just how much he loves you.

Jesus did not care what it cost him—you were worth it. He loved you all the way until his end when he breathed his last. He loves you as much as love can love, all the way to the end.

APRIL

Clap your hands, all you nations;
shout to God with cries of joy.

Psalm 47:1

Seek truth

Pastor Mike Novotny

It's hard to know what to do when you don't know what is true. I felt that way when COVID first hit. As the globe was scrambling to figure out what COVID was and how it worked, I laced up my shoes for some needed exercise. But as I trotted down my usual path, coming straight toward me was . . . a human! What should I do? Hold my breath as I run past her? Stand on a stranger's lawn so she can walk past with a six-foot buffer? I wasn't sure because it's hard to know what to do when you don't know what is true.

The same thing applies when your friend feels an attraction to her same sex. Or when one YouTube video tells you to pray the rosary and another tells you the rosary is wrong. Or when you're trying to find a good church, but the churches in town don't say the same thing. It's hard to know what to do when you don't know what is true.

Jesus once prayed to his Father, **"Your word is truth"** (John 17:17). In a world of feelings, emotions, opinions, traditions, partisan spins, man-made traditions, incomplete data, and conflicting sources, Jesus knew where to find a solid source of truth—the Word of his Father.

Few things in life matter more than making the time to seek the truth passionately through a dedicated study of God's Word. Because once God helps you figure out what is true, you'll know exactly what to do.

My truth? Maybe!

Pastor Mike Novotny

Have you heard phrases like "be true to yourself," "live your truth," or simply, "my truth"? They seem to be the most popular doctrine of modern culture, appearing as the moral of most stories we find online. What would God say to that? Would he agree that you should look within to find truth?

Maybe. In speaking of the Gentiles who lacked the Scriptures, the apostle Paul once wrote, **"The requirements of the law are written on their hearts, their consciences also bearing witness, and their thoughts sometimes accusing them and at other times even defending them"** (Romans 2:15). Notice where God's law/truth was found—Their *hearts*. Their *consciences*. Their *thoughts*. All three of which are *within*.

Christian, if you are a Bible lover like me, you might recoil instinctively at the idea of "my truth." My first reaction is to push back, pointing out the selfishness that exists in the human heart that is all too willing to twist the truth to get its way. But perhaps we should first listen, searching for common ground, finding every spot where the conscience is correct.

If we believe the Bible is the truth (John 17:17), then let's believe that this verse is true too. That first step might lead to a conversation about the Word, where the whole truth can be found.

My truth? Maybe not . . .

Pastor Mike Novotny

I have a love/hate relationship with my heart. I love it because, by God's grace, it has a lot of Scripture stored up in it. After years of church services, home devotions, and sermon podcasts, you can squeeze my heart and Bible will come beating out of it. The Holy Spirit has helped me treasure up God's Word and ponder it in my heart.

But I also hate my heart. Despite the services and sermons, I have noticed that when my heart feels cornered or criticized, it suffers from scriptural amnesia. It forgets everything that is good and true and of God. Instead, my heart goes into defensive mode, proudly pumping words toward my lips and producing detailed spreadsheets of all the things I do right and all the things my critics do wrong. That sin is part of my nature.

You too? The apostle Paul knew why following your heart or being true to yourself wouldn't lead you to the God-honest truth. He wrote, **"You must no longer live as the Gentiles do, in the futility of their thinking. They are darkened in their understanding and separated from the life of God because of the ignorance that is in them due to the hardening of their hearts"** (Ephesians 4:17,18). Notice the source of the problem—"In them."

The humbling reality is that our hearts cannot be completely trusted. So listen to your heart, but never let it get the final vote. Always bring it back to the Word, the only certain source of truth.

Your truth = The truth?

Pastor Mike Novotny

The other day I studied every appearance of the word *truth* in the Bible. In my English translation, the word showed up 137 separate times. The question I wanted to answer, however, was how often *truth* was defined as "the truth" and how often it was described as "my/your truth." In other words, how did the inspired writers of the Bible think about the concept of truth?

The results were fascinating. Out of the 137 uses of *truth*, 99 of them had the word *the* before them. "The truth" was the most common way, by far, for the Bible to talk about the concept. What about "my truth"? From Genesis 1:1 to Revelation 22:21, that phrase showed up . . . 0 times. Never. Not once.

What about "your truth"? That combination actually did show up three separate times, which might lead some to think that truth could be subjective and personal. However, all three of those times were when the Bible's authors were speaking directly to God himself! In other words, those three "your truths" were actually another way of saying "the truth."

The point of this research is that the Holy Spirit wants you to have a sure and certain source of truth. He never wants you to guess about good and evil or wonder about what's right and what's wrong. When it comes to God, especially his love for you and grace toward you, he wants you to know the truth. This is why Jesus prayed, **"Sanctify them by the truth; your word is truth"** (John 17:17).

The gift of now
Christine Wentzel

Listening to the news and the watercooler gossip about the news, there's a pretty good consensus that everyone's positive everything's bad in the world. Trying to find any goodness and mercy in these stories is like searching for the proverbial needle in a haystack mixed with cow manure. Spend too long in the mire, and you're going to need a bath.

Allowing ourselves to take in this constant conscious or subconscious drip, drip, drip of negative messages undermines the daily work of the Holy Spirit. And this actually grieves the Holy Spirit. Before we know it, we're preoccupied by the past "should haves" or fearful of the future "what ifs." When we're distracted like this, it makes it more difficult to receive and make use of the God-given gifts that enliven and enable us to live a life pleasing to him—full of meaningful purpose, peaceful contentment, and joyful thanksgiving.

Let's accept today as a gift for what it is, a time of God's grace. Remain steadfast in this faith walk so that by it others may witness and seek out the Good News of salvation, now more than ever!

"You know that when you were unbelievers, every time you were led to worship false gods you were worshiping gods who couldn't even speak. So I want you to know that no one speaking by God's Spirit says, 'Jesus is cursed.' No one can say, 'Jesus is Lord,' except by the Holy Spirit" (1 Corinthians 12:2,3 GW).

Left on read
Linda Buxa

For today's high school and college students, the worst thing you can do is leave them "on read." Let's pause a moment for a quick lesson because I'm guessing a number of you have no idea what this means. When you text, Snapchat, or DM someone, you can see if they have opened and read your message. If they don't answer quickly—or at all—you are left "on read." This is especially devastating when it comes to young romantic relationships. Leaving someone on read tells them you aren't actually interested in them.

It may sound silly to you when it comes to electronic communication, but you do know the great hurt that comes from feeling like you weren't being heard or answered—especially when it comes to God and your prayers. What if you've been praying and praying and he isn't answering the way you want him to? Maybe you feel like he's ignoring you. Perhaps you wonder if he is really invested in you.

God promises that, instead of worrying, you can rest assured that **"this is the confidence we have in approaching God: that if we ask anything according to his will, he hears us"** (1 John 5:14).

He listens. He hears. He acts.

P.S. To be fair, he doesn't always answer your prayers the way you think he should. That's the hard part about being mature when it comes to faith. God does hear you, and he does respond, but sometimes what is for your best and for his glory isn't the answer you were praying for.

You are normal
Pastor Mike Novotny

When you find yourself addicted to destructive behavior, you might assume that you are not normal, the only one who struggles so deeply, so regularly, so pathetically.

But you'd be wrong.

The apostle Paul can relate to you: **"I do not understand what I do. For what I want to do I do not do, but what I hate I do. And if I do what I do not want to do, I agree that the law is good. As it is, it is no longer I myself who do it, but it is sin living in me. For I know that good itself does not dwell in me, that is, in my sinful nature. For I have the desire to do what is good, but I cannot carry it out. For I do not do the good I want to do, but the evil I do not want to do—this I keep on doing"** (Romans 7:15-19).

The human struggle versus the sinful nature might vary in its specifics (you lust, she worries, he gets angry), but we all have this in common—we don't do what we want. Not yet.

This truth is what drives us back to Jesus, trusting that only he can make us good enough to stand before the Father. And it drives us to each other, trusting that fellow Christians get it and would love to pray about it (James 5:16).

So don't let the devil convince you that you are too abnormal to belong. You belong here, in God's family, at the foot of the cross.

The most important of all
Pastor David Scharf

Name some of the most important people and positions in our world. What did you come up with? Maybe you said, "The president, corporate CEOs, pro athletes, famous actors." Did you even think of a baptized child who lives for Jesus by helping others? Did you consider as most important a Christian mother who does the dishes or a Christian father who changes a diaper? What about an employee who tries to make his boss' company the best it can be? Did you think of yourself?

Jesus did. Jesus thought of you as he left the glory of heaven, where he received his due praise as King of kings and Lord of lords, to become your servant, to become human. Jesus valued you enough to serve you by living the perfect life of service God requires and then dying on a cross for all our service failures. Now Jesus thinks of you as "great" whenever you use your gifts to serve others. And it does not need to be feats of philanthropic proportions but the everyday opportunities that Jesus gives you as a parent, child, friend, coworker, etc.

Jesus said, **"Whoever wants to become great among you must be your servant"** (Matthew 20:26). The world has it all backward when identifying the most important people and positions. But you know what Jesus considers most important! God bless you today as you carry out your work of serving—the most important work of all!

The day a tree stops growing
Pastor Daron Lindemann

One of the largest and longest-living trees in the United States is the Seven Sisters Live Oak in Mandeville, Louisiana. This massive tree is estimated to be over one thousand years old.

And it's still growing!

Actually, there is no such thing as a full-grown tree. The day a tree stops growing, it dies. There is no such thing as a full-grown Christian or a full-grown church either.

We don't graduate from learning more about life and God and this world. We don't graduate from loving God and others more thoughtfully with resources we never knew we could employ. As a church we don't graduate once we've reached a certain size.

We don't graduate. We grow personally and organizationally. We keep growing, like a tree, reaching deep, wide, and high.

"Physical training is of some value, but godliness has value for all things, holding promise for both the present life and the life to come. Be diligent in these matters; give yourself wholly to them, so that everyone may see your progress" (1 Timothy 4:8,15).

We must not use the free gift of salvation as an excuse, because it is everything but. We are *not* required to grow in order to be saved, but when we are saved, then we are required to grow.

It's still grace. It's still a gift. Grow in godliness. Give yourself wholly.

Which is better?
Pastor Clark Schultz

Which is better? Coke or Pepsi? LeBron or Jordan? Dairy Queen or Culvers? Okay, that last one is a trick question because all ice cream or custard is the best. These debates happen at the lunch table, watercooler, or even on the playground. We compare ourselves to others, and we do one of two things. We look down on the car they drive because ours is better, or we drive the minivan with the window sticker that reads, "I used to be cool."

Which side of the coin are you on? Do you look down on others, or do you use social media to look at what others have and think you've been ripped off in life?

Jesus' disciples had the "who is better" debate too. Imagine this conversation:

"Hey, Andrew!"

"Yeah, Peter."

"Remember that time we saw Jesus transfigured?"

"No, Peter. I don't."

"Oh yeah; that's right. You were at the bottom of the mountain. Stinks to be you brother!"

Jesus reminded his disciples and us that true greatness is not found in status or keeping up with the Joneses. Instead he said, **"Anyone who wants to be first must be the very last, and the servant of all"** (Mark 9:35). Jesus demonstrated this by showing the ultimate act of service and humility by living and dying for us all.

In a society of "me," Jesus' words are the best advice to follow.

It's just a thing

Pastor Jon Enter

Do you know what happened to the first light bulb ever invented? After hundreds of hours of working by Thomas Edison, his errand boy dropped and shattered it. Edison went back to work making another. When it was completed, he gave the second light bulb to the same boy. Edison forgave that boy, showing him visible forgiveness.

If a loved one is in a horrible car accident but walks away unharmed, what often is the response? "I don't care about the car; I'm relieved you're okay." But if that same person backed up the car into a light pole, severely denting the bumper, what often is the response? Frustration. Anger. Yelling about how irresponsible the driver was.

Who carelessly damaged or destroyed something you care about? Did they apologize? Did you forgive them or make them feel terrible? Paul encourages us that no matter what someone does, **"you ought to forgive and comfort him, so that he will not be overwhelmed by excessive sorrow"** (2 Corinthians 2:7).

That's exactly what Thomas Edison did. That's exactly what Jesus does for you. That's exactly what Jesus wants from you. A dented car is just a thing. A new smartphone with a shattered screen is just a thing. A lost piece of jewelry is just a thing. We should be careful with the things God has given us, but things should not be more precious than pouring out forgiveness. Whom do you need to show visible forgiveness to?

Self-control is a "fruit"
Pastor Mike Novotny

I wish self-control was a microwavable meal. Pop in a prayer request, wait a minute or two, and your self-control comes out, steaming and ready to resist sin.

But Paul didn't call self-control a microwavable meal. He called it "fruit." **"But the fruit of the Spirit is love, joy, peace, forbearance, kindness, goodness, faithfulness, gentleness and self-control"** (Galatians 5:22,23). The Holy Spirit can give you the strength to control yourself, even in a world where sin is always one second away, but he will produce that strength in you just like produce is produced.

First, you plant a seed of truth (grudge bearing or anger or drunkenness is bad; I am a holy child of God; I don't want to do this). Then, you water it with prayer (your prayers; the prayers of your closest allies). Next, you immerse that seed in the warm promises of God's love (during home devotions, while at church, through your worship playlist). And then, in due time, self-control shows up.

Forget about "fruit" and you'll get frustrated that you're not sin-free after a few weeks. Remember that this is "fruit" and you'll keep nourishing that seed until you become the kind of person you weren't before.

A person who enjoys the fruit of self-control.

Keep confessing
Pastor Mike Novotny

There is only one thing more agonizing than confessing your more embarrassing sins to another Christian. That *one thing* is confessing your embarrassing sins to another Christian *again*. Here's why I say that—It takes tremendous courage to confess to a friend. However, after your confession happens, the temptation isn't over. Sometimes the tempter triples his efforts the very night that you brought your struggle into the light. And sadly, sometimes that temptation works. You fall. You fail. You take two steps back hours after that one bold step forward.

What do you say to your friend in that moment? How mortifying is it when that conversation didn't "work," not even for a week, perhaps not even for a day? The embarrassment is enough to make you avoid the issue altogether, to vaguely claim, "I'm doing pretty well this week . . ."

Please don't. When James wrote his classic verse on confession, his original Greek said, **"Keep confessing your sins to each other"** (James 5:16). The God who inspired his words knew that confession isn't a one-and-done sort of thing. It's a lifestyle, a habit, like going to the gym week after week, trusting that the repetition will produce real results.

So keep confessing. Whether it was a good week or a bad one, keep this part of your life in the light. This practice will give your inner circle another chance to encourage you, pray for you, and tell you the best news in the universe—Through Jesus you are already perfect.

An opened mind
Christine Wentzel

While reading a study book on the 23rd Psalm, I was dangerously close to sleepwalking through the entire book. The author's study questions and answers were such familiar territory until I came to the author's chapter on the fourth verse. There her insight caused this sleepy-eyed student to stub her toes against a chest of treasure.

"Even though I walk through the valley of the shadow of death, I will fear no evil, for you are with me" (EHV). After I read through the verse, the author instructed me to go back and intentionally take note of the words *walk, through,* and *shadow.* She pointed out that I am not running in fear, not standing in terror, and not lost in the dark. Where there is shadow, there is light, and the Light in this valley is Christ, and he is with me!

The author of the study used a widely known portion of the Bible to highlight the faith-building treasures laying there for all to see. How many times do I miss the wealth of godly knowledge because I read and do not see?! The Lord's Spirit opened my mind to receive this treasure at the perfect time and also reminded me that his Word will accomplish his purpose. God's Word is alive, powerful, and true.

"If you search for it like silver, if you hunt for it like hidden treasure, then you will understand the fear of the LORD, then you will find the knowledge of God, because the LORD gives wisdom" (Proverbs 2:4-6 EHV).

God is worth it
Pastor Mike Novotny

Every advertisement in the world has the same goal—to convince you that _____ is worthy. The word *worthy* essentially means "worth it," which is why marketing gurus want to convince you that this car is worth a year's wages and this phone is worth an increased monthly payment and this makeup is worth a trip to the mall. Is all that stuff actually worth it? Maybe, maybe not.

But God is. Just ask the Magi. These mysterious travelers from modern Iran showed up in Israel, searching for the newborn King of the Jews, a journey that probably took one to two months on the bumpy back of a smelly camel. Once they found Jesus, they opened up costly treasures of gold, incense, and myrrh. Were they disappointed by 30+ nights away from their families, friends, and the comfort of their beds? Did they grumble as they got back on their camels and journeyed home, gold-less, after meeting Jesus?

Not a chance. **"When they saw the star, they were overjoyed. On coming to the house, they saw the child . . . and worshiped him"** (Matthew 2:10,11). The Magi worshiped Jesus. They declared that he was absolutely worth it.

In this life, following Jesus will cost you a lot. You will have to pay the price of calling your own shots and doing what is natural, easy, and selfish. But Jesus is worthy! One day, when you see his smiling face, you will also lock eyes with the Magi gathered around Jesus' throne. There you will shout, "You were right! It was worth it! He is worthy!"

Truth lasts forever
Pastor David Scharf

There is a legend told about a feast thrown by King Darius of Persia (the Daniel and the lions' den king). He gathered 127 governors from India to Ethiopia for a huge celebration. Part of the festivities was a contest among four young wise men who were to describe in one sentence the strongest thing in the world. Each wrote his sentence and submitted it. The first one said that wine is the strongest. The second, the king; the third, women; and the fourth, truth. The fourth wise youth explained his reason like this: "Wine, the king, and women are strong, but they are also wicked, and they perish. But truth endures forever. It is the strength, kingdom, power, and majesty of all ages."

As Christians, we couldn't agree more. Jesus said, **"When the Advocate comes, whom I will send to you from the Father—the Spirit of truth who goes out from the Father—he will testify about me"** (John 15:26). Jesus kept his promise to send the Spirit of truth at Pentecost. And what is the Holy Spirit's favorite topic? Jesus said, "He will testify about me." Just as on Pentecost when the disciples proclaimed the gospel in languages they did not know, so the Holy Spirit has been speaking truth in every language. And that truth has never changed. **"For God so loved the world that he gave his one and only Son"** (John 3:16). That truth lasts forever!

Spiritual food
Pastor Clark Schultz

What is the most unique thing you have ever eaten? Let me take you to the island of Antigua. I was there on a mission trip to help the church there. Prior to departure, I was told to respect the culture and above all eat whatever was put in front of me. My first island stop was at a church member's home, where she served fungee and pepperpot. This dish is a vegetable stew with salted meat and fungee—bread balls made with cornmeal. I remember the taste of my first bite to this day.

Matthew 3:4 tells us that John the Baptist's diet consisted of **"locusts and wild honey."** His attire, like his diet, was unique. This matched his message: **"Repent, for the kingdom of heaven has come near"** (Matthew 3:2). The word *repentance* means "to turn from the direction you are heading and go in the opposite direction."

Sometimes we find ourselves eating the "food" the world around us is serving. Dishes that include ingredients that cause us to look everywhere but to God for happiness and hope. But these things fail—they don't taste good at all! Are you eating the spiritual food of the Word of God? John's message is just as valid today: Repent and turn to the unique Savior Jesus—the Bread of life.

April 18

Easter earthquake
Pastor Daron Lindemann

Some of the worst earthquakes in our world's history have killed 200,000-300,000 people in each incident. The Bible says there was an earthquake when Jesus died, and then another earthquake when he rose to life.

"There was a violent earthquake, for an angel of the Lord came down from heaven and, going to the tomb, rolled back the stone and sat on it" (Matthew 28:2).

The earth's job is to hold people up when we're alive and then to hold us in when we're dead. However, it was forced to do the opposite to Jesus.

Roman soldiers sunk the bottom of a cross into the ground and crucified Jesus on it. The earth was holding Jesus up when he was dead. It convulsed at this moment. The innocent Son of God died!?

Jesus was buried in a tomb on Friday, and he came to life on Sunday. At that moment the earth was holding Jesus in when he was alive. It convulsed again. The living Son of God buried alive!?

These were the best earthquakes in history. These moments saved millions and millions of people because Jesus did the miraculous, the unearthly. He accomplished what normal and natural moments cannot.

The Bible says that Baptism connects believers to the death, burial, and resurrection of Jesus (Romans 6:4). These moments save you from the natural instincts of sin, from physical limitations, and even death.

Earthshaking news!

Spring = new life
Andrea Delwiche

"May God be gracious to us and bless us and make his face to shine on us—so that your ways may be known on earth, your salvation among all nations. May the peoples praise you, God; may all the peoples praise you. The land yields its harvest; God, our God, blesses us" (Psalm 67:1-3,6).

This psalm of thanksgiving and request for God's blessing reminds me of Easter. The psalmist calls on God to renew the graciousness and favor that he has promised and demonstrated since the beginning of time. And then the psalm celebrates a culmination: "The land yields its harvest; God, our God, blesses us."

The goodness of earthly harvest suggests pumpkins, apples, and the harvesting of crops in the fall. But the earth also yields its increase in spring—birds hatch, lambs are born, and seeds that have lain dormant all winter sprout and push their way through the cold earth.

For Christ followers, spring brings remembrance of our own new life, given early one spring day more than two thousand years ago when Jesus returned to life, giving all humanity a spring beginning.

This new life, our spring, benefits us now. We won't reap the full harvest until we ourselves are raised from physical death, but as we live out our time of grace here on earth, we soak in God's love and live fruitful lives, blessed by God and blessing others.

Thanks be to God for his indescribable gift of love!

Unzip that baggage
Pastor Clark Schultz

As a child of the 1980s, there were some interesting fashions: parachute pants, shoulder pads in sports coats, and my favorite—KangaRoos shoes, which were sneakers that had zipper pockets on each shoe. Why wouldn't you want zipper pockets on your feet?

While attending a big grade school basketball tournament, my mother gave me a roll of quarters to use for my food money. So Mr. Brainy here decided to shove all five dollars of quarters in both of his zipper shoe pockets. Never did it occur to my sixth-grade brain that I was walking around with a lot of extra weight. It also never dawned on me that while I played carrying all that currency in said shoes, that I was slower and couldn't move as quickly.

While diving for a ball, my shoe zippers burst open and quarters went rolling all over the wood gym floor. I can still see the officials tucking the quarters into their pockets and my coaches wondering, "Did he really have quarters in his shoes?"

"You will again have compassion on us; you will tread our sins underfoot and hurl all our iniquities into the depths of the sea" (Micah 7:19). What past sins are you lugging around? What keeps you awake at night with regret?

Friends, unzip the extra baggage and let it roll away. Christ reminds us that it is finished. Our sins are atoned for. You and I are free to hop around with joy—dare I say like kangaroos?!

None.

Pastor Mike Novotny

When I was studying New Testament Greek at Bible college, I can't say that I always loved it. Conjugating verbs and translating obscure words wasn't nearly as fun as playing FIFA on my Xbox.

But sometimes that effort brought back serious blessings. Like Romans 8:1. The English itself is glorious: **"Therefore, there is now no condemnation for those who are in Christ Jesus."** Just after admitting his constant struggle with sin in chapter 7, Paul declares that Christians like us are already saved through Jesus Christ.

But the Greek is even better. The Greek begins, "None, therefore . . ." Paul can't wait to tell us how much condemnation is left after the death and resurrection of Jesus—None! In English, we have to wait until the fifth word of the sentence (*"no* condemnation"), but Paul wanted the Romans to get the good news faster.

Isn't that amazing?! How much condemnation is hanging over your head right now? None. How much disapproval is left in God's eyes when he looks down on you? None. How many minutes do you need to worry about going to hell, falling from grace, or being rejected when heaven's feast begins? None.

If you are discouraged today, read how intensely Paul struggled in Romans 7:14-25. Then smile wide as he begins chapter 8 with a glorious word—
None!

April 22

Jesus is worthy of the center spot
Pastor David Scharf

Is Jesus at the center of your life today? Or do you need to take care of many other things before you can get to him? In a Berlin art gallery, there once hung an unfinished picture by Adolph Menzel of Frederick the Great talking to his generals. There was a small bare patch in the center of the picture where a charcoal sketch indicated the artist's intentions. He had painted in all the generals, but he had left the king for last.

That seems lifelike to us, doesn't it? We carefully put in all the generals (work, family, house, car, etc.) and leave the King for last, with the hope that someday we may still get the King in the center. Menzel died before he could finish his picture. You can get to heaven without a house or family or riches, but you can't get there without Jesus.

The apostle Paul confessed, **"I consider everything a loss because of the surpassing worth of knowing Christ Jesus my Lord, for whose sake I have lost all things. I consider them garbage, that I may gain Christ"** (Philippians 3:8). Many dedicate their lives to gaining what Paul calls garbage and a loss. Is he going too far? Not at all. On your deathbed, nothing else matters except the knowledge of Jesus.

He is everything. The One who died that I might live is worth the center spot in my life and yours. Everything else pales in comparison!

God's hands and feet
Andrea Delwiche

"Give the king your justice, O God, and your righteousness to the royal son! May he judge your people with righteousness, and your poor with justice! Let the mountains bear prosperity for the people, and the hills, in righteousness! May he defend the cause of the poor of the people, give deliverance to the children of the needy, and crush the oppressor!" (Psalm 72:1-4 ESV).

This psalm was written asking God's blessing for a king of Israel. We can incorporate these godly standards into our prayers for our own elected leaders.

We can also prayerfully consider our own "kingdoms," the places in our lives where we have authority and make decisions as citizens not only of our country but as citizens of the kingdom of heaven. How are we doing as being faithful stewards of the responsibilities God has given us?

Are we working for justice in our relationships? Are we defending the cause of the poor or giving deliverance to the children of the needy? Do we work to combat systems that oppress other people? Are our neighbors, no matter their ethnicity, preferences, or theology, precious in our sight?

We are God's hands and feet in this world. While God can act supernaturally to bring about change, mostly he chooses to work with you and me, giving us the privilege of loving and defending others. Ask the Holy Spirit to give you insight into how you can be the heart, hands, and feet of Jesus in your community.

You are not a black sheep
Pastor Mike Novotny

When Ananias reached out his hands toward the serial killer, I wonder if they were trembling. God had spoken directly to Ananias, sending him to the house where Saul of Tarsus was sitting, praying, and waiting.

Ananias knew what every believer in Damascus did, namely, that Saul was a bad man. He was obsessed, violent, and relentless, the kind of guy who would walk six marathons to travel from Jerusalem to Damascus to find a Christian, arrest a Christian, and kill anyone who dared to claim that Jesus was the Christost.

So when Ananias met that Saul, the Saul who came to kill him, what would he say? Acts 9 tells us, **"Then Ananias went to the house and entered it. Placing his hands on Saul, he said, 'Brother Saul'"** (verse 17).

No joke. The first word out of his lips was *brother*. "Saul, you are my brother in Christ. Saul, you are part of my Father's family too. Saul, despite what you have done, you belong at the table as my brother in faith."

If you have been struggling with sin, whether drinking too much or worrying too much or losing your cool too much, it's tempting to wonder which word Christians would use to describe you. *Weak? Self-destructive? Embarrassing?* But that is not who you are. In Christ you get a new name, purchased at the cross and guaranteed by the empty grave.

Through faith in Jesus, you are my brother or my sister, my sibling in the holiest family on earth. Believe it and live according to it.

DEBT: A four-letter word
Pastor Jon Enter

Debt can make you do spiritually dumb things. Debt causes stress, affecting your relationships and your waistline. Debt causes fights over spending habits. Debt causes lying and deception. Debt causes unfaithfulness in offerings to God. Debt destroys.

Jesus came in humility, showing that the most valuable things aren't things. Jesus was born into a poor family, in a backwater town, to a conquered people. As an adult, Jesus lived as a wanderer, couch surfing the countryside. But Jesus was no lazy leech. He chose not to focus on money but on making his Father pleased with his perfect living. He taught us to focus not on money but on our Maker.

"It was not with perishable things such as silver or gold that you were redeemed . . . but with the precious blood of Christ" (1 Peter 1:18,19). God has forgiven you and released you from the control that money desires to have over you. You were not saved with perishable things, so don't live to save up perishable things.

There are nearly 2,200 Bible passages dealing with money and materialism. How do you step free from its control? A.B.C.

Acknowledge all you have comes from God. Use it well.

Budget God's money. Use it well.

Control your spending. Use it well.

When you do, the stress of debt will stop pulling your focus off God. Control your money so your money doesn't control you.

How many motives?

Pastor Mike Novotny

If I made you write an essay listing all the reasons to avoid sin, how long would your essay be?

I wouldn't give you a minimum word count or force you to cite your references in APA style (I'm not a monster!), but I wonder if you could find a pen and scribble down all the motivating reasons that pop into your mind. Fix your eyes on all the good things that God loves and that sin threatens, reminding your heart that our Father truly knows best. Go ahead. I'll wait.

To get you started, let me list my top two. Second on my list is the drama that sin causes in my life. King David wrote, **"Those who run after other gods will suffer more and more"** (Psalm 16:4). The false god of pleasure asks me to sacrifice too much—my integrity, my time, my honesty, my intimacy. The more sin I run after, the more I suffer.

But even more motivating than such loss is Jesus' love. **"For Christ's love compels us"** (2 Corinthians 5:14). The more we meditate on Jesus' love, the love that gave up all pleasure and endured such pain, the more we don't want to sin. We have found something more satisfying, more enjoyable, more interesting than sin could ever provide. We have found a love that never fails.

Reflect on those two reasons and add a few of your own. God motivates us in many ways to say no to sin and yes to him.

Reassurance
Christine Wentzel

"For I am convinced that neither death nor life, neither angels nor demons, neither the present nor the future, nor any powers, nor height nor depth, nor anything else in all creation, will be able to separate us from the love of God that is in Christ Jesus our Lord" (Romans 8:38,39).

My Savior has my back! I picture Jesus looking over my head, holding all those deadly bullies at bay with one blazing, glorified stare. Praise the Lord!

Sadly, there are times I take this for granted by handling business on my own. When I'm at this too long, I'm tempted to drift away from consistent worship, study, and prayer until the next day, next week, next month, or, God forbid, the next year.

On my own, doubt creeps in when my broken-down, aging body no longer follows orders from my frustrated brain. My frustrated brain loses control of my disappointed heart. My disappointed heart demands justice according to my sense of fairness. Before long I'm tempted to become uncertain that Jesus is still there.

It's not just the outside enemies trying to steal me away; it's the enemy within as well. It's time to go back to Romans 8. By God's grace, Christ my King is still there. I look into his blazing eyes of compassion. I sink to my knees in repentance in the realization I allowed pride to usurp his sovereignty over this new life he gifted to me.

Nothing will separate me, not even myself!

Why, God?

Pastor Clark Schultz

A friend, colleague, husband, and father is suddenly called home to heaven. Why, God? Bluntly speaking, life stinks. When we grieve, and trust me, we will, we go through the following steps: denial, anger, bargaining, and depression.

We deny that God could take our dad, child, or best friend. "No, you have to be kidding." Soon we realize there will be no more text messages between us or a warm embrace. We become mad—mad at the world and at God. Why, God? This leads to thinking we have some control over the matter. "If I had just told him not to go on the snowmobiling trip, he'd still be here today." Or, "If I had done a better job at being a dad, I would have noticed the symptoms earlier." Wrong! When this proves hopeless, depression can set in. The devil works overtime during this period to get us to think God does not care.

Where are you on this grief roller coaster? Grief and mourning are real. I have said this before, and I echo it again. It is okay to ask for help. Yes, of course, from your Father in heaven, but also professional help and help from others who have gone through this. Then the final stage of acceptance can take place and you can say with the psalmist: **"My times are in your hands; deliver me from the hands of my enemies, from those who pursue me"** (31:15).

Dispel our doubts
Pastor David Scharf

Fill in the blank to describe this well-known Bible character: _____ Thomas. I bet you got it: Doubting Thomas. He wasn't there that first Easter Sunday evening when the risen Jesus appeared to the other disciples. Can you imagine the disciples saying to him, "Jesus really showed up! It was awesome!" Well, Thomas refused to believe it. A week later, Jesus appeared again. This time Thomas got to see him with his own eyes and touch him with his own hands. Jesus said, **"Reach out your hand and put it into my side. Stop doubting and believe"** (John 20:27). Thomas was no longer Doubting Thomas!

I had a friend in high school who always struggled with some challenge to what the Bible says. He would wrestle with it, and God would lead him to understand, but then another doubt would pop up. I thought, "Why does that happen to him?" A better question might be, "Why does that happen to us?" It has to do with our approach to what Jesus says. We don't believe it because we can prove it. We believe it because the powerful and risen Son of God says it. It's true. Living in that truth dispels our doubts! When we have doubts, where do we turn? Right back to our Savior who encourages, **"Blessed are those who have not seen and yet have believed"** (John 20:29).

The truth
Pastor Clark Schultz

If I hold up three fingers and ask you, "How many fingers am I holding up?" I'm hoping you say three. It would be foolish to see the three fingers and say, "I don't believe you; you have four fingers up." Or what if I say, "I'm holding up three fingers," and you still insist I'm holding up four fingers? That would be a complete denial of what's in front of you—the truth. I know this is an odd analogy, but hear me out. There's a point; I promise.

Why is it when God tells us we are **"fearfully and wonderfully made"** (Psalm 139:14), instead of praising him like the rest of that verse says, we often insist it's not true? We look in the mirror and feel ashamed. We scroll on social media and compare ourselves to others. We take the lack of likes on our Facebook posts to mean we're failures. We think we have no purpose or no special gifts or talents to contribute anything to anyone.

Dear friend, believing these lies is like holding up three fingers and saying there are four. When you see three fingers held up, that's the truth . . . three fingers. The same is true about what God says about you. He made you—fearfully and wonderfully! He loves you—enough to send his only Son to save you! He gave you unique gifts and talents to be used to his glory—yes, he did! (See 1 Peter 4:10 or Romans 12:6-8.)

You can praise God with all of Psalm 139:14: **"I praise you because I am fearfully and wonderfully made; your works are wonderful, I know that full well."**

God doesn't make junk; that's the truth.

MAY

I am the vine; you are the branches. If you remain
in me and I in you, you will bear much fruit;
apart from me you can do nothing.

John 15:5

Jesus woos, not woes
Pastor David Scharf

In one of Aesop's fables, the wind and sun prepared to make a man shed his coat. The wind used its violence and force to tear the coat off, but the man only bound himself all the more within it. The sun gradually used its warmth on the man, and he voluntarily shed the coat himself. In a way, the sun wooed him to want to take off his coat.

This is how Jesus wants to win you. Jesus said of the people of Israel, **"How often I have longed to gather your children together, as a hen gathers her chicks under her wings"** (Luke 13:34). Sadly, they were not willing. But here is the point. Jesus does not shame you with woes. He does not force or intimidate you. Instead, he longs to gather you by warming your heart with his love and reminding you of what he's done.

No matter how many times you and I try to scurry away from Jesus, he gathers us back under the wings of his forgiveness. How? He woos us with his words, *"Then neither do I condemn you . . . surely, I am with you always . . . in my Father's house are many rooms."* No matter how often we stray, Jesus woos us back by showing us just how much he loves us. Far more than any hen for her chicks. Jesus suffered hell on a cross so that you and I would go to heaven. Now we are safe under Jesus' wings!

How's your journey going?
Andrea Delwiche

Some biblical scholars believe Psalm 71 was written by King David in the later years of his life to reflect upon the journey that he had taken with the Lord from conception onward. From these verses, we get an intimate sense of how David viewed his lifelong relationship with God:

For you, O Lord, are my hope, my trust, O LORD, from my youth. Upon you I have leaned from before my birth. . . . So even to old age and gray hairs, O God, do not forsake me, until I proclaim your might to another generation, your power to all those to come" (verses 5,6,18 ESV).

How would you chronicle your history with the Lord? Can you look back to childhood and see, especially with the benefit of years, how God taught you? Or do you remember a point in your teenage years or adulthood when you first realized that God was walking with you and guiding you?

Perhaps even now you are contemplating how to trust God and let him teach and guide and protect your every step. David's testimony gives us an example of what wholehearted faith looks like and sounds like. David's relationship with God was mature and well-tested.

How would you describe your journey? What if you sat down and wrote a psalm of praise to God for the work he has done in your life? Ask the Holy Spirit to guide you as you contemplate the journey that you've been taking with the Lord.

Seek and save
Linda Buxa

"For the Son of Man came to seek and to save the lost" (Luke 19:10).

In October 2021, a hiker was lost in Colorado. As part of their search, rescuers called the hiker's smartphone but never got ahold of her. You know why she didn't answer? Not because service was bad but because she didn't recognize the number! That's right. She was lost, but because she didn't know who was calling, she didn't answer the phone.

It's an amusing story because ultimately it turned out okay, but it made me think about people who are spiritually lost. Maybe, just like the lost hiker, they won't answer a spiritual rescue call from a stranger. When people are lost, they might not be open to talking about sin and grace, heaven and hell, with a stranger. Honestly, I don't blame them. Who wants to open up about such deeply personal things with someone who hasn't earned the right to have that conversation?

Ah, but when the same message comes from someone who knows them, loves them, and cares for them, it has a far bigger impact. They will be far more open to it when a friend says, "I was lost too, and Jesus came looking for me. Mind if I share my amazing story of being rescued?"

You know someone who is lost. Start by making the call. There may not be much time left.

Pray for people
Pastor Mike Novotny

I hear a lot of confessions about pornography. Both men and women, young and old, married and single schedule a time to talk and, for the first time, bring their darkness into the light.

My response to these courageous confessions is almost always the same. First, I tell them God loves them. Second, I thank them for trusting me enough to talk about it. Third, I try to figure out how intense their struggle is. Fourth, I ask them a question: Whom in your life could you talk to about this?

For some, that question is easy to answer. But for others, it's met with silence. It's hard to know who would respond well to their sexual sin, whom they could trust, and who would want to help them fight for self-control.

How about you? Whom in your life could you talk to about this sin (or any other)? If someone immediately comes to mind, praise God! Reach out today and keep confessing. But if you are unsure, here's where to start—pray for people. Pray that God would open your eyes to a person who is fully capable of walking with you, someone in your church or in your circle of friends, someone who would be honored to pray for you so you may be healed.

"Ask and it will be given to you; seek and you will find; knock and the door will be opened to you. For everyone who asks receives; the one who seeks finds; and to the one who knocks, the door will be opened" (Matthew 7:7,8).

Stage presence
Christine Wentzel

Everyone has stage presence in the virtual world of social media. There we can create our own realities while interacting on a global scale like never before. It's in these digital settings we usually don't hesitate to tie ourselves up in knots like we might in face-to-face situations. We share our thoughts, actions, and whereabouts in the most excruciating, even hyperbolic detail. False courage grows in this so-called safe setting.

Let's reevaluate our stage presence. Who is the star? Is it real? Who makes guest appearances? Do we text, tweet, pin, or email **"whatever is true, whatever is noble, whatever is right, whatever is pure, whatever is lovely, whatever is admirable"** (Philippians 4:8)?

Our fingertips are a tap away from posting some of the most uplifting Christian faith stories! Let's grab the opportunity to share how awesome the work of Jesus is. Provide information that will send people seeking answers to their lives from Bible-believing ministries like Time of Grace. There they will discover Jesus in every platform available. Use the Word of God to speak power that enlivens dead souls for heaven's sake!

Whether our audience is a few or in the millions, there are lost souls in our circles who need to know a personally invested Lord and Savior is their Morning Star in this dark world. Let's step aside and announce Christ has the center stage.

"Whatever you have learned or received or heard from me, or seen in me—put it into practice. And the God of peace will be with you" (Philippians 4:9).

Lipstick and a toilet brush
Pastor Daron Lindemann

A high school principal was frustrated by the repeated lipstick graffiti on the girls' bathroom mirrors.

One day she asked a group of girls to assemble in the bathroom. She showed them the lipstick graffiti and explained how much extra work this was for the custodian.

Then she asked the custodian to dip a toilet brush in a toilet and clean the mirror with it. The girls didn't use their lipstick on the mirror again!

I would add one more thing. After the custodian cleaned off the lipstick with the toilet brush, I would have him shine up the mirror and make it dazzle. Then I would have each girl look in the mirror, and I'd ask, "Whom do you see?"

I'd answer, before they could say a word: "A daughter of God." I'd teach that daughters of God are princesses in his kingdom—very precious, perfectly pure, desired by Jesus Christ himself.

The attention-getting graffiti and validation of peers isn't needed because the goodness of God and gifts of God are true.

"Don't be deceived," the Bible says. **"Every good and perfect gift is from above, coming down from the Father of the heavenly lights, who does not change like shifting shadows"** (James 1:16,17).

What lies of the devil do you believe most often that cause you to seek filthy attention and sin? Don't be deceived. Live your true identity as a child of God. That identity is a good and perfect gift.

Who does that?

Pastor David Scharf

"Who does that?" That question can be a wonderful compliment, like when you hear a story of someone donating their kidney to a total stranger. Or the question can be shocking disbelief in a negative way, like when someone shows unusual cruelty to another who didn't deserve it.

The Bible writers consistently look at God and ask, "Who does that?" Only it's never in the negative way. What do you do for people who are born enemies, whose lives give evidence of that inborn hatred, who walk away from you with their thoughts, words, and actions—who don't fully admit the sin in their lives?

God's answer? You die for them. You forgive them. It is what lead Micah the prophet to burst out, **"Who is a God like you, who pardons sin and forgives the transgression of the remnant of his inheritance? You do not stay angry forever but delight to show mercy"** (Micah 7:18). Think of how unlike anyone or anything our God is. Every other "god" of every world religion teaches salvation by good works. In order to please their gods, they must do good works. Adherents are forced to ask, "What must I do?" In Christianity, we do good works *because* God is already pleased. Christians instead ask, "What has God done?" We are compelled to look at Jesus' cross in awe with the Bible writers and ask, "Who does that? Who is a God like you who pardons sins?"

A daily reminder
Pastor Clark Schultz

Allow me to introduce you to my number-one enemies—anxiety and doubt. How often I forget the words
of God when a crisis or problem hits close to home: **"Do
not be anxious about anything, but in every situation,
by prayer and petition, with thanksgiving, present
your requests to God"** (Philippians 4:6). The apostle
Paul wrote this while under house arrest in Rome. One
could argue he had a right to be anxious or upset

"Being anxious" means to be distracted or pulled
in several different directions at once. Our lives offer
myriad opportunities and excuses to fret. God doesn't
tell us to divvy up the big stuff for him and leave the
little piddly stuff to ourselves. We can go to him in
prayer. We can bring everything to him with thankful
hearts because we are approaching him as our dear
Father in heaven. Jesus has seen to that!

In a world where time-saving technology seems
to quicken life's frantic pace and add to its frenzied
distractions, in a society that emphasizes and acclaims
self-achievement, when our broken selves crave the
idiocy of solving our own spiritual problems, we need this
reminder from Paul—to focus on God as the one source
of everything we have and are. Jesus alone gives peace
to our worried hearts, and we need to keep reminding
ourselves of that daily!

The uniqueness of Jesus
Pastor Mike Novotny

Decades ago, at a European conference, scholars discussed the world's religions, wondering if there was anything unique about the Christian faith. Was it prayer? No, almost every religion prays. An afterlife? No, most religions believe in some sort of heaven and/or hell. Doctrine? Too common. Commandments? Standard. Men in fancy hats? The norm.

But then, according to church legend, C. S. Lewis entered the room, the Oxford professor who had converted to Christianity in his early 30s. What's unique about the Christian faith? "That's easy," Lewis replied. "Grace."

That's true. The earliest followers of Jesus Christ were uniquely infatuated with grace. Study the loaded word *grace* in the New Testament and you'll learn that grace reaches people, appears to people, and is poured out on people so that they find grace, receive grace, believe by grace, and share in grace. Christians, the Scriptures say, are people chosen by grace, called by grace, saved by grace, justified by grace, living in grace, and living under grace. Grace is with us, works in us, and sufficient for us. Grace overflows, increases, reigns, strengthens, and gives access to God. That's why we set our hope on grace, grow in grace, and preach the glorious grace of God. In fact, the very last verse of the entire Bible says, **"The grace of the Lord Jesus be with God's people. Amen"** (Revelation 22:21).

Grace gets the last word because the Christian faith is about grace. Undeserved love. Surprising favor. I can't imagine believing any other way. Can you?

Quiet; be still
Pastor Jon Enter

I've never been in a boat in rough water. Have you? I almost drowned when I was about ten, so choppy water makes me anxious. I couldn't imagine how bad the storm must've been for the disciples for them to cry out to Jesus, **"Don't you care if we drown?"** (Mark 4:38).

What storm is pummeling your life, causing you to doubt God's power? No matter what you've done, no matter how hard you've tried to rise above, you sink further into despair that your situation is hopeless. The pounding of the waves of worry are relentless when the storm surrounds you. It's easy to be overwhelmed.

For the disciples, Jesus was physically right there, but they doubted his concern for their lives. What's amazing is how Jesus responded to their accusation: **"He got up, rebuked the wind and said to the waves, 'Quiet! Be still!'"** (Mark 4:39). Notice that Jesus didn't rebuke the water; he told the water to be still. Jesus rebuked the wind that caused the chaos. When the wind's power over the water was removed, the water was calm.

When you struggle to see God's power and even when you come to him unsure of how he will intervene, you still come to him. You know he is the only way peace can come, even if you don't understand how. Jesus will rebuke and remove the sin and uncertainty overtaking your life. When it's gone, quietness and calm will come.

You shine!

Pastor Daron Lindemann

In the rural hill country of Texas, miles away from city lights, many more stars appear in the night sky. It puts my constellation skills to the test. Where exactly is the North Star?

If you can locate the outer edge of the Big Dipper's bowl (the edge farther from the handle), draw an imaginary line extending from the star on the bottom through the star on the top. This line takes you directly to the North Star.

It takes a bit of knowledge and practice—or an app on your phone—to identify constellations. But there is one star you have no problem identifying. The sun! Same with the moon at night. Much more obvious.

You probably even know how the moon shines light. The moon doesn't generate its own light, like the sun, but reflects the light of the sun.

The Bible says that Christians are **"children of light"** (Ephesians 5:8). We don't generate our own light, like children don't bring themselves into existence. We reflect a greater light. The light of God.

God shines. Believe in him, and you are enlightened by him, like the moon. You shine too. Others can look at you and say, "I see a reflection of God." No, you aren't God. Just like the moon is not the sun. But you do shine with God's light.

The Bible calls both Jesus and his believers **"the light of the world"** (John 8:12; Matthew 5:14). So go shine today!

The cure
Christine Wentzel

I am one of over 14 million people who suffer from some form of autoimmune disease. If you add those who suffer from the thousands of other diseases and disorders, there are few left untouched by chronic illness.

However, there's one fatal disease we all have in common—it's called sin. Every person experiences variations of hate, sadness, conflict, intolerance, illness, disregard, brutality, and overindulgence, and all of it ends in death. We adopt various lifestyles, choose the latest health fads, chase down scientific studies, and enact societal laws to pursue a paradise lost on the earth.

"Nevertheless, I will bring health and healing to it; I will heal my people and will let them enjoy abundant peace and security" (Jeremiah 33:6).

Out of love, God promised to send the cure while we were still sinning against him. His Son, Jesus, willingly laid aside his immortality for a mortal life lived in perfect obedience for us. He fulfilled all the Old Testament prophecies predicting his coming rescue for humankind. He took the sin of all humanity upon himself. He destroyed the power of the grave by walking out of his.

Our hope for all that is broken and dying is found in only one cure, Jesus. May we triage people's sickness of sin with his Spirit-driven, love-joy-peace-patience-kindness-goodness-faithfulness-gentleness-self-control Good News medicine!

Guardrails
Pastor Mike Novotny

Over a decade ago, I heard a brilliant teaching on the need for adding rules to the Bible.

If that sounds bad, it wasn't. It was wise. The pastor talked about personal "guardrails," rules that keep us far from the edge of a tragic fall into sin. For example, if you struggle with drunkenness, limiting yourself to one drink (or no drinks!) might be a guardrail that keeps you from going over the edge and hurting the people whom God loves so dearly. There is no passage that demands, "You shall have no more than one drink," but there is wisdom in knowing yourself and acting accordingly.

"Be very careful, then, how you live—not as unwise but as wise" (Ephesians 5:15).

What would a wise guardrail look like in your life? If anger is your issue, which triggers could you avoid that too often lead to your outbursts? Is it watching certain channels or visiting certain websites? If so, have the wisdom to cut temptation off before it even arrives.

You will never regret looking back and playing it safe with your holiness. So be a student of your own story, note the times/places/situations that are most often connected to your sin, and make the bold choice to stay far from the cliff of temptation.

That's how wise people live.

What's your secret?
Pastor Jon Enter

Hello. My name is Jon Enter. Husband. Father of four. Pastor. Coach. Sin addict.

And so are you. You may not see it. You may not be willing to admit it. But you are. You have sins you know are wrong, but you do them anyway. You want to stop. You can't or, really, you won't stop. You're an addict. And so am I. You can't keep your dirty little obsession a secret forever.

Just ask the family of Diane Schuler. In 2009 she hid her alcohol addiction from her family. She drove intoxicated into oncoming traffic resulting in her own death and the deaths of seven innocent people. Then her family and the nation learned the truth.

What is it?

What's your addiction? The devil is unoriginal. He uses the same tired temptations against you. Why? It works. It works so well because the excuses flow freely. "I can stop at any time." "It's not that bad." "No one knows." "I'm in control." "It's not as bad as . . ."

Addiction makes you do irrational things, like making excuses over what you know is hurting you physically, emotionally, and spiritually. It's hard to admit you're powerless to temptation that's trying to squeeze the life out of your soul. **"Humble yourselves before the Lord, and he will lift you up"** (James 4:10). God will lift you up because he lifted up his Son upon a cross to pay the price for you to free you from the clutches of the devil. Humble yourself. And you will be lifted up.

God is with you
Pastor Clark Schultz

It was mid-July. A discussion broke out in our car between our two older boys regarding when school was going to start.

"Not soon enough," mumbled the parents under their breath (☺). But being the adults, we told our middle child that school would be starting in less than a month. His five-year-old response cracked us up: "A whole month? That's like a whole week away!"

"But do not forget this one thing, dear friends: With the Lord a day is like a thousand years, and a thousand years are like a day" (2 Peter 3:8). Is this saying our God is on toddler time? I mean, think about it. When you were younger, summers seemed to last forever, but then you grew up and thought, "Where did the time go? It seems the days are speeding by." There are days when you feel like you're trapped in the eternal car ride of sickness, bills, and fights with siblings. Those days don't seem to speed by quickly enough.

We live in a broken world. Sin makes the miserable times seem like eternity and the good times like catching water in our hands. In both cases, God is God. His timetable is not ours, and he is not bound by the minutes and seconds we hold so dear. While this can seem frightening, remember Hebrews 13:8: **"Jesus Christ is the same yesterday and today and forever."**

Months, weeks, yesterday, today, and tomorrow you are with God.

How much does Jesus love you?
Pastor Daron Lindemann

I need to choose from my many shoes and shirts which to wear each day. As a matter of fact, I have to choose which closet I go to. When I'm hungry, I stand in front of the fridge, not for lack of food but because the options take time to consider.

How much does Jesus give to you? How much healing and hope? How much mercy? How much provision and power? How much of his personal presence?

When he suffered and died for you, did he throw his hands in the air and say, "Enough! I can't take anymore" and bail out? How attentive is he when listening to your prayers? Does he watch the birds flit around for entertainment while you are droning on and on about your troubles?

How much does Jesus love you? More than you need.

"I have come that they may have life, and have it to the full" (John 10:10).

Jesus miraculously fed over five thousand hungry people so full that his disciples collected leftover food. He fills your life with more than you need. Follow him and you'll find more than morsels.

Jesus miraculously turned water into not just any wine but the best of the best wine. He abundantly turns your empty hopes and dreams into the best of his best blessings. Drink from him and you'll be filled.

Jesus gives you more than necessary, more than you need, more than enough. Be satisfied with him more than everything else.

A conversation with God
Andrea Delwiche

Here's an honest conversation with God:
"When my soul was embittered, when I was pricked in heart, I was brutish and ignorant; I was like a beast toward you. Nevertheless, I am continually with you; you hold my right hand. You guide me with your counsel, and afterward you will receive me to glory. Whom have I in heaven but you? And there is nothing on earth that I desire besides you. My flesh and my heart may fail, but God is the strength of my heart and my portion forever" (Psalm 73:21-25 ESV).

It seems the psalm writer had been harboring bitterness toward God. We get an intimate look at his thought process—first the grievance and then a slowly developing realization that opens like a rosebud. This psalm becomes a heartfelt cry of love for God.

These words could be an entry point into a deeper relationship with God. Sometimes we're opposed to God. Our hearts feel like wood blocks. But beneath the emotions lie hope and longing for a relationship with God.

It's good to have a conversation with God about disappointment and anger. He can handle it. The Holy Spirit may guide us into fuller understanding.

Yes, there is inequity, injustice, and brokenness. And yes, God is with us. We live and have our being in God's intimate company. The words of the psalmist are our own: **"I am continually with you; you hold my right hand. You guide me with your counsel, and afterward you will receive me to glory."**

Temporary residents
Pastor Clark Schultz

While visiting Charleston recently, I heard the unique legend and mystery of former Vice President John C. Calhoun's grave. Calhoun was buried in Washington D.C. and then exhumed and moved to Charleston to a "strangers" grave—one for people who were not Charleston natives.

Then during the Civil War, his body was again exhumed and moved to an unmarked grave in a "friendly" graveyard as a precaution against any Union troop desecration. This graveyard was reserved for members of the congregation who were born in Charleston. According to legend, after the war Calhoun's body was moved back to its current sight—the "strangers" graveyard.

The Bible reminds us that we are **"aliens and temporary residents"** (1 Peter 2:11 EHV). Some Bible translations use the word *strangers*. There's even a popular hymn by Thomas R. Taylor that says, "I'm but a stranger here; heaven is my home."

For the believer, there will be no shuffling from grave to grave, just this: **"For the Lord himself will come down from heaven, with a loud command, with the voice of the archangel and with the trumpet call of God, and the dead in Christ will rise first"** (1 Thessalonians 4:16). The war is over. The battle is won. We are on the winning side, and Jesus himself says, **"I have called you friends"** (John 15:15).

My grave or yours, be confident that the only time we will be moved is when Jesus welcomes us home.

Your activity is not your identity
Pastor Mike Novotny

Years ago I tapped into my Bible nerdery and tried to count all the names that Christians are called in the New Testament. In some verses, we are called "sinners," "weak," and "of little faith" while in other verses we are called "saints," "strong," and "loved" by the Lord.

For souls who are already perfect in Christ but not yet perfect in our behavior, this makes sense.

What shocked me, however, is the ratio of bad names to good names. If my unofficial tally is correct, I found 72 bad names (sinners, weak, etc.) in the New Testament and—you ready for this?—610 good names! 610! For every one time that God calls us "sinners," nine times he calls us "saints"!

I wonder if this is what Paul alluded to when he wrote, **"But where sin increased, grace increased all the more"** (Romans 5:20). Yes, our sins are many, but his grace is more. Much, much, much more.

So as you go through the daily battle to deny self and honor God with your life, feel free to call yourself a sinner. The Bible does. But if you want to be biblically balanced, then call yourself all the other names too— Holy. Pure. Loved. Chosen. Justified. Sanctified. Redeemed. Blameless. Spotless.

That's not me trying to make you feel better about yourself. That's God reminding you of your incredible identity in Christ Jesus.

Don't just get by
Pastor Clark Schultz

A famous superhero claims that his shield is made from the strongest metal on earth. Nothing can break it! In Ephesians 6:16, the apostle Paul reminds us that we have something stronger: **"the shield of faith."**

The object of our faith is Jesus, and he is the strongest of all. How much are you connecting to him? A small amount of faith saves, middle-of-the-road faith saves, and all-hands-on-deck faith saves because of the object of that faith—Jesus.

But for those of us who look to "just get by," what happens when the wind and waves of debt, divorce, or depression come crashing? A faith like that may be penetrable.

I'm not saying the object of our faith lets us down, but our connection to him can be knocked a bit off balance if just-getting-by faith is all we strive for. Sometimes folks who had enough faith to just get by walk away from the faith when the first battle came to test them.

Stay connected! The fact that you are reading this right now is a great start. Continue to stay plugged in. What are other ways to connect? Prayer, personal Bible study or with friends, a Time of Grace video or devotion.

When the waves of life hit, and they will, you have the strongest defense. It's not your works, looks, or bank account, which all fail or falter. You have Christ! He's the real superhero, and by faith so are you!

Your audience of one
Pastor Daron Lindemann

The audience gathers eagerly. The eighth-grade band students are dressed in their best backstage, nervously waiting for each of their names to be called for a solo performance.

Like professional performers, they will be on stage under the lights all by themselves, and judges will issue a score.

Amber has prepared for this but still feels her nerves fluttering. She paces back and forth until she hears her name. The curtains open, and for a split second she considers turning around and running. She can't do this! She's going to make a mistake!

But she nervously takes center stage and raises her violin.

As she begins, she sees in the audience the smiling, approving face of her mother—no judgment, no fear, just a bunch of mom pride and eager excitement for the best performance in the world.

And that's what Amber does, performs her best in the world. Her mom is her audience of one. When Amber saw her mom, it changed everything.

"Whatever you do, work at it with all your heart, as working for the Lord, not for human masters. . . . It is the Lord Christ you are serving" (Colossians 3:23,24).

Serve Jesus as your audience of One in whatever you do.

In mercy he forgives you of everything and smiles approvingly at everything you do for him—no judgment, no fear, just a bunch of heavenly pride and eager excitement for your best performance in the world.

Free stuff
Linda Buxa

Every August in Madison, Wisconsin, moving days are a bargain shoppers' dream. As apartment leases end, college students fill the sidewalks and curbs with possessions they no longer want. As the residents are moving out, other people flock in looking for a free dining table or couch or bookshelves or lamp. It's the whole "one man's trash is another man's treasure" concept. People flock to free.

God does this too—except instead of setting out his trash, he gave us his treasure: **"He who did not spare his own Son, but gave him up for us all—how will he not also, along with him, graciously give us all things?"** (Romans 8:32).

God sent Jesus, his own Son, to earth and allowed him to be treated like trash—rejected, scorned, beaten, and crucified in our place. Jesus suffered the punishment we deserved so that God could give us peace, joy, life, and eternity as free gifts.

Because the Father's treasure is now our treasure, it changes how we live: **"Let us run with perseverance the race marked out for us, fixing our eyes on Jesus, the pioneer and perfecter of faith. . . . Consider him who endured such opposition from sinners, so that you will not grow weary and lose heart"** (Hebrews 12:1-3).

Sitting shotgun with Jesus
Pastor Mike Novotny

Once upon a time, Jesus pulled a 15-passenger van into a man's driveway. He honked the horn, rolled down the window as the door opened, and smiled, "Hey, it's me, Jesus. I got room if you want."

The man looked around in disbelief, "Me? You're inviting me? Um, yeah! Give me a second to pack all my stuff."

"Oh, wait," Jesus said. "We don't have room for that, but we have room for you. You in?" But the man looked back and saw the home he loved, his leather chair, his new 65" TV, and the evidence of his comfortable life. He glanced back at Jesus, who was still waiting, still smiling, but the man's face fell. Without a word, he quietly closed the door.

Did you know that something like that happened once? You can read the story in Mark 10, but here's the saddest part: **"At this the man's face fell. He went away sad, because he had great wealth"** (verse 22).

I won't lie to you. Jesus wants all of you. He wants you to follow him, no matter what dreams, goals, or comforts you might have had before he showed up. This is why so many people break eye contact with Christ and quietly close the door.

But don't! Because Jesus wants you to follow him. He wants your life to be lived at the side of the Son of God and Savior of the world.

What an offer! What a blessing, no matter the cost, to be with Christ!

Take the world, but give me Jesus
Pastor David Scharf

It is amazing how many giants of music and the arts today weren't recognized as giants when they were alive. Schubert couldn't find steady employment. Rembrandt died in bankruptcy. Mozart worked himself into a state of sickness that finally killed him. Van Gogh's paintings were spat on by respectable people in his homeland of the Netherlands, and he struggled with poverty.

Jesus is the ultimate example of not being appreciated in his day for who he was: *the* Way, *the* Truth, *the* Life. By and large, Jesus was rejected by his contemporaries, and yet the works of our Savior still change lives and eternities today. Jesus once said of himself, **"The stone the builders rejected has become the cornerstone"** (Luke 20:17). What do you see when you look at Jesus? Do you see the cornerstone that gives direction to the many things in your life, or do you see Jesus as just one of many things that take up your attention in this world?

The reformer Martin Luther had a test to find out if Jesus is really your cornerstone in life. Here it is. When the chips are down in your life, what do you look to for vindication? financial success? family? career? If so, that *underappreciates* what you have in Jesus. Instead, look to the cross. There you find not only your forgiveness but the foundation for every aspect of your life. Take the world, but give me Jesus!

Seed, sword, Spirit, life
Pastor Mike Novotny

For those who are new to the Old and New Testaments, the Bible might seem like an encyclopedia, a dry and dusty text that people own but rarely read. But the Bible is more. So much more.

The Bible is like a seed, so small you could miss it or entirely dismiss it, yet so packed with potential it could produce, according to Jesus, **"a hundred, sixty or thirty times what was sown"** (Matthew 13:23).

The Bible is like a sword, the weapon that keeps you alive in this spiritual war **"so that you can take your stand against the devil's schemes"** (Ephesians 6:11).

The Bible is full of the Spirit, working invisibly, powerfully, and supernaturally, leading Paul to state that **"faith comes from hearing the message, and the message is heard through the word about Christ"** (Romans 10:17).

The Bible is life itself, prompting Peter to resist the done-with-Jesus crowds and confess, **"Lord, to whom shall we go? You have the words of eternal life"** (John 6:68).

There is no other book that is worthy of so much of your limited time in this life. You are no fool if you begin or end each day (or both!) in the God-breathed, Spirit-filled, life-changing Scriptures.

Because these Scriptures are seed, sword, Spirit, and life.

The Word is a seed

Pastor Mike Novotny

I told Ricardo, one of my soccer teammates, about a Bible app that people at my church loved. A year later he said, "Mike, I'm almost done reading the Bible on that app you told me about."

He was in the homestretch of his first-ever time reading the Scriptures! Even better was what he told me about his soul: how the Word had been changing him, especially in his attitude at home and the way he handled stress at work. I was given a fresh reminder that the littlest moments can turn into the biggest blessings in the kingdom of God.

Because God's Word is like a seed. When we read the Bible, hear the Bible, pray the Bible, share the Bible, or discuss the Bible, God is scattering seeds in our hearts. These seeds are potential-packed truths that grow into some of our biggest blessings.

Jesus taught, **"But the seed falling on good soil refers to someone who hears the word and understands it. This is the one who produces a crop, yielding a hundred, sixty or thirty times what was sown"** (Matthew 13:23).

Downloading an app or opening a Bible might seem like a small habit to some, but to those who have tasted and seen that the Lord is good, the Bible is electric in its potential. Today you might read a devotion or get back to Bible-reading, but these are enormously important in the way God works.

Your devotional life might seem small. Seeds are too. But they don't stay that way.

The Word is a sword
Pastor Mike Novotny

My friend Ben realized he had forgotten his Bible when we were a state and a half away from home on the way to a Christian conference. To Ben, a Bible-less start to the week was a big problem.

I can see Ben's point. You and I are in a spiritual war against the devil, the world, and our own sinful nature. No wonder Ben wanted a sword in this fight.

"Take up the shield of faith, with which you can extinguish all the flaming arrows of the evil one. Take the helmet of salvation and the sword of the Spirit, which is the word of God" (Ephesians 6:16,17).

Imagine hand-to-hand combat without a sword. A helmet and shield would help, but it's hard to win a fight without a sword. Thank God that the Spirit inspired one.

The Bible is the way we battle for God's blessings. When the devil swings his sword of shame at our throats, we raise the Bible and quote, **"There is now no condemnation for those who are in Christ Jesus"** (Romans 8:1). When the father of lies declares we are too far gone for God, we decapitate the deceiver with a Braveheart-esque cry, **"It is by grace [we] have been saved!"** (Ephesians 2:8).

Ben was no fool to fidget without his Bible. Neither are you. Take up the sword of the Spirit, which is the Word of God, and stand your ground today.

The Word is Spirit

Pastor Mike Novotny

Sometimes I like to think about the connection between eternal treasure, the words of the Bible, and the work of the Spirit. In the epic closing of John 6, our Savior said, **"The words I have spoken to you—they are full of the Spirit"** (verse 63).

If the Bible had a list of ingredients on its back cover, the Holy Spirit would be the first on the list. He fills the pages of Scripture, taking words off a page (or a screen) and planting them like seeds in your heart and your mind. Because he is divinely working, the Bible grabs you in one verse, slaps you to your senses in the next, and allows you to be still and know that he is God before your devotion is over. Have you experienced this?

Throughout the centuries, humans have sought to find the treasure of God's truth through rituals, pilgrimages, and mountaintop experiences. But our Father, in his mercy, didn't hide the truth about his love and your salvation on the top of Mt. Everest.

Instead, he "hid" it in every Spirit-filled, Christ-centered page of the Holy Bible. We understand what a treasure Jesus is and how much he treasures us when we read his words and listen to our God talk to us over and over again. You may never become a millionaire. But whenever you hold the Scriptures in your hands, you are rich indeed.

"The law from your mouth is more precious to me than thousands of pieces of silver and gold" (Psalm 119:72).

The Word is life

Pastor Mike Novotny

Somewhere in Somalia, Christians risk their lives to read the Bible. After sunset, a brave disciple retrieves a hidden Bible from a cave, sneaks back into the village, and leads his small group in studying it. Before sunrise, this disciple reverses the process before his neighbors discover the secret and demand his death.

Why take such a risk? Jesus knows: **"The words I have spoken to you—they are full of the Spirit and life"** (John 6:63).

"Life" is one of the ways the Bible talks about being with God. Death is, essentially, distance between you and God, while life is the full enjoyment of his presence.

Without the good news revealed in the Word, no sinner could claim a spot in God's presence. But the words that Jesus spoke are full of life because they are full of access to God. Despite your transgressions, the Bible promises you, a believer in Jesus, the unimaginable— God himself.

Shortly after declaring that the Word of God is **"alive and active,"** the author to the Hebrews writes, **"Let us then approach God's throne of grace with confidence, so that we may receive mercy and find grace to help us in our time of need"** (4:12,16).

Approach the King of kings with confidence. Find mercy for every one of your sins. Find grace. God is not annoyed by your request or bothered by your presence. In fact, he wrote an entire book to tell you just the opposite.

Don't believe me? Read the Word. It is full of the Spirit and life!

Taps
Christine Wentzel

"Taps is a military bugle call played slow and solemn to invoke a feeling of remembrance and respect for the soldiers who have died in battle. On a trumpet, there are no valve movements, only tone changes made with the pursing of the lips" (*Naval Bugler*, 1974).

This haunting tune and loud rifle volleys echoed within our heavy hearts as we drove away from our family's funeral service in Arlington National Cemetery. We viewed orderly rows of identical white headstones. The only marked difference was an engraved religious affiliation symbol.

There are faith stories behind those fallen saints with crosses on their stones.

It is said there are no atheists in foxholes. Whether in hell on the front lines or in the PTSD mind, "Oh God!" was a common cry among sinner and saint alike. From the saint to the sinner came the gift to share the divine comfort about their personal rescue from eternal death. Out of love, God sent his Son. The gift of faith and a re-birth in the Holy Spirit awaited their confession from a repentant heart. In that moment of grace, the sinner became the saint and eventually arrived safely in heaven.

We will never forget your sacrificial service to God and country.

Onward, then, ye faithful; join the happy throng,
Blend with ours your voices in the triumph song:
Glory, laud, and honor unto Christ the King;
This through countless ages saints and angels sing.
("Onward Christian Soldiers")

Overflowing
Pastor Daron Lindemann

"Excuse me, sir?!" I was trying to exit a coffee shop as a kind lady behind the coffee bar continued, "I was listening to your Bible study about the Holy Spirit."

Apparently, the awkwardness of eavesdropping didn't concern her. She launched into her faith story while mixing up a latte. She quickly reviewed her upbringing as sad, abusive, and relying on addiction to numb the pain. These behaviors continued into her adult years, but four years ago she got in some trouble and God rescued her.

Throughout this story, she never stopped smiling and never stopped steaming the milk. She wasn't ashamed. She wasn't a victim looking for sympathy. She cared more about God and his words coming to life in her than she cared about anything else in that moment. She was consumed by it. Captivated by the One who changed her life, forgave her, loved her, freed her.

And she had to tell me about it. Just because. Like coffee aroma always overflows through the shop.

People whose lives have been transformed by God's Word and work just have to talk about it. Today, live up to these words, telling God that this is what you want to do:

"My soul is consumed with longing for your laws at all times. Your statutes are my delight. . . . Never take your word of truth from my mouth. . . . See how I love your precepts; preserve my life, Lord, in accordance with your love" (Psalm 119:20,24,43,159).

JUNE

Whether you eat or drink or whatever you do,
do it all for the glory of God.

1 Corinthians 10:31

If things are going well
Pastor Mike Novotny

If things are going well in this season of your spiritual life, I want to praise God with you. And I want to quote God to warn you.

God once said, **"So, if you think you are standing firm, be careful that you don't fall!"** (1 Corinthians 10:12). Sometimes success makes us feel like we're standing so firm that we don't need to be careful anymore. We can forget that God blessed us with success *because* we were working his steps to victory.

Have you ever met someone who decided to stop taking their medication because they were feeling mentally healthy? They forgot that they are healthy *because of* the medication.

Have you ever met a teenager who was raised in the church and decided that they didn't need to attend while in college because their faith was so strong? They forgot that they were strong *because of* church.

Don't take that bait when it comes to your spiritual habits. If you have a few weeks of obedience under your belt, praise God and keep working the steps. If praying, confessing, and filling your heart with the Word has been working, then keep doing what's been working.

Stand firm in the process that God is using to produce the fruit of self-control in you. That is how you stay standing and avoid an unexpected fall.

If things aren't going well
Pastor Mike Novotny

If things aren't going well in this season of your spiritual life, I want to grieve with you. And I want to quote God to encourage you:

"As the rain and the snow come down from heaven, and do not return to it without watering the earth and making it bud and flourish, so that it yields seed for the sower and bread for the eater, so is my word that goes out from my mouth: It will not return to me empty, but will accomplish what I desire and achieve the purpose for which I sent it" (Isaiah 55:10,11).

Sometimes failure makes us feel like the Word is not working. But God often is working in ways our eyes cannot see.

If someone told you that snow produces grain, you might laugh. The snow falls and sits and melts and . . . nothing. But beneath the surface, the melted snow is soaking into the soil and preparing the ground for the seeds that are soon to come.

Your journey with Christian living is like that. You might not see immediate results. All these devotions about God's love and the power of prayer might not produce instant change. But God swears that his Word "will not return to me empty."

Yesterday's message might be exactly what you need two months from now. Last week's devotion might pop into your head in a fierce moment of temptation or a lonely evening of self-loathing. The Word is working. It has to. God said it.

And God never lies to his children.

Keep the party going
Pastor Clark Schultz

Is there a party in your future? A graduation, wedding, anniversary, or retirement? Do you know what makes a party successful? Planning, people, some presents, and quality entertainment.

God planned the birthday of his New Testament Christian church with all the same elements in place. Ten days after Jesus went up to heaven, folks from all over the Mediterranean gathered in Jerusalem for the Old Testament harvest festival. Here God had the Holy Spirit come on his disciples, and they were able to speak in other languages. We call this Pentecost in the Christian church. A crowd heard the disciples and were amazed: **"Then how is it that each of us hears them in our native language?** (Acts 2:8).

What do you think happened next? Those folks heard the gospel for the first time in their own language and took it back to their homelands. The gospel spread like fire. How far? All the way to you, dear reader. The challenge for you and me is this: can we keep the fire burning and the party going? That Pentecost morning, some felt this was a gimmick or the disciples were drunk. We too can slip into excuse after excuse of why it is someone else's job to spread the Word.

Party checklist requirements: 1) you have an awesome God who loves you and equips you with unique gifts, and 2) more important, you have the same Holy Spirit who gives you power through the Word. So keep the Pentecost party going!

You are the plan
Pastor David Scharf

There is an old legend—and I stress it is merely a legend—that illustrates a good point. The legend is that after Jesus ascended into heaven, the angel Gabriel asked him, "Who is going to carry on your work now?" And Jesus answered, "I have left it to John and Peter and Andrew and the others." Gabriel then asked, "What if they don't do it?" Jesus answered, "I have made no other plans."

In other words, you and I are the plan. Jesus said, "*You* will be my witnesses." He does not use angels; he uses us. Why? Because the angels have never known what it is like to be forgiven, to go from hell to heaven in a moment. We do. So did Isaiah the prophet. Isaiah thought he was going to die, but God forgave his sin. Isaiah records: **"Then I heard the voice of the Lord saying, 'Whom shall I send? And who will go for us?' And I said, 'Here am I. Send me!'"** (Isaiah 6:8). Isaiah went from "Woe is me" to "Here am I. Send me!"

Jesus came to pay for your sin with his life and death. Jesus suffered hell so that heaven is now yours. Jesus lives to bless you today beyond all that you ask or imagine. Jesus is with *you*. Now he asks, "Who will go for me?" What else can you do but respond, "Send me!" After all, you are the plan!

Don't forget to breathe
Pastor Clark Schultz

Somewhere between a pike press, a plank, and high knees, the instructor shouted, "Don't forget to breathe!" "Who's the idiot who forgets to breathe?" I wondered. Mere moments later, I was the one feeling light-headed and dizzy. Yup, you guessed it; I didn't breathe.

When you exercise and your muscles work harder, your body uses more oxygen and produces more carbon dioxide. To cope with this extra demand, your breathing has to increase from about 15 times a minute when you are resting to up to 40 to 60 times a minute during exercise.

Life is a series of breaths. From the moment God created man—**"the LORD God . . . breathed into his nostrils the breath of life, and the man became a living being"** (Genesis 2:7)—to when we take our last breath, a **"person's days are determined"** (Job 14:5).

But what about all the days in between? Stress, work, family, depression—many times we want to hold our breath. Spiritually, physically, and mentally we become light-headed. When those moments come, don't hold it in. Take a breath and let it all out on God because he reminds us to **"call on [him] in the day of trouble"** (Psalm 50:15).

Deep breath in and now out . . . God's got this.

Good enough for God?

Pastor Mike Novotny

About ten years ago, I met a young woman who was a good person. I mean, a really good person. One of those people who got along with everyone at her high school—the athletes, the musicians, the math kids, everyone. Soon after we met, I asked her if she thought she was good enough to get into heaven. "I'm not sure," she confessed. But she came to church and then to Bible class, listening to Jesus' words, his standards, and his promises. Not long after, I asked her the same question I had posed months earlier: "Are you good enough to go to heaven?"

"Oh, I'm sure," she smiled, a smile that reflected a change that had happened in her heart. She met Jesus, the real Jesus, the only Jesus who could make her not just good but Good, Good enough for God.

The earliest Christians put it this way: **"Salvation is found in no one else, for there is no other name under heaven given to mankind by which we must be saved"** (Acts 4:12). They believed that there was one name that could save them, the name of Jesus Christ their King.

So are you good enough for heaven? Good enough to have God think about you and smile? Good enough to live in his presence both now and forever? Through Jesus, the answer is an undeniable Yes! His name was given so that we could be saved from every spiritual danger and enjoy every spiritual blessing. What a name!

Pop-up storms
Andrea Delwiche

Have you experienced a pop-up storm on a sunny summer day? Within a few moments, your activities must change as you respond to new conditions.

Each day of our lives contains pop-up storms of different magnitudes. And our outlook may suddenly shift too, making each situation loom large. As believers, we are not immune from suffering or anxiety. We may bob in a sea of despair, each wave threatening to fill our lungs with water as we pray for breath to survive.

But we don't need to face life barely treading water. **"Blessed be the Lord, who daily bears us up; God is our salvation"** (Psalm 68:19 ESV). The Lord comes beneath us and "bears us up" so that we don't drown. And while Jesus very clearly tells his followers, **"In this world you will have troubles"** (John 16:33), he also reassures us, **"Peace I leave with you; my peace I give you. . . . Do not let your hearts be troubled and do not be afraid"** (John 14:27).

God is our salvation. We share in Christ's resurrection and will live with him forever. God is also our salvation in the nitty-gritty of daily life. He wants to lead us into the way of love and trust as we come to understand his steadfast character, praise him, and work with him to bless others.

What evidence of God's support can you see when you examine the last 24 hours? God is daily investing in and supporting the well-being of your body and soul.

Blink first
Christine Wentzel

If you've lived long enough and squabbled often enough, you know by now that pride starts every conflict but never ends it. By nature, we thrive on pride. Nothing stirs that dark nature more than seeing someone we don't like getting something we believe is undeserved. In friendships, we keep mental scorecards on our giving and their taking. It takes a confrontation on pride for humility to win, and that conflict ended in victory two thousand-plus years ago.

It took an incredible act of love on God's part to win that war. Jesus chose to blink first by laying aside his sovereignty and becoming small enough to fit into the confines of bones and flesh. He overcame every temptation the devil could throw at him. He allowed himself to be crucified by the very people he came to save. He defeated death by rising from the grave. His victory makes us free and eager to blink first in any stare down to joyfully show the character of true love.

Not budging an inch with your spouse? Blink first.

Not seeing eye to eye on a church issue? Blink first.

Haven't talked to a friend in a long time? Blink first.

"Therefore if you have any encouragement from being united with Christ, if any comfort from his love, if any common sharing in the Spirit, if any tenderness and compassion, then make my joy complete by being like-minded, having the same love, being one in spirit and of one mind" (Philippians 2:1,2).

They sharpen you
Pastor Mike Novotny

By nature, we become dull. Just ask the knives in your kitchen drawer. As time passes and meals are made, they don't naturally become sharper but instead lose their edge. To stay sharp, they need to be acted upon aggressively by an outside force.

The same is true for you. By nature, we become dull to the realities of God, forgetting how glorious he is, how serious sin is, and how loved we are. Like a farmer working in a cow barn who has gotten used to the smell or a woman who lives by the ocean and is no longer moved by its beauty, we too can grow complacent. We forget.

This is why we need Christian friends. The classic proverb reminds us, **"As iron sharpens iron, so one person sharpens another"** (Proverbs 27:17). I love that picture. To stay sharp and effective, an iron tool needs the help of another iron tool. For Christians to stay sharp in their thinking and effective in their living, we need the help of other Christians.

Today is a great day to ask someone to keep you sharp. Have the courage to ask them, "What do other people think of me? What don't I see?" Warning—The answers might cause some friction. But please remember that it takes some friction for dull things to become sharp again.

Your life matters. The way you live matters. May God give you the humility to ask honest questions, to consider candid answers, and to stay sharp in your faith.

Lost in translation
Pastor Clark Schultz

A while ago, I took a trip to Germany. In addition to the historic sites, the food was amazing. I'm not sure if you know this, but in Germany most folks speak German. Kidding aside . . . there were moments, when asking in my broken German, that simple phrases like "where is the bathroom" or "may I have an ice cream cone" got lost in translation. I knew what I wanted. The person on the other side of my conversation knew what he or she wanted, but we couldn't communicate it clearly.

Biblically that is true too. God loves us. God wants us to have a relationship with him, but due to sin, it gets lost in translation. We have our own pity parties, make God out to be a bad guy, and think that God just doesn't care about us.

When Jesus prayed to heal a deaf man, this phrase stands out: **"He looked up to heaven and with a *deep sigh* . . ."** (Mark 7:34). This was not a father frustrated with his children sigh. This sigh was similar to the tears Jesus shed at his friend's funeral or the compassion he showed to the widow who lost her only son. It's the same empathy he shows to you. His heart goes out to you. Jesus is not some far-removed God who is too busy to know or care about you. He gave his life for you!

"Because he himself suffered when he was tempted, he is able to help those who are being tempted" (Hebrews 2:18).

The dumpster story
Pastor Mike Novotny

There was once a man who had a secret stash of pornographic magazines. One day when his wife was gone, he indulged his sinful nature but immediately felt the shame of his hypocrisy. So he took the whole stack of magazines down to the dumpster for their apartment complex and threw them away once and for all.

Well, not exactly once and for all. Something within him didn't want to give up those fleeting moments of pleasure, so before his wife returned, the man decided he would get the magazines back. He reached over the edge and—ready for this?—fell headfirst and broke his arm, leaving him stuck at the bottom of the dumpster and unable to escape until his wife came home.

Seriously. That happened.

Any sin, on its worst days, can feel like that. You love it, you hate it, you love it again, and you sometimes end up broken and bottomed out. There are moments when there are no logical explanations for our sin, just the intense shame of our addictive choices.

This is why Romans 5:20 is worth memorizing: **"But where sin increased, grace increased all the more."** When your sin feels so overwhelmingly big, remember what is always bigger—the grace of God. When our Father finds you in the dumpster of immorality, he doesn't walk away in disgust. Instead, he offers a hand, cleans you up, and stays by your side to nurse you back to health.

He cares that much. He is a perfect Father after all.

Get in the wheelbarrow
Pastor Jon Enter

Where are you struggling to trust the power and protection of God?

Years ago a tightrope walker did amazing stunts at tremendously scary heights in Paris. An American promoter doubted his ability and challenged him to tightrope walk over Niagara Falls. He did. Then the daredevil walked the tightrope again blindfolded and pushing a wheelbarrow. He asked the promoter, "Now do you believe I can do it?"

"Yes, of course," the promoter said.

"Good!" the stuntman replied. "Then get in the wheelbarrow!"

It's one thing to say, "I trust you." It's entirely different to have your life and well-being directly in the hands of another.

It's one thing to say, "God, I love you." It's entirely different to have your life and your eternity in the hands of Jesus. James challenges you to go beyond words in expressing your faith: **"Faith without deeds is dead. . . . I will show you my faith by my deeds"** (James 2:26,18).

Jesus is the object of your faith, but what is the objective of your faith? Get in God's wheelbarrow (so to speak), and trust God will not let you fall. If he has power to create wind and the gentleness to calm its force, if he has power to destroy the grip of death and the gentleness to dry the tears of those who weep, he has the power to protect you and the gentleness to comfort you. Nothing is too big or too small for his love.

Trash talk?
Pastor Daron Lindemann

I was bullied as a kid. He would stalk me after school and trash-talk: "I'm gonna punch you in the face!" I was too scared to trash-talk back.

Learn to be a better trash-talker. Why? Because your fiercest enemies are trash-talking all the time. If you listen to them, you will lose.

The Bible teaches you to respond with trash talk of your own and put these enemies in their place. Well, it's really not trash talk but truth talk because it comes from God.

Here it is: **"'Where, O death, is your victory? Where, O death, is your sting?' The sting of death is sin, and the power of sin is the law. But thanks be to God! He gives us the victory through our Lord Jesus Christ"** (1 Corinthians 15:55-57).

Take a cue from the Bible for some truth talk!

"Hey, sin, Jesus died and rose so you can't curse me, you don't make me dirty, and Jesus' empty tomb empowers me to say no to you, sin!"

"Hey, death, do you really think you win? Jesus rose, and you are dead. New life from Jesus with my name on it is in charge, and I'm going to live that life now and in heaven!"

"Hey, devil, sure you're real, but I'm not afraid of you trying to intimidate me and manipulate me. You are full of lies, but Jesus is my truth and life. He is Lord, not you!"

You must not love God enough
Linda Buxa

A friend was going through a really hard time and told me some of the "encouragement" she received from other Christians. "You didn't have enough faith." "If you had been in a closer relationship with God, this wouldn't have happened." "You must not be praying hard enough."

Those comments reminded me of a Bible story involving a man who was born blind. **"[Jesus'] disciples asked him, 'Rabbi, who sinned, this man or his parents, that he was born blind?' 'Neither this man nor his parents sinned,' said Jesus, 'but this happened so that the works of God might be displayed in him'"** (John 9:1-3).

When we look for reasons why bad things happen to other people, it's like we are asking the same question as those in Jesus' inner circle: Who sinned?

I think we say those things because if we can find a reason why bad things happen, then we can take action to ensure they won't happen to us. The truth is simply that in a world that is no longer perfect (the way God created it to be), bad things will happen to "good" people.

This means that bad things will happen to you and me too.

Instead of asking who sinned and accusing the people around you of not praying or believing enough, we simply sit by them, hug them, and remind them that even if we don't know what God is doing, we trust that God's work will be displayed in their lives.

Best chapter ever?
Pastor Mike Novotny

In the early 1600s, Thomas Goodwin, an English preacher, wrote a lot of words about God. A lot of words. When put together, Goodwin's work filled 12 volumes, over 500 pages each, in small font with the lines squished together. But volume 2 was the most interesting. In volume 2, Goodwin didn't cover 1/12th of the Bible, as you might logically assume. Nor did he narrow his focus to one book of the Bible. Instead, Goodwin spent an entire volume, 500 tiny printed pages, trying to explain just one chapter of the Bible! Which chapter was that? Ephesians chapter 2.

Have you read it? You should. If you wonder why the world is so messed up, why people are so messed up, or why you sometimes are so messed up, it's in Ephesians chapter 2. And if you want to know how to fix it, you won't need to turn the page. If your life could use a little more grace, mercy, and kindness, leave your bookmark in the same place because Paul is proud to cover that too.

I don't have room to reprint the whole chapter here, but let me inspire you to open your own Bible to that epic page by quoting these epic words: **"Like the rest, we were by nature deserving of wrath. But because of his great love for us, God, who is rich in mercy, made us alive with Christ even when we were dead in transgressions—it is by grace you have been saved"** (Ephesians 2:3-5).

Pray the psalms
Andrea Delwiche

"Make haste, O God, to deliver me! O Lord, make haste to help me! Let them be put to shame and confusion who seek my life! Let them be turned back and brought to dishonor who delight in my hurt! Let them turn back because of their shame who say, 'Aha, Aha!' May all who seek you rejoice and be glad in you! May those who love your salvation say evermore, 'God is great!' But I am poor and needy; hasten to me, O God! You are my help and my deliverer; O Lord, do not delay!" (Psalm 70:1-5 ESV).

The words of this ancient psalm are compact and suitable to the daily challenges we face. Each day we need God's deliverance and protection. Each day we have reason to rejoice in God's greatness.

Early Christians and some Christians still today memorize psalms to use as prayers. Christ himself certainly knew the psalms by heart and used them as he battled temptation. He used the psalms to express his heart to his Father as he hung on a cross.

For us also the psalms can be prayers ready for us not only in moments of crisis but as blessings to pray over our ordinary moments. Situations change, but God's faithfulness and eagerness to spend time with us and to rescue us is new each day.

We're no angels
Christine Wentzel

"Do not fail to show love to strangers, for by doing this some have welcomed angels without realizing it" (Hebrews 13:2 EHV).

"BC" was a societal outcast; an older man with untreated mental illness, stronghold addictions, and physical disabilities. He was homely, disheveled, and unwashed. He was prone to angry outbursts and untethered joy. He possessed an infectious smile overlaying dirty teeth. He was outwardly unique in our Christian congregation. Was he our visiting angel?

Soon after my prodigal return, God worked on my residual worldliness. BC was one of many faith-building lessons. When I first spotted BC, I had a knee-jerk, sin-filled reaction of distaste. One Sunday service, I walked passed him to reach the very last pew. It was empty enough to accommodate my personal space from the rest of the flock. Just as I settled in, BC climbed over me, sat at my hip, and grabbed the hymnal out of my hands. My eyes watered from the alcoholic fumes; I was ready to bolt. Suddenly, Hebrews 13:2 spoke as a whispered memory and instantly convicted my pride-filled heart.

"God, forgive me for this sin of self-righteousness. Help me see BC as you see him, as you see me. Help me love BC as you love him, as you love me. Amen."

I turned to face BC and asked, "Will you share that hymnal with me?" Together we worshiped our triune God. We were no angels. We were a family in Christ. We learned and grew under God's care. One day we will be united in heaven and live in loving harmony forever.

God is with us
Andrea Delwiche

Life continues day in and day out, morning and evening. Seasons emerge and fade. Leaves color and fall and then months later slowly emerge. Children are born and grow. Our family members grow old and leave us. Power is accumulated and disintegrates. Governments rise and fall. Illness has us in its grip and then loosens its hold. We savor tears of joy and are caught in the grasp of grief. The words of Ecclesiastes 3:1 resonate with nearly everyone: **"To every thing there is a season, and a time to every purpose under the heaven"** (KJV).

We can feel powerless in our own lives, unable to stop time, unable to effect change, unable to pursue the good that needs to be done for Christ, for our neighbors, for our families. "Who is in control?" we ask. "Who is working for us?"

The confession of this psalmist, writing during the destruction of every other certainty, can be our hope as well: **"For God is my King of old, working salvation in the midst of the earth"** (Psalm 74:12 KJV). Can you stop for a minute and focus on this certainty? Can you picture it in your head? Our God—Father, Son, and Spirit, who spoke our world into being—still stands in our midst, protecting, guiding, working. As his beloved child, he holds you close to him.

God is never absent from his earth. He who formed it continues working in it, alongside and on behalf of his beloved people. His arm is strong. His wisdom is unsurpassable. His goodness never ends.

Rooted in Jesus
Pastor Clark Schultz

Last summer we planted pine trees on our property. A tree is a symbol of stability and of home. A mature tree on an old farm might remind visitors of the generations who have lived there and the roots they laid down. We planted our trees thinking of the shade or beauty they will provide.

"In those days and at that time I will make a righteous Branch sprout from David's line; he will do what is just and right in the land" (Jeremiah 33:15).

We are rooted and established in God's Word. Here we are safe and at home, a part of God's family tree. In Christ this family tree is branching out. The church won't be done growing until Christ returns. Be motivated by the love that this Righteous Branch showed toward you personally. He died for you! He died to give you life.

When Jesus told his disciples and us to go and make disciples of all nations (Matthew 28:19,20), it wasn't a chore or a command but a request by our loving Savior to reveal to people God's love and promise to them in Christ Jesus. Each time the precious Word of peace and hope in Jesus is spoken in our homes, communities, churches, and neighboring nations, the "tree" branches out and grows. Stay rooted in the Word, keep your eyes focused on Jesus, and open your mouth to share the gracious promise and fulfillment our God and Savior has given to us.

Being a Christian is hard!
Pastor David Scharf

"Why is my life as a Christian so hard? It wasn't this hard before." That has been spoken or thought by many new Christians. Maybe you've thought it too. Before there was no pang of conscience when you did whatever made you happy. There were no strange looks, but now you see them on your friends' faces when you go to church. There were no conflicts in your conversations, but now you feel the "archaic" and "close-minded" labels being pinned to your back because of Scripture. You realize that striving to please self (before) was a whole lot easier than striving to please Jesus (now). Being a Christian is hard.

Jesus said as much. **"For whoever wants to save their life will lose it, but whoever loses their life for me will find it"** (Matthew 16:25). A wise theologian once commented, "When Christ calls a man, he bids him to come and die." In other words, the more I live in Christ's words, the more I die and the more he lives in me. That's the goal of the Christian life. I want my weakness, my sin, my insecurity, my _____ to die. In its place, Jesus fills me with his strength, his forgiveness, the confidence that comes from him, and . . . he exchanges the cross I carry in this life as a Christian for the crown of heaven.

So, yes, being a Christian is hard but worth it! God's blessings as you lose *your* life today and find it *in Christ*.

Stop playing it safe
Pastor Daron Lindemann

I am a safety-holic and don't take enough risks. I asked some guys at church if they wear safety glasses for yard chores like I do. They kinda looked at me funny.

Okay, so I need to skip my vitamins once in a while. I need to talk to people about Jesus with more passion and less concern that they'll look at me funny. I need to trust Jesus more and my own control and comfort less. You need to trust Jesus more too. He called his disciples not to a sterilized, quarantined safety zone but to a stormy, life-changing mission.

Jesus appeared to his disciples, seeking safety in a locked room after he had died. **"'As the Father has sent me, I am sending you.' And with that he breathed on them and said, 'Receive the Holy Spirit. If you forgive anyone's sins, their sins are forgiven; if you do not forgive them, they are not forgiven'"** (John 20:21-23).

Will Jesus' mission for you be safe? Actually, it will be a whole lot safer than you locking down the status quo and staying tied down to what makes you comfortable (so that you don't need Jesus).

Jesus gives you three reasons to take more God-honoring risks for him. He is sending you so the mission is holy. He gives you the Holy Spirit so that God himself is in you. People need forgiveness, and you can assure them of it.

Stop playing it safe!

Billy Graham, a glimpse of God
Pastor Mike Novotny

Billy Graham's daughter Ruth, in her book on for-giveness, recounts the day when her father gave her a stunning glimpse of our Father.

After a messy divorce, Ruth fell in love again. Her children didn't like her new boyfriend, and her parents had deep concerns. But after only six months of knowing this new man, Ruth followed her heart and married him. A day after their vows, however, she realized she had made a mistake, finally seeing the red flags that others had pointed out. She moved out within weeks, knowing the marriage was over.

She knew she had to drive home and face her parents. Ruth tells the story: "As I rounded the last bend in my parents' driveway, I saw my father standing there, waiting for me. . . . As I turned off the ignition, Daddy approached. I opened the car door and . . . he spread his long arms wide, wrapped me in his tight embrace, and said, 'Welcome home.' . . . I was wrapped in grace. Un-merited. Undeserved. Merciful. Generous. Billy Graham was not God, but he modeled God's grace for me. Never again would the theological definition of *grace* be just an academic concept for me. It was now a personal experi-ence" (From *Forgiving My Father, Forgiving Myself*, p.74).

How incredible to feel a glimpse of God's amazing heart. **"Praise be to the God and Father of our Lord Jesus Christ, the Father of compassion and the God of all comfort"** (2 Corinthians 1:3).

An acceptable time
Andrea Delwiche

God has a particular plan in mind for each of us. He always works the circumstances in our lives for good. Sometimes it can be hard to see the good immediately. But waiting on God and his timing is much easier when we trust him—when we know that although we are dangling out over the ledge of life, God has us by the hand and won't let us go.

In Psalm 69:13, David wrote, **"But as for me, my prayer is to you, O Lord. At an acceptable time, O God, in the abundance of your steadfast love answer me in your saving faithfulness"** (ESV). His trust in God was strong, even during severe trials, because the foundational work of building a relationship with God had been done. David had practiced meditating on the works and promises of God. He knew that the deliverance and the answers he sought would come from God "at an acceptable time."

Try spending a few minutes with this section of Scripture. Let your mind and heart stay with it. Read it again and start to picture what these words meant to David, what his frame of mind might have been as he was writing them. Read it a third time and consider how these words can bring comfort and understanding to your own life. This is your own foundation work.

Ask God to let his words soak into your soul. Talk with God about the ways you are trying to understand his "acceptable time" in your life. May your time together be blessed!

Get dressed!

Pastor Clark Schultz

Get dressed! This phrase starts and ends our days. Children fighting to take off their pajamas in the A.M. are arguing 12 hours later to put those same pj's back on at the end of the day. "Why is it always a fight?" my wife and I ask.

The world is evil, and for the Christian there is always a fight. The apostle Paul tells us in Ephesians 6:11-17 to get dressed. But what do we wear? Paul has excellent fashion advice. **"The helmet of salvation"**: where your head goes, you go. Is your head on straight? Perhaps life makes you shake your head, but you are saved! No matter what happens, God has saved you! Let that soak into your head.

"The breastplate of righteousness": a breastplate protects the vital organs. Many in this world will take their stab at you, ridicule you, or try to tear you down. You are right with God! Christ made you righteous no matter what others hurl at you.

"The belt of truth": a belt holds up and holds close. You want the truth? God in his Word holds you up! God through his Son's sacrifice holds you close.

Finally, **"your feet fitted with . . . readiness"**: where you go, there you are. Your mission in life is not to get rich or die trying. Whatever occupation, whatever road you are on, you take the gospel with you to share with others. This peace you have of sins forgiven can be shared with others who need to get dressed!

Why Paul loved grace (and we do too)
Pastor Mike Novotny

The apostle Paul was the poster child for grace. If the internet would have been invented two thousand years earlier, he immediately would have reserved the website grace.com. If Paul would have gotten married and been blessed with daughters, I bet he would have named them Grace, Gracie, and Baby Grae-Grae.

Why do I think that? Check out this data—Paul wrote 28% of the total words of the New Testament (he wrote 13 of the 27 books, but they're often rather short). Yet Paul is responsible for 73% of the occurrences of the word *grace* in the New Testament! Of the 114 total occurrences of *grace*, 83 of them are from Paul. In fact, every letter that Paul wrote starts with grace and ends with, you got it, more grace. An editor might have encouraged him to spice up his writing with a few synonyms, but Paul insisted in book after book and verse after verse on talking about the grace of our Lord Jesus Christ.

Here's why: **"But by the grace of God I am what I am, and his grace to me was not without effect"** (1 Corinthians 15:10). Grace both made Paul and changed Paul. Grace was his everything.

Meditate on the meaning of grace, and you might feel the same way. Undeserved love. God's smile when you assume he would scowl. Favor and blessing, even if you've fallen and blown it. Picture God's face, shining upon you because of Jesus, and you'll get addicted to grace too.

Can I trust God's power?
Pastor David Scharf

"I trust God, but some things just seem insurmountable even for God." You have probably never said it out loud, but we have all thought it. The evidence is that we doubt and worry. But does it even make sense to worry? God is the One who made *everything*, and he is in control of *everything*. So what are we really worried about? I suppose we are worried not so much that God doesn't have the power but that he doesn't love us enough to use that power for us. Look at the cross and see God's love for you. The One who invested his own blood in your salvation is not going to withhold his power from you!

Do you remember Gideon? Unsure Gideon needed assurance after assurance. God told a trembling Gideon, **"With the three hundred men . . . I will save you and give the Midianites into your hands"** (Judges 7:7). Someone once said that "with a penny I can do nothing, but with God and a penny there is nothing I cannot do." How do you think Gideon felt in the book of Judges with an army of 300 going up against an army of 450,000? That 300 must have felt like he had a penny, but he trusted God's power. And you can too. Just look at Jesus' love for you on the cross for the proof that there is nothing he is not willing to do for you! You can trust God's power!

The best version of you
Pastor Daron Lindemann

You are the best version of yourself when you believe that what God says about you is true.

When you consume others' social media posts and compare yourself to them or you accept the powerful propaganda that only you can decide your identity—this is not your best identity.

Instead, praise God for designing you: **"You created my inmost being; you knit me together in my mother's womb"** (Psalm 139:13).

My college roommate had an afghan blanket knitted by his mom. Woven into it were all his favorite sports, hobbies, nicknames, family names, and some dates. Nobody else fit under that blanket. It was uniquely him.

God knit into you everything that is uniquely you . . . with no mistakes. God brought into being his version of you.

"My frame was not hidden from you when I was made in the secret place, when I was woven together in the depths of the earth" (Psalm 139:15). "The depths of the earth" is ancient language saying, "That's so far away nobody knows how to get there except God."

It's an intimate, secret place where it was only God and you. He didn't check Pinterest. He didn't Google nose shapes or personality mixes. Secret. Just you and God. His eyes were only on you.

There and then he created, designed, sculpted, and brought into this world his version of you. Which is the best version of you. And nobody is a better you than you! So. Be. You.

They comfort you
Pastor Mike Novotny

Have you read the *Scarlet Letter?* A woman named Hester is pregnant; no one knows the identity of the father except Hester and the pastor. Too ashamed to confess his sin, the pastor smiles and preaches, but the secret of his affair kills him inside. He can't live with the lie but is afraid to speak the truth. In my favorite quote, the pastor says, *"Had I one friend . . . to whom . . . I could daily [go to], and be known as the vilest of all sinners, [I think] my soul might keep itself alive."*

That quote brings me to tears, not because I have had an affair but because I know how good it is to have friends like that. God has surrounded me with a small group of Christians who know me fully yet love me completely. I can tell them I am a sinner, the vilest sinner I know, and yet they don't run away. They listen. They love. They bring me back to Jesus.

Do you have friends like that? James writes, **"Therefore confess your sins to each other and pray for each other so that you may be healed"** (5:16). While God loves to hear our honest confessions, he also loves overhearing our confessions to others, an act that allows fellow believers to imitate our Father and forgive us completely.

It's hard to preach the gospel to yourself, but it is easy for them. Tell them what happened. Then listen when they tell you what happened at the cross.

But I

Pastor Mike Novotny

There are three words that have changed my life in amazing ways—*GOD is here!* But there are two words that have changed my life in agonizing ways—*But I.*

But I is my two-word description of what the Bible calls our "flesh" or "sinful nature." Paul writes, **"All of us also lived among them at one time, gratifying the cravings of our flesh and following its desires and thoughts"** (Ephesians 2:3). The human problem is that our flesh has thoughts, desires, and cravings and we tend to follow and gratify them. God says _____, and we respond with, "But I . . ."

Love your neighbor. "But I don't like him." Honor your father. "But I don't think he's worthy of honor." Forgive 77 times. "But I have the right to be bitter." Flee from sexual immorality. "But I have needs." Don't let unwholesome talk come out of your mouth. "But I need to vent sometimes."

But I. Those two words can kill you because they separate you from the God who is life. This is why I want to encourage you today to call out your flesh. When you find yourself thinking in opposition to God, repeating the devil's absurd claim that God is wrong (Genesis 3:4), drag your flesh into the light before it's too late.

The flesh can kill you. But God is in the business of making you alive. **"But because of his great love for us, God, who is rich in mercy, made us alive with Christ"** (Ephesians 2:4,5).

A double-edged sword
Pastor Clark Schultz

A parody of the game show *Jeopardy* had guests who were not the brightest misreading the categories, much to the frustration of the host. One category in particular was "(S) words," and the guests kept saying, "I'll take Swords for $400, Alex."

The apostle Paul reminds us to take a sword—**"the sword of the Spirit"** (Ephesians 6:17). This is our offensive weapon. We use this to pierce the hearts of others with God's law and God's gospel. A seminary professor told me both law and gospel need to be there, like wings on an airplane. You can only get so far with one wing on an airplane.

Some think speaking the law isn't loving. But nothing could be further from the truth. If I let my kids do whatever they want, while I may win "Coolest Dad of the Year," I will not be showing them love because it may cause them more harm than good. Also, to take the law out of the equation is to forget why we need a Savior. If we don't need Jesus, what's the point of his suffering and dying?

As I write this, our society is hurling (s) words, four-letter words, and you name it. Perhaps it is time that Christians share this sharper double-edged sword (Hebrews 4:12), showing others their sins in a truthful and loving way. More important, showing them their Savior because that is the best parting gift one could have in this game called life.

JULY

Jesus replied: "Love the Lord your God with all your
heart and with all your soul and with all your mind."

MATTHEW 22:37

Called out, not kicked out

Pastor Mike Novotny

If I were Jesus, I would have eaten the Lord's Supper alone. Why? Because I would have kicked out all the apostles long before that Thursday night! Read through the gospels and you'll find Peter, James, John, and the boys saying and doing such absurd things that you expect Jesus to stop his journey, pull out his hair, and scream, "Enough! I've had enough! You all are done!"

But Jesus didn't do that. He often called them out, but he never kicked them out. For example, when James and John wanted to torch the ungrateful Samaritans, Luke writes, **"But Jesus turned and rebuked them. Then he and his disciples went to another village"** (Luke 9:55,56). He called them out ("rebuked them") but didn't kick them out ("he *and his disciples* went"). That's the tough yet tender love of our Savior.

He's the same way with you. Through his Word and his people, Jesus might call you out. There will be some tough moments indirectly (through a sermon/written devotion) or directly (face-to-face with a concerned Christian) when God will expose your sin and call you to repentance. But the goal is never to get rid of you. With a tender heart, God will forgive you for your sins, offer his Spirit to help you change, and continue to walk with you "to another village" in your journey to heaven.

Christianity is not a religion of unconditional acceptance. It is, however, a faith filled with unconditional love. That was true for James and John, and—thank God!—it is still true for me and you.

Faith to believe
Pastor Matt Ewart

The early Christians were heartbroken. A great persecution had broken out against them, and many of them were losing their lives. First it was Stephen. Then they lost James. Now Peter was in prison, and it seemed he would soon be gone too. Heartbroken, the church did the only thing they could do.

They prayed.

We are not told what they prayed for, but we know they had faith to pray earnestly during an intense time of uncertainty.

What's ironic is that even though they had the faith to pray, they did not have the faith to believe God could answer their prayers.

Acts 12 records Peter's miraculous escape from prison. Once freed, he went to the house where these Christians were praying. He knocked on the door and called out to the servant on the other side of it. Then this happened:

"When she recognized Peter's voice, she was so overjoyed she ran back without opening it and exclaimed, 'Peter is at the door!' 'You're out of your mind,' they told her. When she kept insisting that it was so, they said, 'It must be his angel'" (verses 14,15).

It's one thing to pray for a miracle to happen. It's another thing to believe that God can do it.

Ask God for a big faith that doesn't just pray for big things to happen. Remember the power of Jesus' resurrection and believe that God can do even more than you ask.

In it to win it
Christine Wentzel

"Do you not know that when runners compete in the stadium, they all run, but only one receives the prize? Run like that—to win" (1 Corinthians 9:24 EHV). If you were baptized, you were given the gift of faith and registered to run a new race, one with a reward to live with Jesus now and forever. Your training routine consists of a steady diet of God's life-sustaining Word using personal devotions, group Bible studies, and worship in Christ.

Jesus warns you this is not easy because your enemies, such as the devil, the world, and your sinful weaknesses, line up along the way to tempt you. They try everything from seductive appeal ("There are multiple, easier ways to reach God") to threatening doubts ("Is there really sin or hell?") to steer you off the road to heaven. As strong as the pull seems at times, the Holy Spirit lives in you to spur you on and increases your faith to know you are in it to win it because of Christ!

Despite the bombardment of temptation, mockery, and hate, Jesus showed you the way to run and win because he did it first. With his joyful eyes on the prize, he ran the race once and for all humanity. He walked through the corridors of hell with fists raised in victory. He stopped the devil from snatching this victory from your hands. May you and I run together with this same joyful confidence and encourage others to follow Jesus.

Who the Son sets free
Katrina Harrmann

Shortly after getting my driver's license, I remember driving around town with my best friend, feeling rather puffed up with my newfound freedom. At one point, I turned onto a road, not realizing it was the on-ramp for the interstate. With hardly any highway driving under my belt, and certainly no experience driving at nearly 70 mph in rush-hour, city traffic, my friend and I shrieked in horrified panic as we careened onto the highway.

Of course, we did survive. But at the time, it felt iffy.

The point is, while I *had* a legal driver's license, there were things I wasn't ready for. My parents didn't want me on the highway yet. They set rules to keep me safe.

As we celebrate the Fourth of July in the U.S., it's important to realize that freedom doesn't mean a stripping away of all rules and expectations. If anything, it's being comfortable *within* a set of rules and expectations.

God—our good Father—expects a lot from us, his obedient children. We aren't set loose with zero expectations! We're expected to show his light to others while operating withing a framework of obedience and love to our Father in heaven.

True freedom doesn't mean a free-for-all existence with no rules, but rather being part of a family with a heavenly Father *who sets rules because he loves us.*

"Now a slave has no permanent place in the family, but a son belongs to it forever. So if the Son sets you free, you will be free indeed" (John 8:35,36).

A strange kind of joy
Andrea Delwiche

Have you ever thanked God for helping you grow through times of testing?

Listen in on this prayer of thanks and praise to God for a time of severe testing: **"Praise our God, all peoples, let the sound of his praise be heard; he has preserved our lives and kept our feet from slipping. For you, God, tested us; you refined us like silver. You brought us into prison and laid burdens on our backs. You let people ride over our heads; we went through fire and water, but you brought us to a place of abundance"** (Psalm 66:8-12).

This same strange joy is discussed in the New Testament book of James: **"Consider it pure joy, my brothers and sisters, whenever you face trials of many kinds, because you know that the testing of your faith produces perseverance. Let perseverance finish its work so that you may be mature and complete, not lacking anything"** (1:2-4).

Where in the last years have you experienced trials that have resulted in your faith being strengthened? In retrospect, are you able to see the growth in yourself? We are so loved by God. Even as he, who knows us best, works to refine us, he is also standing with us, desiring to be intimately involved in nourishing us as we grow through difficulties.

Holy Spirit, please reveal to me where you have been at work in my life, refining me. Help me see! Help me be open to your work. Help me grow! Amen.

Which lie knows your name?
Pastor Mike Novotny

Do you have an untrue thought that you think a lot? I do. About 75% of Sundays when I'm preaching, I think, "Mike, you are terrible at this. Look at all those empty chairs. Look at all those bored faces. This sermon is terrible. You should just shut up and sit down." That thought is so common that I have a name for it—the Sunday blues. I know it isn't entirely true, but it doesn't stop me from thinking it all too often.

Do you have a thought like that? Some stubborn lie that shows up and hunkers down in your head week after week? Maybe it's that your pain is pointless or that you won't make it to heaven or that you have no spiritual gifts or you are too damaged for God to delight in you. Whatever lie knows your name, listen to Paul's words: **"We demolish arguments and every pretension that sets itself up against the knowledge of God, and we take captive every thought to make it obedient to Christ"** (2 Corinthians 10:5).

We take thoughts captive. That's Paul's way of saying, "We think again. We don't trust everything in our heads. We open our Bibles and preach to ourselves, telling our thoughts what to think."

That's what I've been doing these days. I printed a sheet of Bible passages that I keep next to my Bible in church. When that old lie shows up in my head, I fight back. I demolish that argument. I tell myself about Jesus. May God help you do the same!

A final assignment
Jan Gompper

As a former college theater professor, wanting my students to succeed was a double-edged sword. One side hoped they would fulfill their dreams. The other side feared they might do so.

God's directive not to be "of the world" is challenging. The religion of secularism bombards us everywhere, and the arts often serve as a powerful pulpit.

Sadly, I *have* seen former students worship at secularism's altar, abandoning biblical teachings regarding marriage, sexuality, worship, etc. Granted, we all sin and fall short of God's expectations, but there is a graver danger when we deliberately and habitually turn a blind eye to God's truths. Without repentance, hearts eventually grow calloused to the forgiveness Christ offers.

If I could go back, I would give my students one final role-play assignment: **"So here's what I want you to do, God helping you: Take your everyday, ordinary life—your sleeping, eating, going-to-work, and walking-around life—and place it before God as an offering. Embracing what God does for you is the best thing you can do for him. Don't become so well-adjusted to your culture that you fit into it without even thinking. Instead, fix your attention on God. You'll be changed from the inside out. Readily recognize what he wants from you, and quickly respond to it. Unlike the culture around you, always dragging you down to its level of immaturity, God brings the best out of you, develops well-formed maturity in you"** (Romans 12:1,2 MSG).

Unseen footprints
Andrea Delwiche

Have you woken up midway through the night to find that the trouble that lurked in the corners before bed is now perched like a bird of doom on your chest? As you try to sleep, the problem grows. God certainly doesn't seem to be present and active. God seems to be missing.

"I cry aloud to God, aloud to God, and he will hear me. In the day of my trouble I seek the LORD; in the night my hand is stretched out without wearying; my soul refuses to be comforted. When I remember God, I moan; when I meditate, my spirit faints. You hold my eyelids open; I am so troubled that I cannot speak. Your way was through the sea, your path through the great waters; yet your footprints were unseen" (Psalm 77:1–4,19).

The psalmist begins to ask some hard questions. Will the Lord never again be favorable? Has God's steadfast love actually failed? Is he so angry that he can't be compassionate?

In that place of questioning, God reminds the psalmist of his trustworthiness. Time after time, God had worked good for his people; yet oftentimes, "his footprints were unseen." God was there. God was powerful. God was quiet.

Where would it be helpful for you to meditate on God's quiet history of rescuing you? Where has God worked for your good, even though his "footprints were unseen"? Let this psalm comfort you. In the dead of night and during dark days, God is present. Don't be afraid to ask him your questions. May insight well up as you seek him.

Jesus is worth it
Pastor Mike Novotny

Jim Gaffigan, my favorite comedian, has this joke about the disciples who had to give up everything to follow Jesus. I forget his exact words, but Gaffigan points out, "It's not like they were investment bankers! 'We have to leave *everything*, Jesus? So, leave the fishing poles here?'"

But the joke doesn't quite work with Matthew the tax collector (aka, Levi). His profession was equally immoral and lucrative, which is why so many people despised him and his fellow tax collectors. Thus, when Jesus invited Matthew, the stakes were high. Following Jesus would mean leaving his luxury home in Capernaum behind and embracing the uncertain life of a traveling disciple.

But Jesus was worth it. **"'Follow me,' Jesus said to him, and Levi got up, left everything and followed him"** (Luke 5:27,28). There was something about Jesus, likely his unconditional love for sinners, that made Matthew believe that Jesus was worth more than "everything" he had.

Jesus still is worth it. Following him might cost you money, time, energy, comfort, popularity, acceptance, pleasure, or countless other things that we all prefer, but walking through life with the only One who can forgive your sins, provide a remedy for death, and offer you a place in the presence of God is so worth it.

No matter what your "everything" includes, leave it behind. Jesus is worth it!

Think again
Pastor Mike Novotny

A few months ago, my mom won an award from the Rotary Club of Madison, Wisconsin. The rotary folks invited our family to a fancy hotel with over one hundred business leaders—lawyers, doctors, and other professionals. When the rotary president stood up to start the meeting, she began by reminding everyone in attendance about how to think. "Ask yourself questions like—Is it true? Is it helpful? Is it kind?" As I listened, I wondered, "Why would highly educated people need this?" Because, apparently, even PhDs need to think about what they think about.

You might be a sharp student, an experienced professional, or just older and wiser, but we still all need the reminder to think again. Paul tells us, **"Finally, brothers and sisters, whatever is true, whatever is noble, whatever is right, whatever is pure, whatever is lovely, whatever is admirable—if anything is excellent or praiseworthy—think about such things"** (Philippians 4:8). Paul is commanding us: "Think like this. If your thoughts about a stressful situation or a difficult person in your life or even about yourself aren't noble or pure, develop the mental muscle to think again."

The next time you sense that you have lost your spiritual joy or peace, think about your thoughts. Are they true? Are they helpful? Are they biblical? If not, think again. Think about the love of your Father, the forgiveness of your Savior, and the presence of the Holy Spirit in your heart. Think about such things.

The results of pruning
Katrina Harrmann

I hate pruning the grapevine in my garden. Cutting off some of the plant always seems counterproductive when what I want is a larger, thriving vine! But if I don't prune, the plant will not produce as well next year.

People are often the same way. How many times have you suffered through a rough season in life only to look back and realize you grew immensely as a result? It happens to us all.

"[God the Father] **cuts off every branch in me that bears no fruit, while every branch that does bear fruit he prunes so that it will be even more fruitful**" (John 15:2).

God trims us back in ways that make us even more fruitful as we move forward. We don't always understand it, but rest assured—*he does.*

"Imagine yourself as a living house. God comes in to rebuild that house. . . . But presently He starts knocking the house about in a way that hurts abominably and does not seem to make any sense. What on earth is He up to? The explanation is that He is building quite a different house from the one you thought of. . . . You thought you were going to be made into a decent little cottage: but He is building a palace. He intends to come and live in it Himself" (C. S. Lewis, *Mere Christianity*).

The next time you think you can't bear the "pruning" God is doing in your life, remember that the Master Gardener always knows what he's doing. And the finished product will be amazing!

Not until you bless me
Pastor David Scharf

Have you ever been desperate in prayer? So desperate you would not stop praying until you got your answer? Jacob in the Bible was desperate. He had stolen his brother Esau's life by stealing his inheritance. Jacob had run away from his brother while his brother was raging like a lion. Years later, as a wealthy man, Jacob was returning to the lion's lair. He was coming back home. What would Esau do to him? It ate him up. He needed assurance.

That night the Lord himself wrestled with Jacob. The Lord said, **"'Let me go, for it is daybreak.' But Jacob replied, 'I will not let you go unless you bless me'"** (Genesis 32:26). And the Lord blessed him. Why? Because Jacob was a better wrestler? No, because God had a purpose for the wrestling. Like Jacob, God uses the "wrestling" in our lives to strengthen our faith, teach us persistence in prayer, and simply because he loves to bless his children. Consider the grace of this thought today: God allows himself to be overcome when we wrestle him in our prayers.

When you feel as though you are on the bottom of the wrestling pile with God, remember that God loves it when you hold him to his promises. And what happens? You will *always* win. He will *always* call you his child. He will *always* forgive your sins. And he will show you that the wrestling was meant to bring you closer. Say, "No, Lord, I won't let go until you bless me."

The tension of being Christ(ian)
Pastor Mike Novotny

If you think about it, the Pharisees asked a fair question as they observed Jesus feasting in the home of Matthew the tax collector: **"Why do you eat and drink with tax collectors and sinners?"** (Luke 5:30). Tax collectors were first-century villains, sellouts who lived in big houses while driving their Jewish neighbors into grinding poverty.

What would be the equivalent today? Imagine scrolling though Jesus' Facebook page and seeing pictures of him with the guy who turned your little sister into a drug addict. Or with the woman who cheated on your best friend, lied to the judge, and got full custody of their kids. Or with the registered sex offender who left someone you love with deep trauma that will not be easily cured. What would you type into the comment section after seeing Jesus with such sinners? You wouldn't be crazy to ask the question that the Pharisees asked: "Jesus, if you are the Messiah, if you love God and hate sin, why are you with them? Don't you care about what they did to us?"

Christ back then and Christians today constantly live with this tension. How do we love the sinner while hating the sin? How do we send a clear message that sin is evil while, at the same time, preach the gospel message that every sin is forgivable?

Meditating on Jesus' brilliant reply is a great place to start: **"Jesus answered them, 'It is not the healthy who need a doctor, but the sick. I have not come to call the righteous, but sinners to repentance'"** (Luke 5:31,32).

When life doesn't make sense
Pastor Jon Enter

Do you have a black belt in planning ahead or a bruised ego from your plans failing? One thing is true. Life goes wrong; plans fail.

During a wedding Jesus attended, something big went wrong. The hosts ran out of wine. In Bible times, wedding celebrations lasted a week. If some heavy drinkers outlasted their welcome . . . well . . . you ran out of wine. Having no wine was a big deal because it was often mixed with polluted water to make the water safer to drink. And everyone needs water!

Jesus has the power to make any problem at any moment of any day go away. Jesus knows all things. He knew the wine at this wedding was running out. Why didn't he fix it *before* it ran out? God knows your pain, your problems. Why doesn't he fix them before they assault your joy?

If Jesus had fixed the wine problem before it happened, those servants, the wedding couple, and his disciples wouldn't have encountered his power and love. This problem pointed their hearts to him because he intervened and interrupted their pain.

When life fails around you, it's not the absence of Jesus' power and love; it's the opportunity to see them clearly. God allows plans to fail and problems to persist, but he uses them so we can experience his power and encounter his love. The wedding couple had a problem. But they also had a friend who could do something about it. And so do you.

Be like them
Pastor Mike Novotny

Paul's words struck me initially as a bit too proud to have a place in the Holy Bible. **"Whatever you have learned or received or heard from me, or seen in me— put it into practice. And the God of peace will be with you"** (Philippians 4:9). But then it dawned on me that Paul was writing a joyful letter from jail. He was falsely accused, unjustly imprisoned, and left to spend some of his prime career years under arrest—and yet he was bursting with joy! I guess he did deserve to be an example for those of us who struggle to rejoice.

Do you know anyone like Paul? Can you think of anyone who is in the same boat as you but has more joy than you? Same school, same never-ending homework, same annoying classmate, but your friend is smiling most days. Same job, same boss, same Monday-to-Friday frustrations, but your coworker isn't checking the clock or saying she needs a drink just to cope. Same pandemic, same mandates, same situation, but your brother isn't afraid or angry. In other words, is there someone who is like you but doesn't think like you?

If so, I have some homework. Interview your Paul. Reach out and ask him, "What are you thinking?" Figure out what's going through his head when challenges come his way. Write down his answers. Put them into practice. And the God of peace will help you restore your joy.

Break free from greed
Pastor Matt Ewart

Everyone wants to be free from guilt.

Everyone wants to be free from anger.

But not everyone wants to be free from greed. Why not? Because in a sense, greed has its benefits.

If you were to walk around your home right now, it is entirely possible that you will find the consequence of greed hidden in plain sight. It might be hanging in your closet. It might be parked in your garage. It might be hanging on your wall. You probably have a very good reason for why you wanted it and why you got it, but that doesn't change the fact that the consequence of greed is right there.

Breaking free from greed can be complicated, but this was a topic that Jesus addressed on many occasions. Here's one of them: **"Watch out! Be on your guard against all kinds of greed; life does not consist in an abundance of possessions"** (Luke 12:15).

The constant pursuit of more stuff will not give you a fulfilled life. It will leave you empty, and that is not the life Jesus wants for you.

What he wants for you, he lived for you. Even though he deserved more than what his life gave him, he defined his life based on what he provided to others. Because of him, you don't need to settle for a life that finds purpose in possessions. You have more than you deserve. You are truly rich.

I hate feet
Ann Jahns

I hate feet. God bless all you podiatrists out there. Seeing the bare feet of others up close really makes me squirm. My husband likes to tease me about it. When we are traveling on the freeway and he sees a vehicle approaching with the front passenger's bare feet propped on the dashboard, he'll announce, "Feet coming up on the left!"

You know who didn't hate feet? Jesus. During his final meal with his disciples the week he died, he shed his outer clothing, got down on his hands and knees, and lovingly washed the grit and grime from the feet of his dearest friends. Feet washing was something typically assigned to a servant or a slave, not to the King of the universe.

Yet Jesus did it. He did it to set an example for all of us: **"Now that I, your Lord and Teacher, have washed your feet, you also should wash one another's feet. I have set you an example that you should do as I have done for you"** (John 13:14,15).

Feet washing can take many forms. The possibilities are endless for us to serve others humbly. We don't need to hijack our coworkers and neighbors with a basin of sudsy water and a washcloth, but we can shovel the snow from someone's driveway, send a message of God's love to a grieving widow, or take a hot meal to a family with a dangerously ill child.

How can you show the love of Jesus by washing someone's feet today?

Sin is a sickness that Jesus can cure
Pastor Mike Novotny

The Christian church should be the most offensive and most beautiful place in our culture. In reply to the Pharisees who were offended that Jesus ate with tax collectors, our Savior answered, **"It is not the healthy who need a doctor, but the sick. I have not come to call the righteous, but sinners to repentance"** (Luke 5:31,32). Do you find his words offensive? beautiful? I say both.

Jesus was saying, "You're right. Matthew and his friends are sick. The way they love money, rob people, and ignore God's Word is so sick that if it kills them, they will end up in hell. But where do you expect to see a doctor? Are you scandalized when a doctor is in the same room as the sick? So why are you shocked to see a Savior and sinners together? Oh, you thought me being here was an approval of their lifestyle? Not a chance. I am here to call them to repentance, to show them that God is better than anything money can offer."

Can you imagine Matthew's face as Jesus said that? Was he offended? comforted? both?

This is what true Christianity is. It confronts our sins, calls our hearts sick, and commands our repentance. In the next breath, it comforts us, offers healing for our hearts, and points us to Jesus. Like surgery for a cancer patient, God slides his scalpel over our souls in hopes of taking out what would otherwise kill us.

Don't run from a church that does the same. You have found one that is just like Jesus.

Under God's dominion
Andrea Delwiche

Do you live in fear of powerful people, or do you find yourself drawn toward following them?

In every age of humankind since the fall, rulers have attempted to position themselves in the place of God. They ruthlessly build their kingdoms, and carnage is their legacy. Yet all the earth's strongmen, both the ones we fear *and* the ones in whom we secretly trust, are under God's dominion.

Contrast these earthly power-grabbers with the awe-inspiring description of our God: **"You are the radiant one. You are more majestic than the ancient mountains"** (Psalm 76:4 GW).

We have the option to meditate on and live under God's rule, even as earthly leaders burn and pillage. God sees. God listens. God is working. Our perspective and possibilities are clearest when we submit to God's reign: **"Make vows to the LORD your God, and keep them. Let everyone around him bring gifts to the one who must be feared. He cuts short the lives of influential people. He terrifies the kings of the earth"** (Psalm 76:11,12 GW).

Our God is the radiant one, more majestic than the ancient mountains. If you find yourself preoccupied with the power dynamics in this world, consider dwelling on the opening words of the Lord's Prayer: "Your kingdom come. Your will be done on earth as it is in heaven."

Pray and work to follow this King, bringing his goodness and power to every circumstance.

Don't hide
Linda Buxa

Tullian Tchividjian is Billy Graham's grandson and a well-known pastor who loves to preach about God's unlimited grace. In 2015 he stepped down after he and his wife had separate affairs.

As you might expect, the news shared that the popular pastor fell from grace. Some believers were disappointed; others were smug. People who don't believe in Jesus pointed to yet another example of believers' hypocrisy.

A month later Tchividjian shared a public message where he admitted he wanted to keep hiding, but he knew that if he tried to hide his shame and fear and anger and sadness, then he wasn't practicing what he preached. He said that it's destructive not to practice what you preach.

Being honest with our failings isn't easy. It's easy to say that Jesus forgives sins, but we aren't always honest about what those sins are. If we deny our weaknesses, we miss the opportunity to share that anything good we do is actually the power of Christ working in us. If we don't share our hurts, others aren't able to follow God's command to carry one another's burdens. So, like Paul, we **"boast all the more gladly about** [our] **weaknesses, so that Christ's power may rest on** [us]**"** (2 Corinthians 12:9).

Admittedly, this is messy and hard. However, if you hide and don't give God the glory when you're broken, other broken people won't know that thanks to Jesus, the Father is ready to run and welcome them home too.

Joy of salvation
Christine Wentzel

"For the joy set before him he endured the cross, scorning its shame, and sat down at the right hand of the throne of God" (Hebrews 12:2).

Dearest Resurrected Lord,

When I think of joy, I think of happiness in the forms of smiles, laughter, and good times with family and friends. Then the spell of happiness is broken when the tears begin to roll over the brokenness in myself and these same relationships. This sadness loves to turn my thoughts inward and away from you, the source of joy.

You took up my cross and broke its deathly hold on me. You didn't do this happily—you knew the pain you would experience in the complete separation from your holy Father because of my sinful heart. You sweated blood for the strain you were under to do this work on my behalf. But you saw beyond your own suffering to what awaited me if you didn't go through with it.

You saw my restoration on the other side of your persecution and death. Your work would bring about my eternal life. So you persevered and removed my death sentence.

That same holy joy is what your Holy Spirit creates in me. A joy knowing you love me that much—that your Father and mine loved me that much. A joy that goes beyond the temporary sadness on this side of heaven. A joy that keeps my eyes fixed on you in this life and to the reward you alone earned for me in the life to come.

Thank you.

Time to dance
Pastor Matt Ewart

"A time to mourn and a time to dance" (Ecclesiastes 3:4).

King Saul of Old Testament Israel was not a godly king. He was taking God's people in the wrong direction; therefore, God decided to make a change in leadership. The prophet Samuel knew this was the right move, but Samuel was hesitant to move on.

God had to prompt him with these words: **"How long will you mourn for Saul, since I have rejected him as king over Israel? Fill your horn with oil and be on your way; I am sending you to Jesse of Bethlehem. I have chosen one of his sons to be king"** (1 Samuel 16:1).

Yes, it was sad, but it was time to move forward. God had a plan. The best was yet to come. The longer Samuel would dwell on the past, the more he would miss out on what God had in store for the future.

I do that sometimes. I get so caught up mourning losses from the past that I can't see the blessings God has prepared for my future. Maybe you do that too. In fact, maybe today you will begin to feel the aching burn of mourning start to grab hold of your heart.

It is okay to grieve. But don't let grief block your view of the greater blessing that God has in store for you. Sometimes the losses we endure in the present allow God to do greater things in the future.

Go to war with the Word
Pastor Mike Novotny

Paul's words about your life of faith sound like war, don't they? **"We demolish arguments and every pretension that sets itself up against the knowledge of God, and we take captive every thought to make it obedient to Christ"** (2 Corinthians 10:5). Demolishing enemies. Taking captives. Paul knows that to win the battle versus temptation you must go to war with the Word of God. You can't sit back and hope that this time your temptation will be different. Put on your armor and get ready for a fight!

So, warrior, keep the sword of God's Word at your side. Maybe a note card would help. Write down God's mighty Word that will help you fight against those familiar temptations. If you anxiously think the worst will happen, write down Jeremiah 29:11: **"'I know the plans I have for you,' declares the LORD, 'plans . . . to give you hope and a future.'"** If you are tired of being a new parent or a caregiver or an unappreciated leader at work, write down Matthew 11:28: **"Come to me, all you who are weary and burdened, and I will give you rest."** If you think you can't be forgiven after *that* sin, smash that stronghold with John 19:30. Jesus cried out, **"It is finished."**

These words have divine power to demolish the sins that have a strong hold on your heart. Let the Word of God fight against the lies you believe, because God's Word is the truth.

Find the cross
Katrina Harrmann

I was in the doctor's office for some tests recently—"scary" tests. Do you know the kind I mean? While waiting for the doctor to examine the results, I got more and more anxious . . . my heart pounding a mile a minute.

Strangely, I happened to glance at the ceiling and noticed how the tiles made a cross where they intersected. Almost immediately, I felt my heart calm down and my breathing return to normal. I even smiled. Scanning the room, I quickly found other places where the furniture or accessories of the room intersected to form crosses.

I was surrounded in a very comforting way.

The cross of Christ can have that effect on people, creating calm where there was chaos and bringing clarity into moments of calamity. The cross reminds us who is in charge and why: God—because of the death of his Son, Jesus, on a cross.

"God did this so that they would seek him and perhaps reach out for him and find him, though he is not far from any one of us" (Acts. 17:27).

And even if bad news HAD been the result of my day (which it wasn't), here is an amazing truth: **"They will have no fear of bad news; their hearts are steadfast, trusting in the Lord"** (Psalm 112:7).

We can live fearlessly because of God's great love for us! But if you're nervous, look for a cross in the room. I bet you'll find a few.

When God's goodness doesn't make sense
Pastor Jon Enter

What is an unexpected gift that you have received? My sister won a Corvette from a radio station once. True story! Jesus changed water into wine as a gift for an unsuspecting wedding couple. True story.

God's goodness is so good, so grand, that it doesn't make sense. Who am I to deserve any gift from my perfect God when I sin and disappoint him? Who am I to get any goodness? And yet, when God gives . . . his grace knows no bounds, his love no limits, his gifts no price tag.

We see this truth in the gift of wine Jesus gave the couple at Cana in John 2. When Jesus gives, he gives generously, because that is what God does and that is who God is.

Jesus changed around 150 gallons of water into the finest tasting wine. That's the equivalent of 750 bottles of wine. His gift was the best; it was abundant. The leftover wine after the wedding could've been sold. What a blessing!

You are blessed! Don't expect a semitruck to unload 62 cases of wine. But you can expect and you have received an endless supply of Jesus' kindness and mercy. Jesus saw this couple in need, and he acted. He knew exactly what they needed, and he fulfilled it. He does the same for you. Jesus gives. Jesus provides. Your life was saved from the spiritual bankruptcy of hell. Jesus never tires of loving and forgiving you. That goodness knows no end!

If you get God, you win
Pastor Mike Novotny

In the magical world of Harry Potter, there's a sport called quidditch where players zip around on brooms trying to throw a big ball through a giant hoop, giving their team ten points. But quidditch has an important addition—the golden snitch, which is a winged, gold-colored ball that zooms around like a nervous hummingbird. Each team has a seeker, a player whose sole job is to catch the golden snitch, which is worth a whopping 150 points. Seeking and catching the snitch is worth more than a dozen goals put together. Seek the snitch and you win.

I thought of that image recently as I read Isaiah's invitation: **"Seek the Lord while he may be found; call on him while he is near"** (Isaiah 55:6). Seek. Don't just stand or sit and wait to find God. Be a seeker. Do whatever is necessary to know him, understand him, and be close to him. Because if you get God, you win.

You might be old enough to realize that the people who have the most money or the greatest popularity don't win at this thing called life. The true winners are those who know Jesus as their Good Shepherd.

The truth is that you are going to "seek" something today. God, in his mercy, is inviting you to seek him. He wants to be found, which is why he isn't flying away from you but instead waiting for you in his sacred Word. I am so glad you're seeking him right now, because if you get God, you win.

A lesson in contentment
Linda Buxa

In July 2021, an F-1 tornado struck half a mile from our house, leaving a trail of destruction multiple miles long.

Thanks to weather forecasters who were insistent this would be a big storm and to God's protective hand, no one was killed. However, a drive to check on our neighbors that morning showed that while lives were spared, homes were not. Houses were shifted from their foundations, roofs were ripped off, garages disappeared, and farm fields were filled with pieces of buildings and lives and memories.

Seeing so much loss was a strong reminder that—as a Christian who lives in the U.S.—it's tempting to pay lip service to the passage, **"But godliness with contentment is great gain. For we brought nothing into the world, and we can take nothing out of it. But if we have food and clothing, we will be content with that"** (1 Timothy 6:6-8).

This is my very public confession: I am not always content with only food and clothing. I want more food and more clothing. I like being content with plenty. Being content when things are hard can often be a bigger challenge. Still, after seeing people lose so very much, it was a reminder that—thanks to the strength the Holy Spirit provides—we can be more like Job, who even though everything was taken away, publicly proclaimed, **"The LORD gave and the LORD has taken away; may the name of the LORD be praised"** (Job 1:21).

Thinking of leaving?

Pastor Mike Novotny

Whenever I hear a story of someone leaving the Christian faith, I'm equally heartbroken and understanding. While it grieves me, I think I understand why people walk away from Christianity, because Jesus will cost you.

The other day, I tried to count up all that Jesus has cost me in my life. I calculated all the hours of going to church, reading my Bible, etc. The sum total was 7,514 hours! That number could double before I'm dead.

Time, however, is the easy part. The hard part of following Jesus is letting him be Lord, that is, letting him have the last word about what is right or wrong, what to rejoice in and what to repent of. There is an absurdly high cost to the Christian faith when you are attracted to your same sex or you are deeply devoted to a certain political party or your parents are almost impossible to honor. Jesus' commands to love God first, love every neighbor as yourself, and trust in the Word as truth make my 7,514 hours seem small.

So why would you stay with Jesus? The author of Hebrews, speaking to suffering Christians who were considering leaving Christ, wrote, **"Therefore, holy brothers and sisters, who share in the heavenly calling, fix your thoughts on Jesus, whom we acknowledge as our apostle and high priest"** (3:1).

Fix your thoughts on those words—*holy, heavenly calling, our high priest*—and you will realize why Jesus is worth whatever he costs you. Stay, fellow Christian, no matter what you must sacrifice. Jesus is worth it.

God's will
Pastor Matt Ewart

He broke up with me. *Must be God's will.*
I lost my job. *Must be God's will.*
Tragedy hit that family. *Must be God's will.*
I made every green light. *Must be God's will.*

I'm not sure who needs to hear this, but just because something happens—whether good or bad—doesn't necessarily mean it was God's will for it to happen. Just read through the Bible and you will find several examples of things that happened that were the opposite of what God wanted to happen.

The good news is that God can still work through things that aren't his will.

"We know that in all things God works for the good of those who love him, who have been called according to his purpose" (Romans 8:28).

When the plans of man result in evil, God's plan is to make everything work out for good.

The same is true of your own life. The regrettable choices you made in the past were not in line with God's will, but through his love and forgiveness, God can tell his story of grace even through your brokenness.

Today you might experience God's will being done in your life, and you might experience what it's like when things run against his will. No matter what happens, his plan is to work all things out for your good.

July 30

Help for the directionally challenged
Jan Gompper

I am *very* directionally challenged. I can turn the wrong way coming out of a restaurant bathroom! Driving before I owned a GPS was an even greater challenge. I'm amazed I made it anywhere.

Now I don't know what I'd do without my GPS. What an amazing gadget! Not only does it give me clear directions to get me where I need to go; it also warns me of approaching hazards or traffic jams along the way.

Wouldn't it be great to have a GPS for our lives—a device that would always guide us in the right direction and warn us of any roadblocks that might divert us from following God's path?

Actually, we do. God has given us a spiritual GPS: **"Every Scripture passage is inspired by God. All of them are useful for teaching, pointing out errors, correcting people, and training them for a life that has God's approval. They equip God's servants so that they are completely prepared to do good things"** (2 Timothy 3:16,17 GW).

Through the Old Testament history lessons, the wisdom of Proverbs, and the teachings of Jesus and his apostles in the New Testament, God gives us a clear road map for our lives to help us arrive at our ultimate destination. And he provides warnings about the hazards we may encounter en route, complete with examples of what happens to those who don't heed his cautions.

I don't go many places without using my car's GPS. I go even fewer places without utilizing my spiritual GPS.

Make me the cotton
Pastor David Scharf

One night at a mission in Africa, the pastor overheard one of the native people praying. The prayer was simple but strange. The person prayed, "Lord Jesus, you are the needle. Make me the cotton. Amen." The missionary asked the man what he meant by his prayer. The man explained that he had visited the mission school that day and watched the women sewing. He noticed that the thread always followed the needle. In the same way, he wanted to follow Jesus wherever he led.

"'Come, follow me,' Jesus said" (Mark 1:17). At first, that sounds daunting! It's not always popular to show we are followers of Jesus. People may disagree with us, hate us, take advantage of us, or worse! How will we get the courage to follow Jesus? Realize who Jesus is. He is the Almighty God who can do anything. He does not need anyone. He does not need to do anything. And yet, what did he choose to do? He chose to love you. He chose to come to this earth to live the perfect life you couldn't live. He chose to give his life on a cross for you. He chose to forgive you and lead you out of hell to heaven. He is the one who says to you, "Follow me."

Our response? We will follow as directly and dependently as the thread follows the needle.

Lord Jesus, make me the cotton today! Amen.

AUGUST

Put on the full armor of God, so that you can take your
stand against the devil's schemes.

EPHESIANS 6:11

Eyewitnesses of Jesus
Pastor Mike Novotny

Do you remember back in the 90s when high school girls' bangs poofed off the front of their foreheads? Or do you recall when the internet first came out and you couldn't be online and make a phone call from your landline at the same time? I wouldn't be shocked if that sounds familiar. After all, it was only 30 years ago.

Just like the gospel of Luke. When Dr. Luke did his thorough research on the life of Jesus, his gospel masterpiece was completed in the 60s A.D., approximately 30 years after the death and resurrection of our Savior. Why does that matter? Because people were still around who remembered what happened. Luke writes, **"Many have undertaken to draw up an account of the things that have been fulfilled among us, just as they were handed down to us by those who from the first were eyewitnesses and servants of the word"** (1:1,2).

In a modern courtroom, few things matter as much to the judge and jury as the eyewitness testimony of the events, especially when the witnesses (1) agree to the story and (2) have little to gain from their testimony. No wonder Luke listened to every word handed down by the eyewitnesses of the Word made flesh. Despite the pain of persecution, they declared that Jesus lived, died, and rose.

You can be confident that every word Luke wrote is true. This is no story. This is the history of the God who came to this world to save you.

Stress facilitates growth
Pastor Matt Ewart

The University of Arizona owns a biosphere that allows scientists to study how plants grow in a controlled environment. One of the first observations they made was that trees grow much faster in the biosphere than they do in the wild. But they also found that the trees in the biosphere collapsed before reaching full maturity.

After some study, they determined that their instability was due to a lack of wind. Wind puts stress on a tree, and the tree compensates for that stress by becoming sturdier.

I'm not sure what the human equivalent of a biosphere is, but if we all had our wish, I'm sure we would prefer a controlled environment where everything went our way. But that kind of place doesn't exist in this world. There are plenty of things that will stress your mind, heart, and body.

But that's a good thing.

Just like trees need a healthy amount of wind to make them strong, we need a healthy amount of stress to make us resilient. Here's how Paul talks about it in Romans:

"We boast in the hope of the glory of God. Not only so, but we also glory in our sufferings, because we know that suffering produces perseverance; perseverance, character; and character, hope" (5:2-4).

Today, like every day, you will encounter some stress. Ask God to accompany you through it so that he can shape and strengthen you through it.

Give up!

Linda Buxa

Most motivational speakers will encourage you never to give up, to hang in there and fight. May I suggest that plenty of things in our lives aren't worth keeping? Maybe we *should* give up.

Give up your burdens. **"Come to me, all you who are weary and burdened, and I will give you rest"** (Matthew 11:28).

Give up your anxiety. **"Peace I leave with you; my peace I give you. . . . Do not let your hearts be troubled and do not be afraid"** (John 14:27).

Give up selfishness. **"As we have opportunity, let us do good to all people, especially to those who belong to the family of believers"** (Galatians 6:9,10).

Give up your life of sin. **"'Then neither do I condemn you,' Jesus declared. 'Go now and leave your life of sin'"** (John 8:11).

Give up your short-term view. **"See to it, brothers and sisters, that none of you has a sinful, unbelieving heart that turns away from the living God"** (Hebrews 3:12).

Give up loving Jesus halfway. **"The Spirit God gave us does not make us timid, but gives us power, love and self-discipline"** (2 Timothy 1:7).

Give up everything. **"In the same way, those of you who do not give up everything you have cannot be my disciples"** (Luke 14:33).

When you fail—and you will—thanks to Jesus, you get a fresh start. Don't give up on giving up!

Lay your burden down
Katrina Harrmann

Our family loves to go backpacking. There's a "little" 22-mile trail we visit for a few days each summer along the Manistee River. The first year we went, my youngest child was only seven.

We each carried backpacks. My daughter's was a Disney backpack weighing less than 5 pounds, containing a change of clothes, fruit snacks, and water.

My husband's professional-grade hiking pack weighed in at 75 pounds and contained our tent, our stove, and most of our food. He hadn't carried such a heavy weight so many miles since his days in the army.

Within the first few miles (my husband trekking along under the weight of a small mountain), my daughter declared that her tiny pack was too heavy. Without a word, my husband took her pink princess backpack, strapped it to his chest, and marched on. Free of her burden, our little girl hopped and skipped blissfully down the trail.

Our heavenly Father invites us to do the same thing—to lay our burdens upon his shoulders. Unlike us, he can take it without flinching or waking up the next morning with sore muscles. **"Come to me, all you who are weary and burdened, and I will give you rest"** (Matthew 11:28).

And in the meantime, we can mimic our Father's love and carry one another's burdens whenever we can! **"Carry each other's burdens, and in this way you will fulfill the law of Christ"** (Galatians 6:2).

Restoration projects
Andrea Delwiche

"Restore us, O God; make your face shine on us, that we may be saved" (Psalm 80:3). We pray this and know that God is eager to work with us to continue the transformation of our hearts and minds to be more and more like Christ. So what does it look like when God takes on a restoration project?

God has a plan in mind. He redeemed us. He loves us right now, as we are, and yet he has a living vision of you and me that we oftentimes can't see. He sees us *living* and *growing* and *thriving* in relationship with him and others.

Restoration is messy. Walls need to come down. Old cabinets get ripped out. Faulty wiring gets replaced.

God is working on each of us right now. Each of us is in the middle of a spectacular remodel. We can catch a sense of God's restoration vision for us through the words of the apostle Paul in his letter to the Philippians: **"This is my prayer: that your love may abound more and more in knowledge and depth of insight, so that you may be able to discern what is best and may be pure and blameless for the day of Christ, filled with the fruit of righteousness that comes through Jesus Christ—to the glory and praise of God"** (1:9-11).

Restore us, O God. Let us be like you.

August 6

When the Bible doesn't make sense
Pastor Jon Enter

Have you read the Bible and said, "Yeah, I don't get it"? That can happen. Often it's because our sinful hearts don't accept the clear commands of God. That's not the Bible contradicting itself; it's the Bible contradicting our sinful nature.

Other times the Bible seems to contradict itself. When Jesus was at a wedding in Cana, they ran out of wine. Jesus' mother said to him, **"They have no more wine"** (John 2:3). His response sounded sinfully disrespectful: **"Woman, why do you involve me?"** (verse 4). If your mom asked you to pass the potatoes and you answered, "Woman, why do you involve me?" how would that go over?

The Bible clearly declares Jesus to be completely, always, only perfect (1 Peter 2:22). It's confusing how his response to his mother wasn't sinful.

When you're confused by a passage, read the context. Read the chapter and then that particular Bible book for the answer. Or search the Bible using the internet. When Jesus was on the cross, he lovingly made certain Mary was cared for by his disciple John. In fact, he called her "Woman" there too (John 19:26). No one sees that as disrespectful. It wasn't. Jesus wasn't disrespectful at Cana either.

When you have a question, search the Bible. When you do, you'll see one truth repeated: *Jesus perfectly loves you!* **"These are written that you may believe that Jesus is the Messiah, the Son of God, and that by believing you may have life in his name"** (John 20:31).

Our thoughts < God's thoughts
Pastor Mike Novotny

Recently, I risked my life to prove the importance of reading the Bible. One Sunday I decided not to sit but instead stand on the stool that is up on stage where I preach. I jumped up on the small seat of that stool, which was a definite insurance risk but hopefully a helpful reminder to read the Bible.

What point was I trying to prove? That the highest, smartest, and wisest of us is not even close to God. As I stood on the stool, I towered above everyone in the room, yet I was still so far below the clouds, stars, and God. I was still exponentially smaller than God. Here's how Isaiah expressed it: **"'For my thoughts are not your thoughts, neither are your ways my ways,' declares the Lord. 'As the heavens are higher than the earth, so are my ways higher than your ways and my thoughts than your thoughts'"** (55:8,9).

This is why we need the Bible. Without God revealing the wisdom of heaven, all we have is the wisdom of earth. Your feelings, my opinions, national surveys, and church traditions might be better and wiser than others, but they are still light-years from the wisdom of God. So if you want true wisdom, turn your ear to the heavens as you turn your eyes to the Word.

Without the Bible, there are only our thoughts. With the Bible, we receive the thoughts of God. And what thoughts they are!

A matter of faith
Christine Wentzel

"Why, Lord, do you stand far away? Why do you hide yourself in times of trouble?" (Psalm 10:1).

I am thankful that the Bible offers many examples of his people asking this same question. To ask is not a sin. To believe he is not who he says he is, is. If people say they don't believe in God because of all the pain and injustice in the world, isn't this a matter of acknowledging his existence? If our existence started from a big bang in space, then why blame God instead of the banality of happenstance?

"But not all the Israelites accepted the good news. For Isaiah says, 'Lord, who has believed our message?' Consequently, faith comes from hearing the message, and the message is heard through the word about Christ" (Romans 10:16,17).

On the matter of faith, it is only possible as a free gift of love given by the Creator of the universe through Christ. He raises faith above our limited human understanding. This faith assures us that God is who he says he is. His Son has our back. His Spirit knows what he is doing. This kind of faith prepares us for the now and grants us the sure hope of the new world to come.

"Now faith is confidence in what we hope for and assurance about what we do not see" (Hebrews 11:1).

Fix your thoughts on Jesus
Pastor Mike Novotny

If being a Christian feels hard during this season of your life (trusting God's plan, forgiving *that* person, not giving up on organized religion, etc.), pay attention to the encouragement that the author of Hebrews gives: **"Therefore, holy brothers and sisters, who share in the heavenly calling, fix your thoughts on Jesus, whom we acknowledge as our apostle and high priest"** (3:1).

Fix your thoughts on Jesus. Don't glance at Jesus or scroll past or spend an hour each week thinking about Jesus. Fix your thoughts on Jesus. The author is convinced that if you do that, you will realize that Jesus is worth it, no matter how hard following him might feel.

Recently, we practiced this at my church. I asked worshipers to stare at the cross in our worship space for a full 30 seconds, which gave us some silence and space to think about what Jesus did on our behalf. Afterward, an every-Sunday worshiper named Tom asked me, "Was the blood always there on our cross?"

"From the beginning," I answered.

"Huh . . ." Tom replied.

There are things about Jesus, glorious things, that you won't notice with a quick glance. So fix your thoughts on his cross. Think deeply about who he is (God in flesh), who you are (a sinner who deserved his wrath), and what he chose to do (prove his love by dying for you). Thoughts of his sacrifice will put your sacrifice in perspective, reminding you that God is still good and that his Son is still worthy of praise.

Think about the gospel
Pastor Mike Novotny

When I was studying to become a pastor, my professors would often remind me, "Preach the gospel every time." Why were they so passionate about turning me into a gospel-focused preacher? Maybe because the gospel isn't something that people can figure out on their own.

God's law (all the dos/don'ts of the Bible) is, for the most part, obvious. Because we all have a conscience, we don't need the Bible to figure out whether or not it's okay to murder our neighbor. But who, without God's Word, would ever think something like this: **"Let** [the wicked and the unrighteous] **turn to the Lord, and he will have mercy on them, and to our God, for he will freely pardon"** (Isaiah 55:7)?

Think about that. Whom is God freely pardoning here? On whom is he promising mercy? The wicked. The unrighteous. This is the most unhuman thought ever. God is inviting the wicked, the worst of us, the blackest sheep, the most prodigal son, to turn to him. "I want you wicked people to be with me," God says. "I want you sinners to become my sons and daughters," the Lord invites.

Isn't that crazy? Our God will freely pardon the wicked. He forgives for free. He forgives the wicked through the blood of Jesus Christ. That's the gospel, the good news that we would never figure out on our own.

Thank God for planning it, Jesus for doing it, and the Holy Spirit for revealing it!

Keep your eyes on the road
Jan Gompper

Can you imagine what it would be like to drive if our windshields were the size of our rearview mirrors? Likely, we'd get in many more accidents. Some of us wouldn't even get out of our own driveways. Thankfully, cars were designed with large windshields so we can clearly see what's ahead of us. The small rearview mirror is only there to see what's behind.

Sometimes people look at their lives through a rearview mirror instead of a windshield. They focus on past incidents, hurts, and/or regrets more than they do on what lies ahead of them. I've done so at times. How about you?

Occasionally it helps to look at the past to remind us of where not to return and/or of how far we've come, but when we stare too long in our rearview mirrors, we can become stuck, depressed, and unable or unwilling to move forward.

Perhaps that's why the apostle Paul gives us this encouragement: **"Forgetting what is behind and straining toward what is ahead, I press on toward the goal to win the prize for which God has called me heavenward in Christ Jesus"** (Philippians 3:13,14). Paul had done a lot of things in his past that could have made him remain in the land of regret, but once he experienced the love of Christ, he chose to stop focusing on his rearview mirror. Instead, he looked through the windshield of his *new* life and saw not only the road immediately ahead of him but, more important, his ultimate destination.

Your road trip isn't over. Focus forward!

Living water
Katrina Harrmann

It's easy to take water for granted.

My family and I realized this during our very first backpacking trip. The first half of the 22-mile trail was up on a bluff—nowhere near water. After hours in the sweltering sun, all our water bottles were empty. Boy were we hot and thirsty!

When we finally made it to Eddington Creek—a sandy-bottomed, fast-moving stream about 8 miles from the trailhead—we cheered! The kids and dogs splashed into the crisp river, and we dropped to our knees and drank right from the stream before filtering water into our bottles.

It brought to mind a familiar Bible passage: **"Whoever drinks the water I give them will never thirst. Indeed, the water I give them will become in them a spring of water welling up to eternal life"** (John 4:14).

Imagine never being thirsty again! It's hard to imagine how much that matters if you've never been DESPERATELY thirsty. Most of us don't have to worry about thirst in this day and age.

But God promises to assuage an *inner* thirst . . . an innate desire for something MORE. Something necessary. Something soul-saving . . . through his Son, Jesus Christ. Maybe we don't know how much we need that because we've known him our whole lives and have taken him for granted. Or maybe we've recently reencountered this Savior named Jesus.

Either way, Christ is the necessary water that offers eternal life, and we will never thirst again!

Grace makes space
Pastor Matt Ewart

It was the late 80s, and my family was experiencing what many other families were experiencing for the first time: a home computer.

I was always a natural at figuring out how to make computers work, even in the days when they weren't so easy to figure out. One day I was surprised that a member of my family didn't know how to make the computer print something out. "It's just logical," I said. At least it was to me.

Have you ever been surprised that other people don't see things as clearly as you see them? Or have you ever been shocked to learn that someone else wasn't able to do something that came naturally to you?

When those times come, it is so easy to think that those who are different than you are inferior to you. So keep this truth in mind: **"We have different gifts, according to the grace given to each of us"** (Romans 12:6).

When you encounter others who are different from you, remember that they are exactly like you. The grace they were given just looks a little different than yours.

And when you remember that you stand as a child of God by grace, it makes it easier to reflect grace to others. Grace means you give other people the space not to be you, and it celebrates the variety of gifts that God gives to different people.

See the King's glory!
Pastor David Scharf

Picture this. King David wrote, **"Lift up your heads, O you gates . . . that the King of glory may come in. Who is he, this King of glory? The LORD Almighty"** (Psalm 24:9,10). King David was describing the Messiah marching gloriously through the temple doors! But David didn't build the temple; his son Solomon did. In addition, the glorious King that he described wasn't going to come into the picture for another thousand years. And yet David described it as though he was there, witnessing the whole thing. David didn't miss the glory.

Do you ever miss it? Do you ever miss seeing the glory because things don't look glorious? Many missed it in Jesus' life. The religious leaders plotted to kill him. The people of Nazareth tried to push him off a cliff. Even his disciples didn't see the glory very often. It's easy to think that today is just another day.

But Jesus is coming . . . today. Maybe not for final judgment, but don't miss the King and his glory. Do you see him? The King of glory is at our worship just as he promised. Jesus is there at your prayers before bed to listen to your requests and your thanks. The King's glory can be seen when you put away someone's guilt and say, "I forgive you." Lift up your head and see! When you realize that the King of glory not only *did* come, not only *will* come, but *is* coming—then you won't miss it.

Stand firm
Linda Buxa

My son and I were driving to school when we saw two birds in the middle of the road. One flew off as I approached, while the other one stood still. It didn't even flinch. We laughed at the bird's bravado; I believe I called it a "flex," if you speak teen lingo. Then I said, "There's got to be a devotion idea in that."

We decided there was, and we found it in 1 Corinthians 15:57,58: **"But thanks be to God! He gives us the victory through our Lord Jesus Christ. Therefore, my dear brothers and sisters, stand firm. Let nothing move you. Always give yourselves fully to the work of the Lord, because you know that your labor in the Lord is not in vain."**

Because Jesus defeated death and gives us credit for that, we get to claim his victory as our own. With our eternal future secure, we get a new perspective on the present. When we do face trouble, which can seem overwhelming (kind of like how huge my car is compared to that tiny bird), we know who gives us the strength to stand firm. We don't fly off when troubles come because we have the courage and power of our Savior Jesus.

Because we aren't moved, we stay focused on the work we have to do: telling others Jesus won the victory for them too. They can stand firm. Thanks be to God!

What can't God give you?
Pastor David Scharf

Abram of the Old Testament was in his 80s and childless, even though God had promised him a son. In a moment of doubt, Abram cried out, **"Sovereign Lord, what can you give me?"** (Genesis 15:2). Have you been there? When money is tight or guilt is raging or loneliness sets in: "Lord, what can you give me?" Listen to God's answer: **"Look up at the sky and count the stars—if indeed you can count them. . . . So shall your offspring be"** (Genesis 15:5).

Think about that. The Creator of the stars is the One who made promises to Abram and to you. Are you worried God won't provide? Look at the stars. God knows each one by name. He knows you and will provide. Are you concerned God won't work things for your good as he promised? Remember the special star he put in the sky at Jesus' birth. He can make your difficult situation work for your good. Are you racked with guilt? The One who promises to forgive your every wrong is the One who darkened the star we call the sun on Good Friday to prove that your sin really is forgiven. Are you scared of death? God made the sun rise on Easter morning to reveal that his Son had risen from the grave! Death is not the end. That's what he will give you!

When tempted to ask, "Lord, what can you give me?" just step outside and look up at the stars . . . and you'll have your answer.

Wait on the Lord
Ann Jahns

There's a stoplight on my way to work that I detest. A left turn arrow, specifically. If you drive up to it as it's turning yellow, you need to wait an eternity for it to turn green again. The last time I pulled up to it, I decided to time it just to feed my righteous indignation. You know how long I had to wait for that arrow to turn green again? Sixty whole seconds.

When did we get this impatient? When did we get to the point where having to wait a mere minute at a stoplight can ruin our morning commute?

Do you ever feel this impatience with God? King David did: **"How long, Lord? Will you forget me forever? How long will you hide your face from me? How long must I wrestle with my thoughts and day after day have sorrow in my heart?"** (Psalm 13:1,2).

We are such impatient creatures. Not only does God sometimes not answer our prayers the *way* we would like, but he also doesn't seem to answer them *as quickly* as we would like. How long until I meet that perfect someone? How long until my kids get older so parenting becomes easier? How long until God delivers me from the nagging sin I can't seem to conquer?

God's timing; not ours. God's plan; not ours. Our heads get it, but our hearts still struggle. Let's also declare with David, **"Wait for the Lord; be strong and take heart and wait for the Lord"** (Psalm 27:14).

Lord, give us strength to trust your timing for our lives.

August 18

God guards your mind
Pastor Mike Novotny

Recently, I tried to barrel through a barrel-chested Hawaiian and a former black ops soldier. John and Tim, two solid guys from my church, agreed to help me teach Philippians 4:7. John probably weighs 225 and looks like he could lift me above his head with one hand. And Tim makes John look small! So when all 175 pounds of me took a running start and tried to get past these two men . . . let's say things didn't go well. I slammed into a wall of muscle that wasn't about to move.

What truth was I trying to visualize? **"The peace of God, which transcends all understanding, will guard your hearts and your minds in Christ Jesus"** (Philippians 4:7). God's peace *guards* our hearts and our minds. God's peace is bigger than we can even understand, and it guards our vulnerable hearts.

When the enemy's lies try to barrel through, they don't stand a chance. Do you think you're too sinful to be loved? too broken to be saved? too unworthy to be heard when you pray? God's peace bounces those thoughts out of your heart. Do you feel like you aren't going to make it, that you won't be able to resist it? God's peace refuses to let those lies live within you. The devil might seem too strong, but he is a skinny devil that doesn't stand a chance against the peace of God. Take a deep breath. You're going to make it today. The peace of God will guard your heart and mind.

The Jesus broom
Pastor Mike Novotny

Not long ago, I preached about the high cost of following Jesus. Denying yourself, putting God first, and allowing the Word to determine how you should live can make you question if you want to be a Christian.

That's why I grabbed some black duct tape and a broom from our church's janitorial closet. I wrapped the black tape around the end of the broom handle, put the taped end in my palm, fixed my eyes on the tape, and attempted to balance the now vertical broom. Within two seconds, it came crashing to the ground.

Next, however, I repeated the experiment but fixed my eyes not on the taped bottom of the broom but instead on the top of it. Same me, same broom, but different focus . . . and very different results. I easily balanced the broom for all to see.

My point? Focus on all the hard parts of following Jesus—denying yourself, repentance, etc.—and your faith will soon topple. But focus on the gifts that only Jesus can give—eternal life, salvation from sin, a way to the Father—and your faith will endure.

Perhaps this is why Hebrews says, **"Therefore, holy brothers and sisters, who share in the heavenly calling, fix your thoughts on Jesus, whom we acknowledge as our apostle and high priest"** (3:1). Fix your thoughts on the Jesus who was sent out from the Father ("our apostle") to offer himself as the perfect sacrifice for our sins ("our high priest"). That focus will make you cry, "Worthy! Jesus is worth it!"

Enjoy the present
Pastor Matt Ewart

"I wish there was a way to know you're in the good old days before you've actually left them."—Andy Bernard, *The Office*

The great irony of life is that most of our thoughts are directed toward things from the past or things in the future. It is almost unnatural to pause and live in the present. And it comes at a cost.

Dwelling too much on the past will either fill you with regret over the way things turned out, or it will fill you with lament that the good times are past.

Dwelling too much on the future will either fill you with anxiety over all the things you can't control, or it will fill you with false security over all the things you think you control.

If any Christian ever wrestled with regrets over the past or anxiety over the future, it should have been the apostle Paul. But he found the secret to living in the present, and he was kind enough to share it with all of us: **"I have learned the secret of being content in any and every situation"** (Philippians 4:12).

Being content in the present creates a peace that no event from your past can take way. Finding contentment in the present makes you resilient to all the anxiety about whatever's in the future.

Contentment begins when you believe that God has forgiven your past and he has a purpose for your future. Take some time today to enjoy the present.

I have great news
Ann Jahns

My husband and I recently became grandparents for the first time. I can't seem to stop telling everyone the amazing news, to the point that I'm even starting to annoy myself. "How am I doing today, you ask? Well, I just became a grandparent! Want to hear all about it?" I want to shout it from the rooftops. I want to plaster it all over social media. I want to go on and on (and on and on) about it to anyone who will listen.

The first Christians also had great news to share. Peter and John, Jesus' friends and disciples, got into hot water with the hard-hearted religious leaders of the day. They healed a man who couldn't walk in the name of the risen Jesus and were then ordered to cease and desist and thrown into jail. Their response? **"We cannot help speaking about what we have seen and heard"** (Acts 4:20).

These two men were on fire for the gospel. The doubts and questions they had while Jesus was on earth with them were now erased, replaced with the zeal and conviction of faith that the Holy Spirit had burned into their hearts on the Day of Pentecost.

As hard as it is to believe, we as Jesus followers have even better news to share than that first grandchild or that long-awaited promotion or that good medical test result. We have the news of the risen Jesus, the greatest good news of all.

Lord, give us the fire to share that good news!

Share your stories
Andrea Delwiche

Have you been tempted to sugarcoat the story of your faith walk with God? In Psalm 78, the writer shares a story. In some respects, it's a tragic story of humanity's failed attempts at self-reliance. But it's also a story of God's provision and persistent work and caring for his beloved children. We can learn a lot from this honest story.

"I will open my mouth with a parable; I will utter hidden things, things from of old—things we have heard and known, things our ancestors have told us. We will not hide them from their descendants; we will tell the next generation the praiseworthy deeds of the Lord, his power, and the wonders he has done" (verses 2-4).

What if, rather than hiding in shame, we shared the contrasting stories of our spiritual failures and successes and God's faithfulness? The psalmist gives us good reason to do so: **"So the next generation would know. . . . Then they would put their trust in God and would not forget his deeds"** (verses 6,7).

We are God's beloved. We share our stories in a spirit of freedom. We all fail; but In Christ, we can grow and change. Our vulnerability becomes a doorway to a haven where others can admit their own struggles and experience God's love.

It's not too late. Jesus' followers begin again each moment. Look at the works of God; see his faithfulness in your life. You are taking a journey with him. Ask for the Spirit's guidance and wisdom as you bear witness to his work in your heart and life.

Church is a chance, not a chore
Pastor Mike Novotny

The founding pastor of my church often said, "Coming to church isn't a 'have to.' It's a 'get to.'" I like that. I suppose you could see gathering for worship as an obligation or a chore that must be done, given what God says in Hebrews 10:25. Church isn't an option according to the law of the Lord.

But I prefer to see it as a chance to hear about God's unconditional love. Just before warning us not to miss church, the author of Hebrews writes, **"Therefore, brothers and sisters, since we have confidence to enter the Most Holy Place by the blood of Jesus, by a new and living way opened for us through the curtain, that is, his body, and since we have a great priest over the house of God, let us draw near to God with a sincere heart and with the full assurance that faith brings"** (10:19-22).

When is the last time your boss told you about the blessings of the blood of Jesus? Um . . . never. What was the last commercial that promised you a place in the very presence of God? Um . . . I can't remember. But when was the last church service that told you about God's love, Jesus' blood, and the full assurance that faith brings? Last Sunday. And next Sunday will too.

I know it takes some time and effort to make it on Sunday, but church isn't a chore. It's a chance to hear the greatest news in the world. It's much more "get to" than "have to."

Slow patience
Christine Wentzel

"The Lord is . . . patient with you, not wanting anyone to perish, but everyone to come to repentance" (2 Peter 3:9).

When God allows lies to speak . . . Grace is patient.

When God allows his teachings to be banned . . . Grace is patient.

When God allows the martyrdom of his people . . . Grace is patient.

When God allows the distortion of marriage and sex . . . Grace is patient.

When God allows global diseases, natural disasters, and violence . . . Grace is patient.

When God allowed his innocent Son, Jesus, to be sacrificed for our disobedience . . . Grace was patient.

When God allowed Jesus to be raised from the dead so we can be raised too . . . Grace was patient.

When God allows Jesus' love to shine through our work in a hate-filled world . . . Grace is patient.

When God allows the free gift of faith in Jesus to jump-start dead hearts . . . Grace is patient.

When God allows us mere immortals to tell this good news in Jesus' name . . . Grace is patient.

When God allows a stay of judgment until that gospel work is done . . . Grace is patient.

"The law was brought in so that the trespass might increase. But where sin increased, grace increased all the more, so that, just as sin reigned in death, so also grace might reign through righteousness to bring eternal life through Jesus Christ our Lord" (Romans 5:20,21).

A Savior for smart people
Pastor Mike Novotny

I have always loved the intellectual side of the Christian faith. Far from "blind faith," the Bible is filled with details that should make smart people pay attention. Perhaps no New Testament sentence says it better than this: **"With this in mind, since I myself have carefully investigated everything from the beginning, I too decided to write an orderly account for you, most excellent Theophilus"** (Luke 1:3,4).

Notice the details: "I myself" refers to Luke, a medical doctor who is writing this paragraph in the classical/complex Greek style. In other words, Luke is an intelligent man. "Carefully investigated" describes Luke's approach to his research, which was the opposite of a quick Google search or a lazy freshman just hoping to turn in an essay at the 11th hour. "Everything from the beginning" points to the thoroughness of this gospel, which begins before the conception of Jesus and walks us all the way through our Savior's return to heaven, the only one of the four gospels that covers that span of events. "Most excellent Theophilus" might refer to Luke's patron, a wealthy man who could have given a research grant so that Luke could dedicate his brilliant mind to this work as a full-time job.

Put it all together and you have even more reasons to read Luke and find certainty in the Christian faith.

When God's timing doesn't make sense
Pastor Jon Enter

In John chapter 2, Mary asked Jesus to help a new-lywed couple at Cana who ran out of wine. Jesus replied, **"My hour has not yet come"** (verse 4). It sounded as if he had no plan and no interest in doing something to help. But then Jesus changed water into wine.

Sometimes it seems as if God has no plan or no interest in doing something to help you or me. Where is God seemingly delayed in response to your prayers?

God has not forgotten you. Have you read about the ten lepers from Luke 17? When they left Jesus, they weren't healed. The healing happened later. In Mark 8, Jesus healed a man born blind. The healing happened in stages. First the man saw shadowy figures. Later he was healed completely. God gives you what you need when the timing is best.

Ultimately, what do you need? It's what the couple at Cana needed. It's the same thing the ten lepers and the blind man needed. It wasn't wine or healing; it was something more valuable.

What do you need? It's something you already have. You need a Savior. And that's what you have in Jesus! When Jesus said to Mary, "My hour has not yet come," he was referring to his death, to his sacrifice that fulfills your greatest need—forgiveness.

Jesus always has your best interests in mind. Sometimes he acts instantly. Other times he uses the pains of this broken world to draw you to him. Either way, you are supported, you are loved, you are his.

Demolish the lies you believe
Pastor Mike Novotny

Back in 2013, I saw the stronghold of Corinth, the ancient fortress perched just above the Greek city where Paul planted a Christian church. After climbing the steep banks that led up to the fortress, I marveled at the towering walls that protected the highest point of the city. What would it have taken to conquer such a place? In an age without drones or bombs, how could someone knock down the walls and conquer this stronghold? Answer—It would take something with immense power.

I wonder if the Corinthians glanced up at the stronghold of their city when the apostle Paul wrote about untrue thoughts. **"The weapons we fight with are not the weapons of the world. On the contrary, they have divine power to demolish strongholds"** (2 Corinthians 10:4). God's Word has divine power. It can demolish the lies that have a strong hold on your thoughts, like the lie that God isn't hearing your prayers or that your pain means that God is mad at you or that you can't patiently parent those kids another day. Since the Bible is full of the Spirit and of life, as Jesus once put it, it can do more for you and in you than you might believe.

Never underestimate the impact of a morning devotion or a Sunday worship service or a Christian song filled with the promises of God's Word. Your Father is handing you a weapon infused with divine power that has the ability to demolish whatever lies have lived in your head for far too long.

The mouse that roared
Katrina Harrmann

One summer, my family and I were enjoying a bonfire. My son was holding our puppy's leash when a tiny mouse scurried out of the woodpile. My son was not small—but he wasn't paying attention. And when the puppy lunged for the mouse, my son went flying off his feet with a look of comical surprise. He wasn't hurt—and we all had a good chuckle. But it really got me thinking.

How often is sin like this?

We might ignore the little sins because we think they aren't much. It's not a big deal. Looking at that won't have a lasting effect. Gossiping like this won't make a difference. Indulging in this or that "tiny" addiction doesn't matter much.

But how often do we underestimate these "little" sins, (it's just a mouse!) until one day, when we aren't paying attention, we get pulled off our feet in a BIG way!

"It does not matter how small the sins are provided that their cumulative effect is to edge the man away from the Light and out into the Nothing. Murder is no better than cards if cards can do the trick," says C. S. Lewis' troublemaking demon in the infamous *Screwtape Letters*.

Small sins DO matter! Because sin is sin! After all, Adam and Eve felled the world with the bite of one piece of fruit. **"Sin entered the world through one man"** (Romans 5:12).

Instead of ignoring the "small" sins, we use them as training grounds so that when BIG temptations arrive, we can stand firm.

The peace of God will guard your heart!
Pastor Mike Novotny

When I was a kid, all the sermons ended the same. I don't know when or how this tradition started, but the pastors in my denomination would always end by saying/ mumbling, **"And the peace of God, which transcends all understanding, will guard your hearts and minds in Christ Jesus"** (Philippians 4:7). And I would yawn. Or I would smile and reach for my jacket, because I knew that church was almost done (I was a sinful kid).

Now that I'm older, I have new thoughts about those words. I believe they are caps-lock, shout-out-loud worthy. God's peace is guarding my heart and my mind today. Yours too! God promises to be with you at your new job, to love you despite your family drama, to forgive you for your sexual sins, to help you with an aging relative, and to strengthen you to suffer well. His words are like burly guards that are ready to bounce any fearful thought or outright lie from your head. God loves you so much that he has ordered his peace to guard your heart and your mind.

Recently, I ended a sermon by having our whole church stand up, spread their arms out wide, and shout these beautiful words. Maybe you could do the same right now. Ready? **"And the peace of God, which transcends all understanding, will guard your hearts and minds in Christ Jesus."** What a thought!

Don't be afraid to repent
Pastor David Scharf

Has fear ever driven your repentance by thinking, "I need to repent to be forgiven?" As Christians, we don't repent to be forgiven. We repent *because* we are forgiven. Look at God's heart for you on the cross. You *are* forgiven! God loves you! Now, what do you want to do? You want to repent, not *so that* God forgives you but *because* he forgives you.

Psalm 25:7,11 says, **"Do not remember the sins of my youth and my rebellious ways;** *according to your love* **remember me, for you, L**ORD**, are good.** *For the sake of your name,* **L**ORD**, forgive my iniquity, though it is great."** The psalmist repented for his sin *because* he knew God's love. He was sorry, not because God would kill him but because his sin would kill the God who loves him. He continued: **"My eyes are ever on the L**ORD**, for only he will release my feet from the snare"** (verse 15).

Never take your eyes off Jesus. You have a lot of things to do today, a lot of deadlines to meet, and a lot of places to run to and from. But always keep your eyes on the Lord. After all, when you remember that he has given you all your gifts and opportunities in life, your ability to work and play, and most important that he gives you himself—when you remember just how much God loves you, then you won't be afraid to repent.

Contentment blues
Christine Wentzel

One day while cleaning the kitchen, I thought I could hear running water coming from the den. I threw down the sponge with a "what now?" thought and cautiously peered around the corner to see sudsy water from the old washing machine doing a slow creep toward the dry carpet. I irritably grabbed a mop and lots of clean towels to sop up the mess. I was so worked up by the time my husband came home from work that I offered him a cup of sour whine. He sighed and went to investigate while I not-so-secretly hoped he couldn't repair it. I wanted a new washer. Then a voice rang out with a happy, "Honey, I fixed it!" (Yay me . . .)

"Keep your lives free from the love of money and be content with what you have, because God has said, 'Never will I leave you; never will I forsake you'" (Hebrews 13:5).

Seeing my husband's tired, relieved face, I was ashamed for the discontent I let roar in my heart and drown my peace and his—again. My hardened heart melted into a hug of real appreciation for his God-given talent that saved us a lot of debt. Contentment slowly settled back in the present because I knew from past experience that my heavenly Father will answer that prayer of want in the way he knows best. For the future, the gift of contentment offers peace in the knowledge that one day there will be no need to clean dirty clothes or fix broken washing machines, because in Jesus, heaven is my forever home.

SEPTEMBER

Submit yourselves, then, to God.
Resist the devil, and he will flee from you.

JAMES 4:7

They see you
Pastor Mike Novotny

One of the hardest truths to see in yourself is your own God-given talent. When something comes so naturally to you, you might assume that everyone is like that, that anyone could do that. "It's nothing," we think. But that's not the truth!

In 1 Corinthians 12, the apostle Paul writes, **"There are different kinds of gifts, but the same Spirit distributes them"** (verse 4). Different. That means you are not like them. Just like the nose has a unique gift and purpose, so do you. So do your brothers and sisters who are filled with the Spirit.

Here's some homework—Point out people's gifts. They won't know how glorious God is unless you point out the glorious gift that he has given to them. Say to your information-loving friend, "How do you read so many books and listen to so many podcasts? That's a gift!" Or to your influential buddy, "How do lead like that? You share your ideas and people follow them. That's a gift!" Or to your bighearted sister, "How do you care so instinctively about people? Everyone else moves on, but you see the hurting people and reach out in love. That's a gift!"

As our scientific knowledge grows, we marvel more and more at the way the human eye or ear works. May our spiritual knowledge grow too so we marvel at the way God made and gifted us.

Afraid of success?
Pastor Matt Ewart

Most people are afraid of failure, but Peter was afraid of success.

He had already been out on the water all night trying to catch some fish, but they just weren't biting. He was frustrated and back on shore when Jesus invited himself onto Peter's boat. Jesus told him to put out the nets one more time. Even though this was the worst time of day to fish, Peter made a miraculous catch. It scared him.

"When Simon Peter saw this, he fell at Jesus' knees and said, 'Go away from me, Lord; I am a sinful man!'" (Luke 5:8).

Peter was afraid of success because it brought attention to how much of a failure he really was. He did not want the spotlight. He considered himself unworthy.

Have you ever felt afraid of success? Do you feel unworthy when people compliment you?

Like Peter, we should acknowledge that we are sinful too. But also, like Peter, we should not let our sinfulness limit what God wants to do through us.

Jesus came into your life not because you were worthy of him but because you were in need of him. Through his work he made you forgiven, holy, and blameless in God's eyes. When he came to you, he had a purpose for you.

There will be good fruit that simply comes from following Jesus. Don't get shy when people notice it. Thank God for what he's doing in you and through you. Honor him in your success.

Your identity and destiny
Pastor Mike Novotny

Have you ever noticed how human beings ache for (1) an identity and (2) a destiny? We try to figure out who we are, where we belong, and what the purpose of our lives is. How about you? Do you know who you are and why you are here?

Perhaps that's why I find the Christian faith so intriguing. Through the name of Jesus, every Christian is given (1) a beautiful identity and (2) a thrilling destiny. Hebrews says, **"Therefore, holy brothers and sisters, who share in the heavenly calling, fix your thoughts on Jesus"** (3:1).

Who are you? You are a holy member of the family of our Father. You aren't average, mediocre, or unimpressive but "holy," because the Holy One shed his holy blood to make you as holy as he is. You don't need to be popular, famous, or known by your next-door neighbor to be someone special, because you are someone to our Father in heaven. You are his beloved child.

And you have a destiny. You "share in the heavenly calling," meaning that God has called you to join him in heaven and, until that day comes, to bring a glimpse of heaven's love here to Earth. You don't need to be a pastor or start a business or launch a nonprofit to fulfill your destiny, because your destiny is simply to love others until you see the face of the One who loved you before the creation of the world.

Identity and destiny. Two of the countless gifts that are yours because of Jesus!

A prayer for mercy
Andrea Delwiche

"O God, the nations have invaded your inheritance; they have defiled your holy temple, they have reduced Jerusalem to rubble. They have left the dead bodies of your servants as food for the birds of the sky, the flesh of your own people for the animals of the wild. They have poured out blood like water all around Jerusalem, and there is no one to bury the dead. We are objects of contempt to our neighbors, of scorn and derision to those around us" (Psalm 79:1-4).

In these opening verses of Psalm 79, we've stumbled into a description of a horrifying scene. It can be appallingly easy to forget those who are suffering when we live in privilege.

What if we let the words of this psalm be raised as both a lament and prayer for mercy for suffering people around the world? Today, take a few minutes to raise your heart and hands in prayer to our God on behalf of others. Pray that they be delivered from evil. Pray that they see Jesus walking with them. Ask the Holy Spirit to give comfort to all who have witnessed and endured harm to their bodies and spirits. Ask the Lord to wrap them in his love and protection. Ask the Lord to stop evil acts for his name's sake.

May we bless our hurting brothers and sisters in this nation and throughout the world with our prayers and our actions.

THE BEST
Pastor Clark Schultz

My family and I recently watched the movie *Twister*. Have you seen that one? Experiencing a tornado live or even witnessing its destruction from afar can be life changing.

In our lives, we sometimes experience tornadoes of different kinds. We might see death happen to another family, but then the winds might hit us directly as we stand by the grave of a loved one. We might hear the howl of a broken marriage with children left to pick up the pieces. Or in the middle of a life storm, we might feel the strong winds of doubt and despair pulling us in every direction. Permit me to show you the Storm Stiller. This is not a story with Jesus in a boat but at a wedding with his disciples where he changed water into wine: **"You have saved the best till now"** (John 2:10).

If Jesus can take simple water and make it into prize-winning wine, think of what he can do and is doing in your life. When you are in the eye of a storm, all you see is the storm. Thankfully, you have the Bible's stories of Jesus' miracles to remind you that the sun is still shining and the Son is still very much active in your life, whether you see or feel him or not. He allowed his body to be twisted and pummeled to give you peace, security, and THE BEST.

Hold on and take cover in Jesus; he's got this and you!

Back to school
Katrina Harrmann

This is my least favorite time of year.

In Michigan where we live, this is the time all the kids go back to school. This has always been hard for me. I like the noise and chaos of my kiddos. And when the house empties out of all their conversation and laughter, my purpose flies right out the door with them. Other moms LOVE the return of peace and quiet, and I understand that too!

I think the struggle lies with routine. It feels like we've just gotten used to summer—sleeping in and enjoying vacation, kiddos rummaging in the fridge at all hours of the day for snacks, coming and going from summer jobs and outings with friends—and then it all changes and we're suddenly waking them up at 5:30 in the morning and trying to find enough hours in the day for school, music lessons, sports, and homework, not to mention our *own* to-do lists! And if we're letting go of college-aged students, it can be even harder!

"Trust in the LORD with all your heart and lean not on your own understanding" (Proverbs 3:5,6).

At times like this when the busyness of life bogs us down or the sudden quiet of an empty home robs us of purpose, turn to Christ and let HIM bridge the gap. **"There is a time for everything, and a season for every activity under the heavens"** (Ecclesiastes 3:1).

When God's commands don't make sense
Pastor Jon Enter

Which command of God doesn't make sense to you? The servants at a wedding in Cana must've been confused by Jesus' command. You can read the whole story in John 2, but some wedding hosts ran out of wine. Jesus' plan to fix this was to have six stone jars filled with water. Why? Water isn't wine. And Jesus wanted a lot of water. Each jar held about 25 gallons, so that's 150 gallons! The servants walked across town, maybe out of town, to haul about 1,200 pounds of water. That's a lot of trips. That's plenty of time to realize this didn't make sense! Then Jesus told them to scoop a cup and present it as wine to the one person who could fire them. They did what Jesus said because Jesus does what he says. Jesus turned the water into wine. What couldn't be, was because Jesus was involved.

What does Jesus say to you and me? **"Come to me, all you who are weary and burdened, and I will give you rest"** (Matthew 11:28). Go to Jesus with your pain and problems. Go to Jesus with your worry, your fears, and your anxiety. Go to Jesus when life doesn't make sense and you don't know what to do. He promises you rest. That doesn't mean he promises the pain will leave, but he promises he will give peace in the pain, perspective to the problems, and the rest you so desperately need. He will. Because Jesus does what he says he'll do.

Show them love
Ann Jahns

As a customer service associate, she wasn't that service-oriented as she silently and sullenly scanned my groceries at the checkout on New Year's Eve. As I got ready to leave, I remarked, "Let's hope next year is better than this year." This year had been yet another year of social unrest and pandemic-related turmoil. "Yes," she replied. "I lost my stepdad two days before Christmas." She went on to share the pain her family was going through.

It just goes to show that we never really know what's going on in people's lives that influences their words, attitudes, and actions. This young woman was just getting through the day, faithfully showing up for a thankless job of serving often thankless people. She needed some love and compassion.

If anyone knew how to show love to the unlovable, it was Jesus. He told his disciples: **"A new command I give you: Love one another. As I have loved you, so you must love one another. By this everyone will know that you are my disciples, if you love one another"** (John 13:34,35). This wasn't a friendly suggestion or something to check off and forget on our to-do lists. This was a command from our Savior for how we are to treat others.

Crabby customer service person? Show her love.

Jerk who cut you off on the freeway? Show him love.

Family member who always says the wrong thing? Show her love.

After all, we have been shown the greatest and most undeserved love of all.

Afflict the comfortable.
Comfort the afflicted.

Pastor Mike Novotny

I hadn't planned on being that intense with her. We were at a coffee shop, and I was loving the conversation with this intelligent, honest, and spiritually curious woman. Eventually I asked her, "If you died today, do you think God would let you into heaven?" She replied, "I do. I try to be a good person. And I have a pure heart." After asking a few more clarifying questions, I replied rather bluntly, "According to Jesus, you are in grave spiritual danger."

During my Bible college years, my professors reminded me that the teachings of Jesus afflict the comfortable and comfort the afflicted. That's a way of saying Christianity confronts people who believe they are good and offers comfort to people who confess they were bad.

Need proof? Read Luke 18:9-14. Notice how Jesus confronted the "good" Pharisee who fasted twice a week and tithed to the church. Notice how Jesus comforted the "bad" tax collector who couldn't even look up to heaven out of his shame.

Do you think you're "good" without God's grace? You're not, and a one-minute video of your worst sins posted online (and the comments from other sinners!) would prove it. Do you think you're so "bad" that God is done with you? Think again. Jesus promised: **"For all those who exalt themselves will be humbled, and those who humble themselves will be exalted"** (Luke 18:14).

On our own, none of us deserves to be with God in heaven. But through Jesus, any of us can be there. What a comfort!

Always have hope
Pastor David Scharf

I once knew a child who would put her hands over her eyes if she did not want someone in the room with her. It was cute but delusional. Covering your eyes doesn't change the reality.

Is that how we view Christian hope sometimes? Like we're just covering up our eyes and refusing to see reality? We cry out to a world filled with war and crime and school shootings and sickness and death: "Our God is good! Our God is in control!" At low times, we wonder if those words seem empty to others and to us too.

The psalmist writes, **"As for me, I will always have hope. . . . You who have done great things. Who is like you, God?"** (Psalm 71:14,19). That's a great question. Who is like our God? He once mercifully spared Adam and Eve when they sinned. He once powerfully divided the waters of the Red Sea so his people could pass through safely. Our God once sent his Son, our Savior, to die on a cross. Who would make himself weak like our God? Our God once did that . . . for you and me. Who, O God, is like you? No one.

Christian hope doesn't come from living life with your hands over your eyes, refusing to see reality. Instead it's taking your hands off your eyes to see the reality of what God has done.

You can *always* have hope!

If he died for you, he wouldn't lie to you
Pastor Mike Novotny

"Pastor, do you ever doubt?" I was sitting across the table from a young mother who had serious doubts about the Christian faith. I tried my best to answer her questions about the Bible, heaven/hell, religion, etc., until she asked if I ever have second thoughts about my faith. After admitting that I do in my weaker moments, I explained an idea that often brought me comfort. If Jesus died for me, he wouldn't lie to me. That sentence is worth writing again—*If Jesus died for me, he wouldn't lie to me.* If Jesus came into this world to suffer for me when I was nothing but a hostile sinner, why in the world wouldn't he tell me the truth now that I am his friend? I can understand how selfish, manipulative men might use religion to control me, use me, and gain something from me. But I cannot understand why a liar would suffer in my place. That just doesn't make sense. Which is why it helps me deal with my doubts.

There are some hard things to believe in the Bible. You might struggle with trusting in the creation account, with the virgin birth, or with the existence of hell. When these tough teachings challenge your faith, repeat the words in the title of this devotion.

"But God demonstrates his own love for us in this: While we were still sinners, Christ died for us" (Romans 5:8). If you ever have doubts about the gospels, remember the gospel. It's the greatest proof that God is always telling us the truth.

Puppy training
Katrina Harrmann

We recently got a new dog . . . a Chihuahua pup that is only three pounds.

I've forgotten what it's like to care for such a vulnerable creature. We've learned to shuffle walk so we don't step on him, and we check the couch before we sit down.

Our yard isn't fenced, so when I take him outside, I *really* have to pay attention—especially at night when it's dark and hard to see. The pup zooms around the lawn, but I lose sight of him in the shadows, and this makes me decidedly nervous because Chihuahuas can get attacked by hawks or owls. I call him back repeatedly to the light spilling from the back porch and sigh in frustration when he sticks to the shadows. He just wants to have fun.

Aren't we often like this zoomy, little pup? We are constantly running from one thing to another, often ignoring the pitfalls and oblivious of the "hawks and owls" of the world, even though our Good Shepherd is always right there trying to call us back into the light and patiently extending his arms.

How often do we zoom right by him, going deeper into the shadows, because we want to do things *our* way? Much too often, right?

But Jesus, the Good Shepherd, never gives up on us.

"As a shepherd looks after his scattered flock when he is with them, so will I look after my sheep. I will rescue them from all the places where they were scattered" (Ezekiel 34:12).

Your every word is heard
Pastor Mike Novotny

"So, Mike, why do you stink at prayer?" the radio hosts asked. We were discussing a book I cowrote with Mark Jeske whose intro began with my confession, "I stink at prayer." I meant those words. I do pray. I just don't pray as much as I'd like to.

Do you feel great about your prayer life? One of the hardest things about conversations with God is that prayer seems so disconnected from life. Sometimes you pray about your health for years but nothing changes. Sometimes you barely pray at all and everything changes. Going to church often gives you a boost of wisdom, and listening to worship music can instantly lift your spirits, but prayer rarely has that immediate impact.

Maybe that's why God sent an angel to speak this good news to Zechariah, the soon-to-be father of John the Baptist: **"Do not be afraid, Zechariah; your prayer has been heard"** (Luke 1:13). That last phrase jumped off the page at me. The angel didn't say that "some people's prayers are heard" or that "your prayer might be heard if God can find the time." No! "Your prayer"—the specific thing that Zechariah personally prayed about— "has been heard." It reached God's ears and heart the moment he prayed it.

That's good news for people who stink at prayer. When you pray in Jesus' name, every word is heard. Don't be afraid your prayer isn't working. It is. Every single time. Pray today, because one day you'll see that God was listening to your every word.

Smashing stuff in church
Pastor Mike Novotny

I recently had one of my most memorable church moments. I built a tall tower out of Legos, so strong and sturdy that the little Lego guy that I placed outside the walls had no chance to get inside. That image represented some of the lies that have a strong hold in our heads that we just can't seem to shake. For you, that might be, "Everything is my fault" or, "Everything is their fault" or, "If I'm not perfect, I'm pathetic." These lies feel immovable, impossible to change, don't they?

But then I picked up a Bible. A big Bible. Holding that Bible like a baseball bat, I backed up from the Lego tower and swung as hard as I could! Boom! Legos flew in every direction as the tower exploded into hundreds of tiny bricks. (Honestly, it was so cool!)

What was my point? **"The weapons we fight with are not the weapons of the world. On the contrary, they have divine power to demolish strongholds"** (2 Corinthians 10:4). The Bible is our divine weapon, and it comes with divine power. What feels impossible for you to change is not impossible for God to change.

So pick up your Bible and swing it at that lie. Smash down your assumptions and take your thoughts captive, comparing them to the unchanging standards of Scripture. Lies won't come out with their hands up. You have to smash some stuff and go get them.

Happy smashing, child of God!

Just for you
Christine Wentzel

The Christmas gift-hunting season is on for those who do some early shopping. For some this is a thrill; for others it's a nerve-racking chore. But whatever the motivation, when the "perfect" gift is found, it's because we expect it will be graciously received. However, there will be times that balloon pops, and we might hear these real-life comments:

"I hope you saved the receipt."

"Here, you keep it—I'll never use it."

"Hey thanks; now I have two of them."

"This IS a joke, right?"

Truth be told, haven't we occasionally been the balloon poppers? The only perfect gifts are those given by our generous Father in heaven. Yet how many times do we grumble over our bodies: too average or too unhealthy; our clothes: too outdated or too few; our work: too boring or too difficult?

"But the wisdom that comes from heaven is first of all pure; then peace-loving, considerate, submissive, full of mercy and good fruit, impartial and sincere" (James 3:17).

The greatest gift God ever gave was Jesus. For us and our grumbling, he gave his Son to be born in this world to live life right—to give and receive in perfect obedience and to pay the entire sin price for us to receive the gift of salvation. He showers us with gifts for every need and prepares a heavenly mansion for the world to come. Even so, some will reject this perfect gift.

Lord, guard our hearts in the wisdom of your presence.

No seat for fear
Pastor Matt Ewart

"You cannot keep birds from flying over your head, but you can keep them from building a nest in your hair."—Martin Luther

Anxiety is becoming more and more of an issue in our world. The frenetic pace of life and barrage of digital distractions have both increased the demands on our lives and decreased our ability to handle them. One of the best ways to deal with anxiety is to prevent it.

Anxiety comes from two things. On the one hand, it can come from ignoring your fears and not addressing them in a proactive way. On the other hand, anxiety also comes from amplifying your fears and making too big of a deal out of them.

Ultimately, you cannot prevent fears from entering your heart, but you can stop them from building a nest. Here is one practical exercise that the apostle Paul taught people to do: **"Do not be anxious about anything, but in every situation, by prayer and petition, with thanksgiving, present your requests to God"** (Philippians 4:6).

Pay attention to fear, but do not let it command your attention. Give fear a listen, but do not give it a vote. Give fear a name, but do not give it a seat at your table.

Jesus makes it safe for you to address the fears that will enter your life. He has taken away the sting of death, and if he was able to do that, no fear can last long in his presence.

Today you have God's blessing
Pastor David Scharf

Jesus had come back home to preach. He stood up and quoted the prophet Isaiah: **"The Spirit of the Lord is on me, because he has anointed me to proclaim good news to the poor. He has sent me to proclaim freedom for the prisoners and recovery of sight for the blind, to set the oppressed free, to proclaim the year of the Lord's favor"** (Luke 4:18,19). After speaking of the promises of freedom, forgiveness, and favor with God, Jesus' next words took his listeners' breath away: **"*Today* this scripture is fulfilled in your hearing"** (verse 21). Not tomorrow. Not someday. Today!

For four thousand years, God's people had been waiting for *someday*. But the wait was over. Jesus had come to fulfill God's promises made so many years before. Because of it, *today* he gives you peace even in the presence of peril. *Today* he gives you comfort even in the chaos of catastrophe. *Today* he gives you forgiveness even in the fear of failure. When it comes to these promises of Jesus, someday is today!

Look into the Word and see. You don't need to hope that someday your health will improve, your wealth will increase, or anything else. *Today* you have freedom, forgiveness, and favor with God. And nothing in your life can change that reality. Nothing can change what Jesus has already given you. Every day you realize these blessings and hang on to Jesus' every word. Scripture is fulfilled . . . today and every day you have God's blessing!

There is joy in aging
Ann Jahns

When I was a kid, I remember paging through a catalog and seeing a product aimed at aging women. They were reading glasses—but with a twist. The lenses of the glasses were hinged, so the wearer could flip one lens down to apply makeup to that eye, while being able to see through the lens of the other eye. They looked, well, silly.

Decades later, I am wondering if they still make these handy glasses and where I can purchase them.

Oh, the indignities of aging! Our bodies and our minds are breaking down. We can now throw out our backs by simply sneezing. At best, we forget why we walked into a room. At worst, we forget how to eat or the faces of even those we love the most.

Is your aging body or mind betraying you? Do you groan with the psalmist, **"Do not cast me away when I am old; do not forsake me when my strength is gone"** (71:9)? I get it. But there can be joy in aging. The older we get, the more serious we become about God's purpose for us with the time we have remaining.

The psalmist also says, **"[The righteous] will still bear fruit in old age, they will stay fresh and green"** (92:14).

Are you still breathing? You are still producing fruit. Even if your mind gets cloudy or you can no longer walk on your own, you can still praise God with your lips and share the reason for the joy you have in Jesus.

First thought = wrong thought?

Pastor Mike Novotny

Have you ever noticed how often your first thought is a wrong thought? Recently, I read every single passage in the Bible that mentions the words *think, thought, thinking,* or *thoughtful* (apparently, I don't have many friends), and it struck me how often people in the Bible thought wrong.

Here are three quick examples: Lot said, "'Hurry and get out of [Sodom], because the LORD is about to destroy the city!' But his sons-in-law *thought* he was joking" (Genesis 19:14). Jesus said, "And when you pray, do not keep on babbling like pagans, for they *think* they will be heard because of their many words" (Matthew 6:7). Jesus asked Mary, "'Woman, why are you crying? Who is it you are looking for?' *Thinking* he was the gardener, she said, 'Sir, if you have carried him away, tell me where you have put him, and I will get him'" (John 20:15). The sons-in-law died, the pagans missed the joy of prayer, and Mary missed a bit of her Easter joy because they all thought wrong.

It is wise for you to think again. Don't trust your first thought, your gut reaction, or your instant opinion. Instead, take all your thoughts to the God who knows all things and wants what is best for you. What does God think about cancer? about dying? about the problems of life? Probably not what you do!

Open his Word, think again, and you will be richly blessed.

Chosen
Jan Gompper

Have you ever *not* been chosen? It may have first occurred in a grade school gym class when two appointed dodgeball captains called out names and yours was the last to be called. Maybe later on you weren't chosen for your high school sports team, play, or singing group. Perhaps still later, you weren't chosen by a person you hoped to date or for a promotion you hoped to get.

Not being chosen can make us feel like losers. If we experience it often enough, we may end up depressed, thinking that we're worthless.

But nothing could be further from the truth, because long before the job promotion, the school play, or the grade school dodgeball team, we already were chosen. **"Before I formed you in the womb I knew you, before you were born I set you apart"** (Jeremiah1:5). God chose you and me to be on *his* team, not based on our physical prowess, musical talent, looks, or intellect. He *chose* us simply because he loved us—from the moment we were conceived in our mothers' wombs.

Isn't that amazing! For *no reason whatsoever*, God *chose* us. Equally amazing is that he promises we will always remain on his team: **"I give them eternal life, and they shall never perish; no one will snatch them out of my hand"** (John 10:28).

"Therefore, as God's *chosen* people, holy and dearly loved, clothe yourselves with compassion, kindness, humility, gentleness and patience" (Colossians 3:12).

Beach glass brokenness
Katrina Harrmann

One of my favorite hobbies is hiking along the shores of Lake Michigan looking for beach glass. We have a few good beaches in our area, and over the years, my collection of glass has overflowed into several jars. The thing I love best about beach glass (besides that perfect moment when you spot a huge piece just lying on the beach within reach) is that it's essentially made from garbage. But when broken glass gets tumbled and churned for years by the waves, it becomes frosted and rounded and beautiful as a glowing jewel.

Think of all the brokenness in your life. Think of the places where you've been smashed and battered and emotionally splintered. Now imagine God singing over you a litany of love and forgiveness and healing so that those most awful, unpresentable aspects become bright as jewels, as brilliant as the sun—as white and clean as Christ himself.

God does this for us, over and over—transforming our awful brokenness into something amazing and priceless. Don't doubt for a moment that he treasures you. Your Creator marvels over you and holds you in his hand just like a piece of broken glass made new.

"And we all, who with unveiled faces contemplate the Lord's glory, are being transformed into his image with ever-increasing glory, which comes from the Lord, who is the Spirit" (2 Corinthians 3:18).

Prayer reaches him and is sweet to him
Pastor Mike Novotny

I had a light-bulb moment regarding prayer. My handy coworker Tom had re-created for me the golden altar of incense, a piece of furniture that used to stand in the temple in Jerusalem. You can Google it to get a visual picture. It was used by the priests to burn fragrant incense every morning and evening, just like God commanded in Exodus 30:1-10.

As I preached the following Sunday on the power of prayer, I lit a stick of cinnamon incense on the altar. Two things became immediately clear. First, the incense smelled sweet. The scent slowly began to spread through the church, a wonderful aroma that, when breathed in, brought a smile to your face. Second, the smoke of the incense wafted up into the air. Unlike smoke from an average candle, the incense billowed up in beautiful ribbons toward the ceiling that we all could see.

That's when it hit me. Prayer reaches God and is sweet to him! Why did God want his people to burn incense every morning and every night? Because prayer reaches him and is sweet to him. Prayer isn't pointless; it reaches him, just like smoke reaches to the sky. And prayer isn't annoying to God; it is sweet to him, like the scent of cinnamon.

Do you struggle to pray? Then meditate on these words: **"May my prayer be set before you like incense"** (Psalm 141:2). Because of Jesus, your prayer reaches him and is sweet to him.

Exult every day!

Pastor David Scharf

Note the word in the title: *Exult*, not *Exalt*. *To exalt* something is to raise something in esteem. Certainly, we can exalt our Savior-God for all he's done. But we can also *exult*, which is to be extremely joyful. When do you exult? Perhaps it's when you're in church, focused on God's promises. But what about on "Start of the work-week Monday" or "Stressed out about kids Tuesday" or "Laid off Wednesday" or "Problems with the marriage Thursday"? Why don't we exult every day? Have God's promises changed? No!

"But in the LORD all the descendants of Israel will be found righteous and will exult" (Isaiah 45:25 NIV84). Jesus has entered through the gates of the heavenly Jerusalem. Do you know who else will be there lining those streets paved with gold one day? You and I will. The books of our lives will be opened, and we will discover to our amazement that Jesus made everything good. Not because we could get to him by what we've done but because he came to us to wipe the books clean of every sin by what he's done. Don't miss what the prophet Isaiah says it means for you. You can *exult*. You can hold your head up high and rejoice no matter what happens during the week or what people say about you or think about you or even what *you* think about you. All that matters is what God says about you. That perspective means you can exult every day!

But for the grace of God
Christine Wentzel

"There but for the grace of God, go I." Perhaps you have spoken these words yourself. They are often attributed to a Protestant Christian martyr named John Bradford. He was burned at the stake in the mid-1550s during the reign of Mary I (Bloody Mary) in England. While incarcerated in the Tower of London for his reformed faith, he supposedly spoke these words as he watched prisoners going to their executions.

When I look back at the road I've traveled, I see corpses of neglected, abused, or rejected gifts of a generous and loving Provider scattered everywhere. My sins deservedly judge me guilty to serve out a death sentence, but for the grace of God.

Through the eyes of faith, I believe my Lord and Savior personally picked up my sin-filled litter from the past, present, and future and hefted the vile bag onto his own sinless shoulders as he willingly allowed himself to die on a cross in my (and your) place. Christ did this so I (and you) can be declared "not guilty!" from an eternal existence in hell.

When I am tempted to judge myself unredeemable, I look up into the same Spirit-powered eyes that provide my gift of faith. I hope to see what God sees through the work of his Son—a clean path with only one thing standing on it: a shining, empty cross reflecting the glory of the grace of God.

"As far as the east is from the west, so far has he removed our transgressions from us" (Psalm 103:12).

What to do with doubt
Pastor Mike Novotny

Recently, I met two women who were struggling with doubt. The first was raised in another religion but had fallen in love with a committed Christian. She was humble enough to learn about his Jesus, but she had her doubts. Was one religion right and the other wrong? Jesus is beautiful and forgiving, but is he true? The second woman faced the same doubts despite a very different path. She had been raised in a Christian church but wondered, as an adult, if Christianity was correct. What about other sincere believers from other religions? What if other faiths are climbing the same mountain toward God, just on different paths?

Two different stories; one similar struggle—doubt. How about you? Do you have doubts about the Christian faith? about Christ himself? Perhaps you wrestled with doubt the first time you had a Buddhist friend or a Muslim coworker or took a college class on comparative religions, experiences that might have turned your exclamation of faith into a hesitant question mark. Or maybe you doubt God's love for you after all you have done in your life?

If so, would you consider reading the gospel of Luke? Listen to how Luke begins: **"I too decided to write an orderly account for you, most excellent Theophilus, so that you may know the certainty of the things you have been taught"** (1:3,4). Certainty. No doubts. That was Luke's goal for his gospel. That's why he wrote an orderly account to Theophilus.

That's why he wrote those 24 chapters for you.

Too crowded to grow
Katrina Harrmann

This past year was our first experiment in raised-bed gardening. We tore out a good portion of our front lawn (yes, our *front* lawn!) and filled it with six or seven raised cedar beds surrounded by a gravel walkway. It's been delightful, but we're learning as we go.

For instance . . . radishes. I planted them for the first time. I was told they were impossibly easy, *foolproof.* But I messed up. I didn't thin them out as much as they needed, and as the plants grew, they began crowding themselves out. In July not a single radish had produced anything more than a pencil eraser-sized bulb.

I'll try again. But it made me stop and think about how often we crowd our lives with the trappings and "stuff" that we have in this world—how often we get so busy that we are overwhelmed and then (oops) we aren't producing *any* fruit. Or worse yet, we've convinced ourselves that 10% of our effort is all God is looking for.

There's an old saying: "If the devil doesn't make you bad, he'll make you busy." Ouch. While perhaps not doctrinally sound, it's an interesting saying that hits hard. We often think of sin as an overt offense against someone, but letting earthly priorities crowd out Christ *can be just as dangerous!*

"Love the Lord your God with all your heart and with all your soul and with all your mind" (Matthew 22:37).

Compensation or restoration
Pastor Matt Ewart

"If you find a perfect church, don't join it. You'd spoil it."—Billy Graham

It's only a matter of time until the people around you do you wrong. Sometimes the "wrong" is a petty offense they're unaware of. But other times it can be something substantially wrong that cost you something dear.

What do you do when that happens? When you confront someone for something they did, what's the goal of your confrontation?

It's easy to make justice the goal. Where there was a wrong, it needs to be made right. There needs to be justice. Usually confrontation happens in a way that seeks compensation from the other person.

But God gives a different way to navigate injustice: **"Brothers and sisters, if someone is caught in a sin, you who live by the Spirit should restore that person gently"** (Galatians 6:1).

God guides you to confront someone, not to seek compensation from them but to pursue restoration with them.

Making restoration your goal reflects the way God loved you. Jesus did not come to seek justice. He came to satisfy it by becoming a sin offering on our behalf. He restored you to God so that your life is now an ongoing offering right back to him.

It is more than likely that someone today will do wrong to you. The way God restored you now equips you to restore the people in your life.

Two gifts to give
Linda Buxa

It's almost time to make your Christmas lists (if you're the kind of person who thinks ahead like that). As you put all the tangible items on your list, might I suggest adding two intangible items? To make these gifts work, you need to start working on them now.

(Because I'm a mom, I'm using that context. To make it applicable, you can replace "mom" with friend, employer, employee, son, daughter, grandparent, etc.)

Here are the gifts on my list:

1. **A content mom.** God put you in your specific situation to be a blessing to those around you. Don't make yourself feel less valuable by comparing yourself to them. And don't make yourself feel better by judging them either. Don't compare your life, home, children, finances, or schedule to theirs. Find your identity as a child of God.

2. **A sinful, forgiven, grace-covered mom.** You probably spend an inordinate amount of time trying to be the perfect mom. You accommodate schedules, plan meals, sign forms, and try to have answers to life's quandaries. None of that makes you a good mom; it just means you're attentive to parenting details. You know what makes good moms? Jesus. Even if all the tasks you juggle were to drop, God would not stop loving you because his love covers over a multitude of sins.

While we can all give good gifts this year, being content and grace-covered will probably bring the most joy.

Why we pray in Jesus' name
Pastor Mike Novotny

There's a powerful truth tucked away in an Old Testament chapter that's tempting to skip or skim. In Exodus chapter 30, God tells Moses to make a gold-covered wooden pillar to burn incense every morning and evening. The top of the pillar had four horns, stylish pieces of wood on each corner, which would be smeared with the blood of an innocent sacrifice once each year.

Do you see the connection to your spiritual life? Probably not. Here's some help. The fragrant incense was a reminder that prayers are sweet to God. Our Father is not like a busy dad hunched over a laptop who wishes his kids would just leave him alone. No, he smiles when he hears our voices.

Second, the smoke of the incense was a reminder that prayers reach the heavens. When you pray, it's never pointless or powerless. Bring your aching joints, your complicated family, your history test, and your pet sin to God. Every request reaches the throne from where he runs the universe.

Finally, remember the blood. In the temple, the blood of an innocent sacrifice made Israel's prayers holy enough for God to accept. It's the same with yours. The blood of Jesus makes your prayers good enough for a glorious God. No longer are you praying as a sinner; you pray as a dearly loved son or daughter. That's the power of praying "in Jesus' name."

Or, as James put it, **"The prayer of a righteous person is powerful and effective"** (James 5:16).

Open your mouth wide
Andrea Delwiche

What if in our walk with God, we aimed to be like newly hatched robins: eyes shut, mouths wide open, crying for God's blessing to be dropped into our mouths to fill us with goodness?

God has given us the ability to care for ourselves, but within that God-given initiative, God *pleads* with us to be like baby birds: **"Open wide your mouth and I will fill it"** (Psalm 81:10). God has more to give us.

We can choose to ignore God's offer, and he will respect our choice. Listen to how he describes what happened in his relationship with his Old Testament people: **"But my people would not listen to me; Israel would not submit to me. So I gave them over to their stubborn hearts to follow their own devices"** (Psalm 81:11,12).

A baby robin doesn't refuse food that it needs to survive, but we refuse God's gifts. We can't survive without God's sustenance any more than a bird can survive without the mushy meal from its parent. Our souls and bodies are incomplete and malnourished and starving without everything that God has to offer us. He has everything we need for body and life.

It's a humbling position for us to be in, but like a tiny robin, we are cradled in a nest woven for us with love. It's our reality whether we want to accept it or not. What would happen if we kept that image of a baby bird in mind? What would happen if we opened our mouths wide so that God could fill them?

OCTOBER

He will command his angels concerning you
to guard you in all your ways.

PSALM 91:11

How low will you go?

Pastor Mike Novotny

When I lead small group Bible studies, we often end with "highs and lows." We talk about a spiritual high (a blessing, sanctified choice, temptation resisted, etc.) and a spiritual low (a mistake, sinful decision, temptation indulged, etc.). Often, these confessions bring Christians closer together.

But there's a question many of us ask ourselves when it's our turn—How low will you go? Will you tell the group *that*? What would they do if they knew about the pills, the pornography, the disordered eating, the divorce, or whatever else feels too messy to confess out loud?

I know those are nerve-racking confessions. But the Bible has a pattern of talking about the lowest of lows. Can you think of King David's sin? Or the apostle Paul's? I can, because the Bible talks about the sins of its saints.

Why does God lean toward specific confessions? So you would know his forgiveness is specifically for you. Paul wrote, **"Christ Jesus came into the world to save sinners—of whom I am the worst. But for that very reason I was shown mercy so that in me, the worst of sinners, Christ Jesus might display his immense patience as an example for those who would believe in him and receive eternal life"** (1 Timothy 1:15,16).

Your honest confession is an example that Jesus is immensely patient and supremely forgiving. Is today the day to talk about *that*? Don't be afraid. You are already safe because of the love of Jesus.

Hear me, Lord
Andrea Delwiche

Have you thought of designating multiple times per day to stop and pray?

"Hear me, LORD, and answer me, for I am poor and needy. Guard my life, for I am faithful to you; save your servant who trusts in you. You are my God; have mercy on me, Lord, for I call to you all day long. Bring joy to your servant, Lord, for I put my trust in you" (Psalm 86:1-4).

Consistent prayer times help make prayer an underpinning of your day, letting the weight of the day rest on your relationship with Christ. Prayer gets woven into all times and experiences of your life. The apostle Paul encourages, "Devote yourselves to prayer, being watchful and thankful" (Colossians 4:2)

In addition, prayer during daily activities grounds you in God. When the day is chaotic, relationships are troubled, or work is maddening, spending a few minutes with God helps you to regain equilibrium. You give space for the Holy Spirit to work within you. You remember whose world it is, whose reality you live in, and how you best operate. You have opportunity to praise God and to ask for his help. In a longer discourse on prayer, James encourages prayer in a multitude of situations: "Is anyone among you in trouble? Let them pray. Is anyone happy? Let them sing songs of praise" (James 5:13).

Prayer lifts the pressures that weigh you down. Lord, help us remember to call on you all day long.

Let this mind be in you: Dependence
Jason Nelson

Early in 2021, a rare infection entered my bloodstream and ravaged my heart. I almost died several times. Teams of heroic doctors scrambled to save my life. Lying in a hospital bed for months withered my body and soul. People suggested God had reasons for allowing me to survive open-heart surgery and serious complications in my lungs, stomach, and kidneys.

At first I was too sick to care. But as I recover, I wonder if the answer is so that I could have one more shot at trying to persuade people to adopt the mind of Christ as revealed in the Bible.

As my own faith has developed, I have avoided asking why when it comes to acts of God. God's thoughts are unsearchable. The apostle Paul says, **"Oh, the depth of the riches of the wisdom and knowledge of God!"** (Romans 11:33). He doesn't consult with anyone but listens to prayer and is willing to change his mind. Jesus didn't know everything God was thinking. Who am I to ask why?

We can identify with King David as he wondered why. His psalms don't explain a lot, but they express the joy and frustration in the restless heart of a flawed and faithful child of God. From the anguish of his soul, David wondered why the nations raged and why God was standing far off. We wonder too during pandemics, wars, social unrest, and grave illness. Our best hope is to depend on great David's greater Son, Jesus, to shepherd us, calm us, and restore us in his goodness and mercy.

A gentle whisper
Pastor Clark Schultz

As I held the kettlebell in one hand, the trainer told me to lift it over my head and take one step forward and one step backward. I took one step and went toppling into the trainer's arms. His advice: "Don't stare at the weight in your hand or at your feet. Instead gaze ahead at a spot on the wall and focus on that." The steps went smoothly after that.

Elijah had taken a few steps forward after a battle with the prophets of Baal on Mt. Carmel. His victory proved who the real God was. But then he went one step backward because the evil queen put a bounty on his head. So Elijah packed his bags for a pity party and went into hiding.

"The Lord said, 'Go out and stand on the mountain in the presence of the Lord, for the Lord is about to pass by.' Then a great and powerful wind tore the mountains apart and shattered the rocks before the Lord, but the Lord was not in the wind. . . . There was an earthquake, but the Lord was not in the earthquake. After the earthquake came a fire, but the Lord was not in the fire. And after the fire came a gentle whisper" (1 Kings 19:11,12).

God reminded Elijah that he needed to focus on the solution—God. Life will be a series of steps forward and back. As you step, focus on that gentle whisper of God who is with you every step of the way.

God's logic in the darkness
Pastor David Scharf

When you want to know someone, you use words. You have a conversation. The apostle John calls Jesus the Word of God. It's how we get to know God as well. John says, **"The Word became flesh"** (John 1:14). If you want to know God, if you want to know how he feels about you, then just look at Jesus.

When something bad happens in our lives, we look for a logical answer to why a loving God would let his child go through something bad. We don't know why, but we still try. We want to come up with logical proof that God loves us in order to make sense of it all. But we don't know him through logic. We learn to know him only through Jesus.

God calls Jesus the Word. The Greek word is *Logos*. It's where we get our word *logical* from. Jesus is the "logic" of God. Do you want proof of God's love? He doesn't give you a logical reason; he gives you a person. Look into the manger. Look at the cross. The answer doesn't come through a logical reason; it comes in Jesus' moaning and sighing, in his groaning, and in his dying. I can't tell you why something happened to you, but I do know this. It is not because God doesn't care about you. If you want to *know* God, look at Jesus. Then you will see God's logic in the darkness.

The symptoms of (and the cure for) greed

Pastor Mike Novotny

According to Jesus, the love of money is a sickness that needs to be cured. Unfortunately, greed is rather hard to self-diagnose, which is why so few Christians confess it. There are, however, symptoms that reveal this common sickness among sinners like us, so let's do a quick checkup.

Do you ever justify wrong for the sake of saving money? Like getting paid in cash to save tax dollars? Or telling the police officer you have no idea how fast you were driving even when you do? Or telling the cashier your children are younger than they actually are just so you can get the cheaper children's rate? Or living with/ sleeping with/having sex with someone who isn't your spouse, in part, because you don't want to spend money on a second rent?

There are more subtle symptoms too, which is why Jesus said that the Pharisees, who donated 10% of their salaries (and garden produce!) loved money. It's like never quite being grateful for what you have. Or always wanting bigger/better/faster/newer/more. Or worrying about tomorrow instead of thanking God for graciously providing today.

If you are sensing greed in your heart, listen to the words Jesus spoke when surrounded by money-loving sinners: **"It is not the healthy who need a doctor, but the sick. I have not come to call the righteous, but sinners to repentance"** (Luke 5:31,32). Confess your greed to Jesus. You are the very soul that this Doctor came to cure.

Side effects of Jesus
Pastor Daron Lindemann

TV commercials for prescription drugs are so amusing. The visuals depict a positive, peppy person living a happy, healthy life with sunny skies and smiley pets. Meanwhile the narrator races through a list of nasty side effects.

Jesus teaches us about the risk of side effects as his followers living in a world that doesn't follow him. He not only warns us about the risks, but he takes the responsibility for the risks himself.

Do you encounter unbelievers at work? Do your children experience an unbelieving, ungodly influence at school, not just from students but the education system itself? Do you struggle as you observe the corrupt immorality spreading through media?

Dangers of unbelief and evil lurk so near, right next to us like weeds growing next to crops in a field. But Jesus owns it all. He wants interaction between wheat and weeds, between believers and unbelievers.

"The one who sowed the good seed is the Son of Man. The field is the world, and the good seed stands for the people of the kingdom" (Matthew 13:37,38). Jesus himself plants the good seeds of wheat. That's you and all believers.

You are who you are and where you are not by accident or a couple lucky breaks or a bad streak of luck or entirely by your own personal choice.

Jesus planted you in just the right place in his kingdom, right where he wanted you in this world. Right next to unbelievers who need you.

Work: A curse or a blessing?

Jan Gompper

On June 28, 1894, Congress made the first Monday in September a national holiday to honor and recognize the work of laborers who helped contribute to America's growth and prosperity. Nowadays most of us look forward to Labor Day simply as a day when we don't have to go to work.

Have you ever felt that work was part of God's punishment after the fall into sin? Certainly, sin affected work, like it did everything else, but work itself was not a *consequence* of sin.

Work was initiated by God before sin entered the picture. After God's "work" of Creation was completed, he commanded Adam and Eve, **"Prosper! Reproduce! Fill Earth! Take charge! Be responsible for fish in the sea and birds in the air, for every living thing that moves on the face of Earth"** (Genesis 1:28 MSG). Talk about a management role!

God intended for his people to be engaged in productive activity, with regular breaks to rest and celebrate his goodness. That's still his desire, even though the infiltration of sin has caused "weeds and thorns" to hinder our endeavors.

Still, there is nothing more God-honoring or rewarding than to follow God's directive to work. He is especially pleased when we recognize our work (whatever the job) as a blessing from him and do it diligently and faithfully.

"That each of them may eat and drink, and find satisfaction in all their toil—this is the gift of God" (Ecclesiastes 3:13).

You get an A
Pastor Clark Schultz

I just read my son's report card. The teacher wrote, "Pleasure to have in class but talks too much, struggles with math, and his handwriting resembles ancient cave paintings." Ok, I exaggerated on that last one, but for fun my mother pulled out my old report cards, and they read almost word for word.

We have moments as parents when we're so proud of our children. We say, "That's my boy/girl!" But what about the days when our children are kicked off the team for breaking training rules or are failing every class? To God that must be what it looks like when he looks at us. He created us to be holy and perfect. But that ship sailed long ago, as Paul reminds us: **"I know that good itself does not dwell in me, that is, in my sinful nature"** (Romans 7:18).

God hates when we don't make the grade, talk too much out of both sides of our mouths, have a me-first attitude, and when our whole attitude toward God and others needs improvement. But Jesus did something about our sloppy sins. He became our substitute. **"God made him who had no sin to be sin for us, so that in him we might become the righteousness of God"** (2 Corinthians 5:21). Through Jesus you get an A on your report card. God is and will always be proud of you!

An encounter with God
Linda Buxa

We all love celebrity encounters. We share the photos of the drumstick caught during the concert. We rejoice that the country singer crossed the street in front of us and briefly made eye contact. We recognize the actress on a flight, tweet about it, and she replies. We frame the professional athlete's autograph. We wave at the presidential motorcade.

It's amazing to me that a celebrity can be near us for maybe seven seconds, and we never forget it—even though that star will never remember it. What's more amazing to me is that every time we are reading the Bible or in a small group study or at a worship service, we are encountering the biggest celebrity of all time, the living God. What's astonishing, though, is that at these encounters, he treats *us* like celebrities! *He* rejoices over *us* with singing. *He* replies every single time *we* pray to him. *He* engraves *our* names on the palm of his hand.

He also promises that he is Immanuel, not "God walked near us" or "God made eye contact with us" but literally "God with us." He assures us that he will always remember us and never leave us. He promises that even if celebrities, the world, or even our own parents forget us, **"I will not forget you!"** (Isaiah 49:15). He reminds us that nothing can separate us from his love, that he will bless us, smile on us, and give us peace, which is way better than a concert drumstick.

You might feel dizzy

Pastor Daron Lindemann

There's a Greek word used in the Bible that means "spinning around and getting dizzy," like on one of those spinning rides at the fair.

It happens when anyone believes **"every wind of teaching"** and buys into **"the craftiness of people in their deceitful scheming"** (Ephesians 4:14). As a result, we are **"blown here and there."** That's where the Greek word for *dizzy* appears.

Man-made opinions about things in this world make people more dizzy than the Tilt-A-Whirl ride at the fair. Like opinions about education, raising children, politics, how to spend or save money, and the best way to address COVID, just to name a few.

Claim that your human opinion is as perfect and authoritative as Jesus' own true teachings, and it's proof you're dizzy, confused, and misdirected. It's okay to have ideas and opinions, as long as you remember that they are human ideas and opinions—not divine truths and answers.

So don't claim to have a monopoly on the truth because it's your opinion. And don't judge others unfairly.

"Speaking the truth in love, we will grow to become in every respect the mature body of him who is the head, that is, Christ. From him the whole body, joined and held together by every supporting ligament, grows and builds itself up in love, as each part does its work" (Ephesians 4:15,16).

Being loving toward others *and* true to Jesus is more important than being right about your opinion.

God is listening
Andrea Delwiche

"Lᴏʀᴅ, you are the God who saves me; day and night I cry out to you. I am overwhelmed with troubles and my life draws near to death. But I cry to you for help, Lᴏʀᴅ; in the morning my prayer comes before you. Why, Lᴏʀᴅ, do you reject me and hide your face from me?" (Psalm 88:1,3,13,14).

Ever end your day feeling like you could have written these words? Ever start a day feeling like these words were already true? You hold the Bible in your hands without flipping a page. You stare at the words on the page without comprehension.

It's okay. This is not a sign that your faith is evaporating or that you don't love God. God meets us in these downtimes and walks with us, interpreting them for us. In addition, we can look to the examples of women and men of faith throughout the ages and learn how God, through his Spirit, reached out to draw them in during the breaking points of life.

These words from James can also serve as encouragement: **"Consider it pure joy, my brothers and sisters, whenever you face trials of many kinds, because you know that the testing of your faith produces perseverance. Let perseverance finish its work so that you may be mature and complete, not lacking anything. If any of you lacks wisdom, you should ask God, who gives generously to all without finding fault, and it will be given to you"** (1:2-5).

God is listening. He is working. He is bringing you through.

Freedom in Christ
Pastor Clark Schultz

On Saturday mornings in the 80s, I remember seeing the *School House Rock* tagline that boasted, "Knowledge is power." One episode of this cartoon was about BILL, who was sitting on Capitol Hill. This cartoon explained to young listeners in word and song how legislation works.

Perhaps another tour of that show is needed because a recent poll cites that 10% of the population knows that the First Amendment protects freedom of speech. About 33% has no clue what the amendment says, and only 19% realizes it protects freedom of religion.

In March 2020 we weren't singing any tunes in church. Churches closed, and some are still closed. I preached my Easter sermon to an empty church, aside from a few cardboard cutouts that some creative members made. Many felt as though our freedoms were taken away from us.

In some respects, yes. In reality, Scripture tells us, **"If the Son sets you free, you will be free indeed"** (John 8:36). Christ has indeed set us free. Is there a pet sin that's holding you down? Fire off the shackles and chains with the victory cry that Calvary's cross won and continues to win for you daily. Buildings and church services can come and go, but that can never take away our freedom in Christ.

You are bad
Pastor Mike Novotny

When I was a kid, *Saturday Night Live* had a skit called "Deep Thoughts With Jack Handy." In one episode, Jack Handy mused, "If a kid asks where rain comes from, I think a cute thing to tell him is, 'God is crying.' And if he asks why God is crying, another cute thing to tell him is, 'Probably because of something you did.'"

That's darkly funny, because many of us think that when we are suffering. Maybe breast cancer is God's punishment for the years of ignoring God and focusing on you. Maybe infertility is payback for your affair. Maybe this difficult season is connected to some sin you committed in the past.

The reason we often make the connection between sin and suffering is because they are often connected. Proverbs is packed with passages like this: **"The wise inherit honor, but fools get only shame"** (3:35). Fools get shame. Alcoholics get failing livers. Gossips lose friends. Sin often has a painful earthly consequence.

Often. But not always. Think of Job, the blameless man from the Bible who lost all ten of his children in a tragic accident. Or David, the man who bravely saved Israel from Goliath and got a murderously jealous king as a reward. Suffering isn't always your fault.

If you want to know why you are in pain, think deeply, critically, and biblically. **"Not only so, but we also glory in our sufferings, because we know that suffering produces perseverance; perseverance, character; and character, hope"** (Romans 5:3,4).

God is bad
Pastor Mike Novotny

"Why, God?" That is the most natural and the most dangerous question to ask when you are suffering. When your dad dies while you're in grade school or you live with depression for decades or a car accident kills someone you love, it is instinctive to ask why. Why did this happen?

While some people look in the mirror and blame themselves, other people look up at the heavens and blame God. After all, God is all-knowing and all-powerful; he is the Lord who once said, "**I am the Lord, the God of all mankind. Is anything too hard for me?**" (Jeremiah 32:27). It would be easy for God to snap his mighty fingers and cure your cancer, fix your family, and pay off every dollar of your debt.

So when God doesn't, it is logical to wonder if God is as loving as he claims to be. How can he look down on his own children in their pain, do nothing, and claim to be good? This is the question that causes many people to question the goodness of God or deny him altogether.

But "God is bad" falls just as short as "I am bad" when it comes to explaining pain. What about the blessings God has given? What about the grace God has shown you? What about the Son that God sent for you?

"**And the God of all grace, who called you to his eternal glory in Christ, after you have suffered a little while, will himself restore you and make you strong, firm and steadfast**" (1 Peter 5:10).

We don't know why
Pastor Mike Novotny

Pain makes us wonder why. Why aren't the kids at school nicer to you? Why isn't God blessing the plans for your career that you prayed so often about? Why did God take your spouse to heaven so early and leave you behind on earth for so long?

For 35 chapters, Job and his friends fiercely debate why God allowed so much pain in Job's life. Was Job bad, a hypocrite who was hiding secret sins? Was God bad, an unjust judge who condemned innocent Job to a life of suffering? If you have (a lot of) time today, read the back-and-forth about one of life's biggest questions. And don't miss the brilliant answer tucked in Job 28: **"Where then does wisdom come from? Where does understanding dwell? It is hidden from the eyes of every living thing. . . . God understands the way to it and he alone knows where it dwells"** (verses 20,21,23).

Where will you find specific answers to your pain? You won't. God alone knows, and he, for some reason, has not chosen to tell you. You can get mad at God, yell at God, question God, even deny God, but there is no Bible passage that specifically explains why you are dealing with _____. Insist on it, and you'll lose your faith in God . . . and still be left with the same pain.

So why would you trust a God who doesn't answer your rawest question about life? Keep reading. The book of Job will tell you.

October 17

We don't know why; we do know who
Pastor Mike Novotny

When I was growing up in church, every Easter service was guaranteed to have a rousing rendition of "I Know That My Redeemer Lives." Ever heard it? It's an eight-stanza marathon of praise to Jesus, the Redeemer who paid the price for our sins before rising, alive, from the grave.

But the life of our Redeemer isn't just an Easter thing. It's a suffering thing. When we are living with chronic pain, waves of grief, and unanswered questions, we need words like these—**"I know that my redeemer lives, and that in the end he will stand on the earth. And after my skin has been destroyed, yet in my flesh I will see God; I myself will see him with my own eyes—I, and not another. How my heart yearns within me!"** (Job 19:25-27).

Job desperately wanted to know why he lost his health, his wealth, and all ten of his kids, but God never revealed the why. Instead, God revealed himself. Job confessed, "I know that my redeemer lives."

I won't claim to know why you are in pain, but I do know who Jesus is. He is your Redeemer, the Savior who personally paid the price for your sins. He is the Son of God, who now lives and reigns, awaiting the day when he returns to end your pain forever. You will see him, even if your body falls apart in this life.

Your Redeemer is alive today. That's something to sing about!

The gap between you and God
Pastor Mike Novotny

In Job 38 we reach the moment we have been waiting for. In Job 1-2, God mysteriously allowed Satan to take away Job's wealth, Job's health, and Job's children. In Job 3-37, Job and four friends argued about why everything fell apart for Job. Was Job bad? Was God bad?

And in Job 38, God finally shows up. What will he say to scab-covered, feverish, childless Job? The answer is not what you would expect. **"Where were you when I laid the earth's foundation? Tell me, if you understand"** (verse 4). **"Have you comprehended the vast expanses of the earth? Tell me, if you know all this"** (verse 18). **"Surely you know, for you were already born! You have lived so many years!"** (verse 21). God tests Job. And Job fails. During question after question (God asks 77 total!), Job just stares up at God. Clueless. Ignorant. Unworthy.

That might seem cruel given all that Job had suffered, but it was actually a sweet display of mercy. Job, who assumed he knew enough to judge God, was on the verge of losing his trust in God's love. Therefore, God had to undo Job's assumption, opening Job's eyes to the massive difference in what each of them understood about life's big picture.

If you have honest questions about your personal suffering, be slow to speak and quick to remember just how much God knows that you don't. Your admission of ignorance just might save your faith in a loving God.

Just trust God

Pastor Mike Novotny

I recently read a blog that recounted a powerful scene from the *Lord of the Rings*. Gandalf, the good wizard, is encouraging Bilbo, his little hobbit friend, to leave behind his powerful magic ring before it corrupts his heart. But Bilbo, under the influence of the dark magic, turns on Gandalf, accusing him of trying to steal his ring; he even reaches for his little sword to fight his old friend. That's when the mighty Gandalf goes off! He towers over the tiny hobbit and threatens, "If you say that again, I shall get angry." Bilbo snaps out of the ring's spell, and Gandalf backs down. "I am trying to help you," the wizard says. "I wish you would trust me, as you used to."

As the blogger pointed out, this is essentially what happens at the conclusion of Job's story. **"Then the Lord spoke to Job out of the storm: 'Brace yourself like a man; I will question you, and you shall answer me'"** (Job 40:6,7).

When we are in pain, the question *why?* is like that magical ring. When we hold on too tightly to it, *needing* to know why God allowed (fill in your most painful moment here), it can corrupt our hearts. That's why God's savage reply is good for us too. God's questions are belittling, and that's the point. God needs us to remember that we are little and he is not.

Then, with compassion in his eyes and pointing to Jesus, your Redeemer, he says, "Trust me, as you used to."

Better than you deserve
Pastor Mike Novotny

Years ago, a Christian named Dave was diagnosed with a brain tumor that would kill him seven months later. His wife, Sharon, would sit by his bed during his final days, caress his hair, and whisper in his ear, talking about their life and their Savior. One day, however, a relative who did not believe in God came to visit, and he was angry. He thought about Sharon being left alone, about Dave's kids not having a dad around, about how such bad things happen to such good people. "Why aren't you angry?" he demanded of Sharon.

This was her response—"My husband deserved hell . . . yet God, in his mercy, forgave him because of the life, death, and resurrection of Jesus. Dave is going to heaven. How could I be angry at God for taking [my husband] to heaven?"

That's the right question. We will get spiritually stuck if we insist that God answer all our why questions. Why did this happen to me? Why did you allow this in my life? Why, God? But if we lay those same questions at the foot of the cross, our anger subsides. We deserve worse than a hard life because of our sins. We deserve hell. If God gives us heaven, even if our lives here on earth are miserable, how could we be angry at him?

"But God demonstrates his own love for us in this: While we were still sinners, Christ died for us" (Romans 5:8).

Love others well
Andrea Delwiche

The Lord has a question for each of us in Psalm 82: **"How long will you defend the unjust and show partiality to the wicked?"** (verse 2). To help us examine ourselves, he continues by stating whom we should be defending and how to defend them: **"Defend the weak and the fatherless; uphold the cause of the poor and the oppressed. Rescue the weak and the needy; deliver them from the hand of the wicked"** (verses 3,4). The prophet Micah records a similar injunction from God: **"What does the Lord require of you? To act justly and to love mercy and to walk humbly with your God"** (Micah 6:8).

Toward the end of his ministry, Jesus was asked, "Which commandment is the greatest?" Jesus replied: **"'Love the Lord your God with all your heart and with all your soul and with all your mind.' This is the first and greatest commandment. And the second is like it: 'Love your neighbor as yourself'"** (Matthew 22:37-39).

God is clear. We are to love our neighbor, defend the weak, uphold the cause of the poor.

Following Christ means following into the work of his kingdom. This work is to love God and to love other people, especially the vulnerable. We may protest inwardly about defending those whose decisions we don't agree with, but we don't choose based on our own criteria. We don't get to pick the weak and the vulnerable; rather, we love others as we have been loved.

Lord Jesus, help us love others well!

Are we imitators of Christ?

Karen Spiegelberg

While running errands one day, I noticed a bumper sticker on the car in front of me. It read, "I like your Christ. I do not like your Christians. They are so unlike your Christ." The credit for the quote was given to Mahatma Gandhi.

Mahatma Gandhi was a Hindu who was responsible for religious and social freedoms in his home country of India. Although as Christians we cannot defend his beliefs, the strong comment he made about Christians does resonate.

In Ephesians 5:1,2, we are told, **"Follow God's example, therefore, as dearly loved children and walk in the way of love, just as Christ loved us."** *Christian* itself means "little Christs," or "little anointed ones." But how can we call ourselves Christians when we don't always act like Christ? First of all, Christ was perfect; we are not. We are vulnerable and sinful, and we fall way short of perfection. But when God commands us to follow his example, it's already been fulfilled in Christ. Ephesians 1:3 says, **"Praise be to the God and Father of our Lord Jesus Christ, who has blessed us in the heavenly realms with every spiritual blessing in Christ."**

So we *can* be imitators of Christ! When we grasp that it is him within us who loves and does all good things, we are capable of being imitators of him!

"Let your light shine before others, that they may see your good deeds and glorify your Father in heaven" (Matthew 5:16).

The defeat of darkness
Pastor David Scharf

In a galaxy ten billion light-years away, you will likely find planets and stars and solar systems that no one will ever see. Jesus made all that. That's how powerful he is. And yet, he became flesh, soft as a baby. The Almighty became weak. The omnipresent became tiny. The immortal became killable. Not only is that incomprehensible, but it doesn't seem like a good battle plan against evil, does it?

John explains: **"The light shines in the darkness"** (John 1:5). You don't solve anything by taking out evil; it just comes back in another way. Eliminating evil is not the answer. The answer is eliminating the darkness. The answer is to rip the darkness that makes him do evil out of man's heart. That's where Jesus said sin comes from, out of man's heart (Matthew 15:19). And in case you missed it, he also means the darkness in your heart and mine.

So Jesus came, not to be crowned but crushed. He came, not to put *evildoers* in the grave but to put *evil* in the grave, which is exactly what he did by bleeding and dying on a cross outside of Jerusalem. Jesus came, not in might to demand service but in weakness to serve you by eliminating your greatest problem—the darkness that's inside of you. That's what happens when light hits darkness—the darkness can't exist. When the light of Jesus comes into your heart, you know your sins are forgiven. Forgiven forever. Darkness is defeated.

God flips it
Pastor Mike Novotny

If you ever read the gospel of Luke carefully, you'll notice a few beautiful themes—God's love for women, God's love for the nations, God's love for the poor, the work of the Holy Spirit, the joy of the gospel, and, perhaps most obvious, the upside-down kingdom. The upside-down kingdom is the idea that Jesus had a way of humbling the holier-than-thous and lifting up the lowly.

Perhaps Jesus grew up singing his mother's song. **"And Mary said: 'My soul glorifies the Lord and my spirit rejoices in God my Savior, for he has been mindful of the humble state of his servant. From now on all generations will call me blessed, for the Mighty One has done great things for me—holy is his name. His mercy extends to those who fear him, from generation to generation. He has performed mighty deeds with his arm; he has scattered those who are proud in their inmost thoughts. He has brought down rulers from their thrones but has lifted up the humble. He has filled the hungry with good things but has sent the rich away empty. He has helped his servant Israel, remembering to be merciful to Abraham and his descendants forever, just as he promised our ancestors"** (Luke 1:46-55).

Reread the lyrics of her song, underlining every "upside-down" moment. Then, humbly confessing your sins to Jesus, remember God's promises. Conclude with, "The Mighty One has done great things for me!" Amen!

Group needed
Pastor Daron Lindemann

Do you ever wonder how much superstars really need their supporting team members, supporting actors, or backup singers?

Make a mental list right now of lead singers who went solo after successful careers with popular groups with platinum hits—but their solo careers never took off. Long list.

The apostle Paul was a spiritual rock star with the talent to go solo. But look what he said to the Christians in Thessalonica on behalf of himself and his fellow apostles Silas and Timothy: **"We also long to see you. Night and day we pray most earnestly that we may see you again"** (1 Thessalonians 3:6,10).

Superstar Paul needed these everyday Christians. Why? Paul already had hundreds of other Christian friends. His close companions Silas and Timothy, the Holy Spirit, and Jesus directly communicated with him.

Paul answered, **"For now we really live, since you are standing firm in the Lord. How can we thank God enough for you in return for all the joy we have in the presence of our God because of you?"** (1 Thessalonians 3:8,9).

Paul couldn't wait to see them standing firm "in the Lord." And they brought him joy in the presence of God. For Paul, needing other Christians was a sign of his spiritual faith and maturity.

Not needing other Christians, therefore, indicates a lack of spiritual faith and maturity. When you love Jesus like Paul did, then you need a small group of Christians who love Jesus too.

Money isn't worth it
Pastor Mike Novotny

I once sat next to a talkative, kind, and very rich man on an airplane. He told me about his home (a waterfront mansion), his family (including his doctor daughter), and, in a much more somber tone, his regrets. Holding up his airline app, he showed me the shimmering gold background, a nod to his frequent flyer status, and mentioned how often work took him away from his family. "It's not worth it," he confessed. "That color isn't worth it."

Money, according to Jesus, is tricky. In his parable of the sower, Jesus taught that some Christians don't mature in their faith because of the **"deceitfulness of wealth"** (Matthew 13:22). Wealth deceives you. It promises you the mansion and the gold status, but it puts all the sacrifices in the fine print. Even after you earn it, save it, spend it, and buy amazing things with it, you might not think it was worth it.

Not so with Jesus. Seeing his face one day is worth it. Knowing that even today he is with you is worth it. No matter what it costs you to follow him, what temporary pleasure or personal plan you have to sacrifice to do God's will today, Jesus is absolutely worth it.

But don't take my word for it: **"Then I looked and heard the voice of many angels, numbering thousands upon thousands, and ten thousand times ten thousand. They encircled the throne and the living creatures and the elders. In a loud voice they were saying: 'Worthy is the Lamb!'"** (Revelation 5:11,12).

Lord, don't be silent!

Andrea Delwiche

Even when we don't realize it, our souls are longing to make a deep connection with God. We need to hear from him, whether we are praying about war, illness, or asking God to shine his light on a decision that needs to be made. Our hearts cry with the psalm writer, **"O God, do not keep silence; do not hold your peace or be still, O God!"** (83:2 ESV).

God desires for us to desire him. He makes this promise: **"You will seek me and find me when you seek me with all your heart"** (Jeremiah 29:13).

When we seek God with all our hearts, we begin to embrace his working in every aspect of our lives. In Acts 17:28, the apostle Paul speaks of our reality: **"In him we live and move and have our being."** Living in God's world, we can feel confident that God wants to walk with us, reassure us, and act on our behalf.

God wants to work with us in everything. Knowing that God is present, active, and eager, we keep praying, "Don't keep silent, God. Don't hold your peace or be still, God." The Lord's Prayer serves as a model for requesting God's assistance for everything from the majestic to the seemingly mundane. In addition, Jesus promised that the Holy Spirit would be available to us to help us discern how to walk with God and to remind us of everything that Jesus has taught us.

Lord God, don't be silent. Give us breadcrumbs of encouragement so we seek after you!

God's watch is the official timer
Pastor Clark Schultz

The ongoing joke with one of the instructors at my local gym is that he can't tell time. When he says we have only 10 more seconds to hold our planks or do an exercise, his 10 seconds really means 30 or (gasp) longer. Others will joke with him and say, "That was longer than 10 seconds."

His response is, "My watch is the official timer."

Now apply this to real life. You're not holding a plank, but you feel pain. Pain caused by a loved one who broke your heart, pain caused by the sin that you can't seem to push away from, pain of watching your parent's memory fade away, the pain of an empty chair at the supper table. You might cry out, "How much longer, God!"

God's response: **"Do not forget this one thing, dear friends: With the Lord a day is like a thousand years, and a thousand years are like a day"** (2 Peter 3:8).

God's watch is the official timer. Only he knows how long our time is on this earth and how long we will endure the effects of sin. Our simple prayer is as the psalmist says, **"My times are in your hands; deliver me from the hands of my enemies, from those who pursue me"** (31:15).

Gym, school, car, work—no matter the time, make this your prayer!

Imperfect vision
Jan Gompper

On June 26, 2021, in Surfside, FL, a condominium high-rise crumbled to the ground, killing 97 people. A few days later, a father and his young son got caught in an undertow at a beach near our home. Another man swam out to try to save them. All three drowned.

When I heard about these two tragedies, I couldn't help but think, "Why?" Why did God not intervene and stop this from happening?

Why? moments in this life are inevitable. It's only human to want answers for why one country attacks another, why hurricanes or earthquakes rip people's lives apart, why our loved one had to die . . .

Asking why is not a sin, but the curse of sin is the cause of all earthly *why?* moments. Satan delights in wreaking havoc and heartache that cause us to ask, "Why?" And he hopes we'll blame God if we don't get an answer.

The apostle Paul had this to say to the persecuted Christians in Corinth who were struggling with their own set of *why?* moments: **"Now we see things imperfectly, like puzzling reflections in a mirror, but then we will see everything with perfect clarity. All that I know now is partial and incomplete, but then I will know everything completely, just as God now knows me completely"** (1 Corinthians 13:12 NLT).

Though our vision this side of heaven will always be impaired, God will one day make it 20/20, and we will never again have to ask, "Why?"

Is your name getting called?

Linda Buxa

My son loves football, so NFL Draft Day is a big deal in our house. Who's going first? Who was supposed to go early but fell to the third round? Who is average but will end up being a superstar? And what about the guys whose names aren't called; what about their futures?

For Christians, judgment day is a big deal too, except it has zero of the questions like those surrounding the NFL draft. We are told exactly what's going to happen. **"For the trumpet will sound, the dead will be raised imperishable, and we will be changed. For the perishable must clothe itself with the imperishable, and the mortal with immortality"** (1 Corinthians 15:52,53).

Everyone is called at just the right time. No one questions the "Owner's" decisions because God has been clear about it for thousands and thousands of years. This is exciting news for people who believe in Jesus, because they will hear their names called and get to wear the Team Jesus jersey. But there's some hard news about paradise too: **"Nothing impure will ever enter it, nor will anyone who does what is shameful or deceitful, but only those whose names are written in the Lamb's book of life"** (Revelation 21:27). Those who do not believe in Jesus will not hear their names called for eternal joy. Instead, they will be eternally separated from the Father.

If you are already on Team Jesus, this means you and I have work to do. Time is short—and eternal futures are at stake.

Reformation freedom
Pastor David Scharf

The events of October 31, 1517, are fairly well known in church circles. When Martin Luther posted his 95 Theses to the Castle Church door in Wittenberg, Germany, the Protestant Reformation was touched off. Those 95 statements emphasized that forgiveness is given through Jesus alone and cannot be bought with money. But do you know what happened six days before?

On October 25, 1517, Luther preached a sermon in Saxony, and Duke George "The Bearded" was in attendance. Luther preached a very Reformation-like message: "Our salvation must always remain our foremost concern. Man can obtain it only through faith in Christ Jesus, not by his own good works."

At dinner that evening, the duke asked his wife's friend, "How did you like brother Martin's sermon?" "Ah," she replied, "let me hear just one more like it, and I can die in peace." The duke was furious. He exclaimed, "I would have paid *not* to hear it. It makes people secure to sin!"

The duke misunderstood the power of grace. Jesus said, **"Very truly I tell you, everyone who sins is a slave to sin. So if the Son sets you free, you will be free indeed"** (John 8:34,36). The grace of God does not make us alive *to* sin but instead makes us alive *from* sin. Sin's chains lay on the floor at your feet. You are truly free. Free to love others as Jesus loved you. Free to forgive as he has forgiven you. Free to serve in a million ways!

NOVEMBER

Ascribe to the Lord the glory due his name;
worship the Lord in the splendor of his holiness.

PSALM 29:2

Who needs help?
Pastor Jon Enter

Have you ever read the book of Judges? It's a fascinating read full of unlikely heroes. That's what a judge is in this Bible book—a seemingly unqualified choice to deliver God's people.

The Israelites needed help repeatedly in Judges. They made terrible life choices and ran from God. They repented, and God sent a judge to deliver them. But then—WHAM!—they fell right back into their old ways.

Who does that sound like? Whom do you love who has a repetitive story line of addiction, destructive anger, habitual lying, or terrible life choices? Who keeps breaking your heart?

It hurts. It's hard. You hurt for that person.

This devotion and the next few devotions are about you being a judge for that person. Not a judge who slams down a gavel and gives a verdict. This is about being a judge (like in the book of Judges) called by God to deliver those trapped and overpowered. God gives us this specific command in Galatians 6:2: **"Carry each other's burdens, and in this way you will fulfill the law of Christ."** God is calling your heart to deliver a message of peace and hope and powerful restoration to that loved one in need. It starts with prayer.

Lord Jesus, someone I love is hurting in sinful decisions. Interrupt any evil plans the devil has against them. Fill them with a yearning for help. I pray this confidently in your name, Jesus, the healer of the helpless and Savior of the needy. Amen.

Using the unexpected
Pastor Jon Enter

In Judges 3 the Israelites finally cried out to God for deliverance from wicked King Eglon. God heard their cries and sent a man named Ehud. He was the unexpected choice because Ehud was . . . left-handed. Wait, what?

Soldiers back then fought right-handed. And being left-handed, Ehud was a military reject. Plus, Ehud was from the tribe of Benjamin—one of the smallest tribes of Israel. Yet God chose Ehud to be the one to bring military-style justice on King Eglon and deliver God's people. That's what God does at times. **"The Lord does not look at the things people look at. People look at the outward appearance, but the Lord looks at the heart"** (1 Samuel 16:7). He uses the unexpected to serve him.

In the last devotion, I encouraged you to be the one God uses to intervene to help a friend leave a sinful habit. I'm guessing you're feeling rather unworthy or unqualified for the job. "I don't know the Bible well enough." "I'm not a counselor to help with emotional trauma." "I'm a mess. Who am I to tell someone what to do?" God says, "You're perfect! You're the one."

You don't need to have all the answers to your friend's questions. You don't need to be skilled in social work, counseling, or grief recovery. Your friend needs a friend. An obvious friend. An intentional friend. Your friend needs someone to lead them to the love of Jesus.

What can you do today to help and encourage a friend in need?

Sin is sin
Pastor Jon Enter

What's the scariest thing you've ever had to do?

For Ehud in Judges 3, the answer would have been obvious.

Ehud brought tribute to King Eglon, which stopped the king from another killing spree of Jews. But later that day—like an Old Testament James Bond—he returned with a sword hidden on his right leg. The soldiers guarding King Eglon only checked Ehud's left leg for weapons because soldiers back then were right-handed.

"Ehud reached with his left hand, drew the sword from his right thigh and plunged it into the king's belly. Even the handle sank in after the blade, and his bowels discharged. Ehud did not pull the sword out, and the fat closed in over it" (Judges 3:21,22). And right there is why you might not know this story; it's not told in Sunday school.

I'm not advocating you hide a sword on the right side of your body. But God's Word is a double-edged sword. It cuts away sin. Sin needs to be removed . . . from our lives and from others' lives. Think of that friend struggling in life, in sin. What message does that person need to hear?

Love that person enough to tell them that sin is sin. Love them enough to help them cut that sin from their life. When they repent, let them know they are forgiven.

One of the best ways to lead your friend into repentance is to model it. What do you need to repent of? When you do, peace will follow!

It gets messy
Pastor Jon Enter

In the last devotion, I revealed how Ehud brought God's judgment upon evil King Eglon in Judges 3. When he plunged a sword into King Eglon's gut, his intestines oozed out. Gross. That's actually how Ehud made his impossible, improbable escape! The smell was so bad that the guards thought the king was in the bathroom, and that gave Ehud time to escape.

Serving God can get messy. I've been encouraging you to be intentional and help someone in spiritual need. The devil won't like this. It'll likely get messy when you talk to your friend about their sinful brokenness. They might get offended and spew hurt/hate just as foul as King Eglon's spilled intestines. Vivid picture, but that's real.

Don't let the possibility of messiness keep you from doing what is right. Focus on helping your friend escape the stink of sin and walk in freedom.

Here's the amazing truth. God will guide you. God will help you. And God will give you what to say if your friend doesn't respond well to your witness. **"But make up your mind not to worry beforehand how you will defend yourselves. For I will give you words and wisdom"** (Luke 21:14,15).

You have nothing to fear. The Creator of the universe will guide your words. Jesus loves the person you love and hurts for your friend who is hurting. He simply needs you to trust and to be a messenger of mercy to your friend who is hurting. Will you go?

Audience of one
Pastor Jon Enter

In Judges 3 after the story of Ehud (who is like a Special Forces operative in the Old Testament), there's a short mention of a guy named Shamgar. **"After Ehud came Shamgar son of Anath, who struck down six hundred Philistines with an oxgoad. He too saved Israel"** (verse 31). Shamgar struck down six hundred men? I want to hear that story! And what's an oxgoad? Google says it's a long wooden pole with an iron spike used to poke an ox pulling a wagon too slowly. Okay, now I want more details on this Shamgar guy!

Do you think Shamgar is in heaven bummed out about only getting one verse, one quick mention in the Bible? Not for a second! Shamgar served God to serve God. He didn't serve for his name to live on but for the name of the Lord to live on. Shamgar lived for an audience of one.

Too often we can wonder if our Christian service is worth our effort. "What do I get out of this? What's this going to cost me? How great of an impact will it make?"

Shamgar is a great reminder that serving God is worth it, regardless of the recognition. If it's good to do good, then do good without counting the cost.

What is left for you to do? What good work has God prepared in advance for you to do that you've been hesitant to fulfill? Be a Shamgar! Be active! Be faithful! And leave the results up to God.

The gospel for productive people
Pastor Mike Novotny

Do you consider yourself a productive person? If those personality tests are true, my life is packed with productive people. My mom, my mother-in-law, my wife, my lead pastor, and many of the Time of Grace team are high-achieving, driven, get-stuff-done Christians. If you are anything like us, your life moves fast and there is little time for silence, stillness, and sabbath rest.

But we all need to slow down from time to time, and Jesus knows it. On the cross, our Savior didn't cry out, "Here's your to-do list!" or "Be productive, and you'll see me in paradise!" Instead, knowing exactly what we needed, Jesus cried, **"It is finished"** (John 19:30). Ah, finished. Such a life-giving word, isn't it? The work of saving us is done. There are no commandments that we must keep to be saved. No list of loving deeds that we need to get done before we die. Jesus did everything that needed to be done in our place.

That doesn't make us lazy Christians. It does, however, offer rest to our running souls. We can slow down. We can be still. We can sit and enjoy the God who didn't make us work for it but instead gives us everything by his grace.

I know you and I will be going after our goals soon enough. For now, how about we both take a deep breath, fix our eyes on the cross, and enjoy the Savior who said, "It is finished!"?

An undivided heart
Andrea Delwiche

God's faithfulness is a fact. It doesn't change. What needs to change is our understanding of God's faithfulness and living our lives under the reality of God's faithfulness: **"Teach me your way, Lord, that I may rely on your faithfulness; give me an undivided heart, that I may fear your name"** (Psalm 86:11).

How does God teach us? Through his Word, which has a description of what God's character is. He also teaches us through our own experience and the experiences that we witness in the lives of other people.

But our hearts are divided; we don't follow in the Lord's way wholeheartedly. We tend to look to our own resources. We decide to abandon the well-marked path that promises to lead us to the foot of the spectacular waterfall and instead crash through the underbrush, trying to get there by approximation. Sometimes it works, but often it becomes just a matter of survival.

The path of the Lord is a difficult path in some ways. But life is more difficult without Jesus. Think of the words of Jesus on the night he was betrayed: **"In this world you will have trouble. But take heart! I have overcome the world"** (John 16:33). By following God and learning to walk with his Spirit, we take advantage of the path that Jesus has already walked.

Under God's guidance, we are capable of great things. It's difficult to proceed without a reliable map or well-walked path. We accomplish good things by following God's path.

Teach us your way, O Lord. Give us undivided hearts.

Let this mind be in you: Bridges
Jason Nelson

I identify myself as being a Christian. I like the best teachings of the reformer Martin Luther. What is better than God's grace alone? In practice, I'd rather try to bring people together than keep them apart.

Some of us went to classes in churches that taught the fundamental beliefs of our group and laid down the markers for keeping other groups at a distance. There was a felt need for churches to differentiate themselves from each other. Those boundaries seemed necessary, like fences in a backyard.

Today, many people haven't come up in any church and are put off by the many Christian groups all claiming to have the truth exclusively. People may admire Jesus, but they can't make sense of the distinctions church folk continue to maintain. So they just stay away.

Jesus taught his followers there was just one holy, Christian church. It grew because the founders of Christianity built bridges to people wherever they went. For them, the one true faith was exactly that. It was centered on the perfect life and redeeming work of God's only Son. In many cases they staked their very lives on it. That was pretty convincing.

I believe that is still the bridge to people's hearts—the clearest telling of the story of Jesus illustrated with our acts of self-sacrifice and humble service. So wherever you go and whomever you meet, see if you can build that bridge.

"As for us, we cannot help speaking about what we have seen and heard" (Acts 4:20).

November 9

The gospel for talkative people
Pastor Mike Novotny

As a man of many words, I hate how right this proverb is: **"Sin is not ended by multiplying words"** (Proverbs 10:19). Like the apostle Peter, some of us say exponentially more than our classmates or coworkers or family members and, in the process, we sin.

Do you ever talk a ton and only later realize that you didn't really listen to anyone else? You told another story, another joke, shared another experience, jumped in and interrupted again, as if everyone in the room is so enamored by you. Do you ever get in the car afterward and only then think, "Why did I say that? Why didn't I listen more or ask more questions?" All of us are proud, but some of us are just proud out loud.

Maybe that's why Peter, the talker, talked about the gospel like this: **"When they hurled their insults at [Jesus], he did not retaliate; when he suffered, he made no threats. Instead, he entrusted himself to him who judges justly"** (1 Peter 2:23). The Word didn't say a word. Jesus suffered, but he didn't spout sinful words at his enemies. He shut his mouth and gave his life so that our sinful, boastful, unthoughtful words were nailed to the cross of Jesus.

That's why Satan won't be able to say a word against you on the day of judgment. That's why your Father says good things about you even today, even if you are the most talkative kid in his holy family.

No ambiguity
Jan Gompper

Not long ago I watched a movie called *Blackbird*. The story revolves around a woman who is suffering from a physically debilitating illness that will only get worse. Rather than lingering in what she feels would be an undignified manner, she convinces her husband, a doctor, to create a medical cocktail for her to end her life. Before doing so, she gathers her children to spend one last weekend with her. Though not in favor of her decision at first, they eventually accept it.

If this isn't depressing enough, immediately after she drinks the death potion, the film ends with her asking her husband, "Where am I going?" He answers, "You tell me."

Her question and her husband's ambiguous answer left a pit in my stomach. Given the premise of the film, it's not that I expected she believed in God, but hearing her voice that question was a wake-up call to pay more attention to people in my life who, facing death, may not know the answer to that question: Where am I going?

Thankfully, believers in Christ have the answer because Christ himself provided it: **"For it is my Father's will that all who see his Son and believe in him should have eternal life. I will raise them up at the last day"** (John 6:40 NLT).

There is no ambiguity for Christ-followers. Where are *we* going? To live with Jesus! **"And if someone asks about your hope as a believer, always be ready to explain it"** (1 Peter 3:15 NLT).

The Lamb covers us
Linda Buxa

Some extended family members own sheep. When we visited their house this spring, a sheep was due to give birth any day. The family was a little concerned because this sheep hadn't been a great mom in the past. Each time she had a lamb, she wouldn't nurse, and the family had to bottle-feed the lamb to keep it alive. (And who wants to take the time to do that?)

My husband asked why the other mama sheep couldn't step in to nurse. (I mean, our barn cats have done that.) As it turns out, sheep are finicky and won't accept another lamb. The farmer told us that this only works if the sheep's lamb dies; then you skin it and place it over the living lamb.

Wow!

The Bible became so much clearer to me that day.

Now when I read what John the Baptist said about Jesus—**"Look, the Lamb of God, who takes away the sin of the world!"** (John 1:29)—I have a far better, deeper, richer picture of exactly what happened when Jesus stepped in to save us. The Father couldn't accept us as we are—because we were not part of his family. However, because he loved us so much, God's Son, Jesus, came to earth to be the Lamb of God. He died, and now his sacrifice covers us. The Father accepts us as his lambs now—and, like the sweet song says, "I am Jesus' little lamb!"

God thinks of you
Pastor Clark Schultz

A young pastor was talking to a seasoned pastor about the heartbreak he felt saying goodbye to his wife at the airport. Her visa had not come, so he had to fly the 13-hour, 20-minute flight to a foreign land alone. There were tears, an embrace, and the whisper of, "I love you and will be thinking of you."

This heartbroken pastor lamented it was the worst feeling he had ever felt. The aged pastor listening to this young missionary put a positive spin on the situation: "How blessed it is that someone cries over you and thinks of you. Many in life do not have that blessing."

How about you, dear reader? Are you like me, where you can be in a crowded room and still feel alone? Like no one gets you?

Or maybe you have one of those big foam hands with the pointer finger pointing directly at you with the words, "Thinking of me and only me."

"I tell you, you will not see me again until you say, 'Blessed is he who comes in the name of the Lord'" (Luke 13:35). In this verse Jesus is mourning over the loss of Jerusalem, but the context is much more. He is showing 100% resolve to show the world and YOU that he is thinking of you! Nothing was going to stop Jesus from saving you, forgiving you, and making death but a sleep for you.

Alone? Tired? Worn out? Know that you are thought of by God and that makes you blessed.

Eternal grip
Karen Spiegelberg

My daddy was my hero. When I was young, I loved holding his hand on summer walks. He was big, strong, and had a very firm grip. As the years went by, his strength weakened. When I held his hand as he labored in death, he could barely even clasp mine. He couldn't hold on to me any more than I selfishly wanted to hold on to him forever.

As my dad and I lost hold of each other that day, God's Word, through the apostle Paul, came through loud and clear: **"What I mean, brothers and sisters, is that the time is short. From now on those who have wives should live as if they do not; those who mourn, as if they did not; those who are happy, as if they were not; those who buy something, as if it were not theirs to keep; those who use the things of the world, as if not engrossed in them. For this world in its present form is passing away"** (1 Corinthians 7:29–31).

Paul's advice was to the Corinthian church, with an eye to the second coming of Christ. The text now instructs us to maintain a Christian end-of-time perspective. Jesus' death and resurrection introduced a new era—that as Christians we have one hand in this world and the other in the kingdom of God, holding lightly to all things of this world.

I'll always remember my daddy's firm grip, but I'll never forget that my heavenly Father's grip is eternal. To that, I hold tightly.

Grace makes no exceptions
Pastor Mike Novotny

A tough-looking guy once approached me in the church lobby right after a service was done. "Pastor, you wouldn't believe the things I have done. The sins you talked about in there don't even come close to my past." I'm not sure if I responded wisely, but I looked him squarely in the eye and said, "I dare you. I dare you to tell me something to make me not love you." The church lobby wasn't the place to sit down for his confession, so I told him my door was always open when he was ready to talk. I hope he takes me up on that offer.

Because grace makes no exceptions. In the kingdom of God, when people approach King Jesus with repentant hearts, there are no sins that he refuses to forgive. **"[Jesus] is the atoning sacrifice for our sins, and not only for ours but also for the sins of the whole world"** (1 John 2:2). What sins could we confess that aren't included in "the sins of the whole world"?

Maybe you, like that man, have some really dark chapters in your personal story, secrets that you have hidden for far too long. I beg you, friend, come into the light. Read 1 John 1 and 2 and allow God to convince you that you can bring your sin, any sin, all your sin, and grace will not make you its exception.

At the cross, we all are forgiven and all is forgiven. Praise Jesus for that!

Comfort in the darkness
Pastor David Scharf

Some parents experience the darkness of losing a child at a young age. How do they move on? As one who lost a sister who was hit by a drunk driver, I have taken comfort in Isaiah 57:1,2: **"No one understands that the righteous are taken away to be spared from evil. Those who walk uprightly enter into peace; they find rest as they lie in death."** The goal of parents is to see their children in heaven. God may have been sparing my sister from something that would have taken her away from the faith, and he wanted her to be safe in heaven with him. We cannot say for certain what God is doing in every instance. We simply need to trust him.

What we do know is this: **"Precious in the sight of the LORD is the death of his faithful servants"** (Psalm 116:15). He cares about each of his children. What we do know is: **"In all things God works for the good of those who love him"** (Romans 8:28). He is in control even of the bad things that happen.

How do the parents move on? They cry. They pray, knowing they have a Savior who hears and sympathizes with them. God knows what it is like to lose a child too. They surround themselves with their Christian family who is there to wrap them up with love and help carry their burdens. They wait patiently for the Lord's deliverance from this pain, knowing that a heavenly reunion awaits.

Sinners get angry quickly
Pastor Mike Novotny

Anger is not an evil emotion. Bible readers know that God occasionally gets angry and that the injustice of our world can anger those who love righteousness. I picture God's anger like a bomb with a football-field length fuse. He does blow up in wrath, but it doesn't happen quickly. As Moses recorded, **"The Lord, the Lord, the compassionate and gracious God, slow to anger . . ."** (Exodus 34:6).

Our problem is that we get angry quickly. It takes two siblings in the back of a van 0.7 seconds to scream at each other when one crosses over that invisible territorial line in the back seat. Grown-up drivers need only 1.2 seconds to go from singing to the radio to raging at less-than-perfect motorists who fail to signal or follow our bumpers too closely. The sad result of our sinfulness is that one comment at dinner, one second of teenage attitude, or one infuriating news story can make us instantly furious. Tragically, when we blow up, the people who are closest to us get hit by the shrapnel of our instant anger.

What's the answer? To walk with God. As Moses noted, God is gracious, willing to forgive our out-of-control emotions. God is compassionate, tenderly holding our hands as we learn how to manage our emotions. God is slow to anger, even when we are throwing another adult tantrum.

Step-by-step we learn a better way, the way of the Lord who is love. **"Love is . . . not easily angered"** (1 Corinthians 13:5).

All of life is worship
Andrea Delwiche

"How lovely is your dwelling place, Lord **Almighty! My soul yearns, even faints, for the courts of the** Lord; **my heart and flesh cry out for the living God**" (Psalm 84:1,2).

It's believed that this psalm was written by God's people traveling to Jerusalem to worship. They sang in anticipation of their first sighting of the temple after a long trip. In our time these words have been used for dedications of special places and inscribed above doorways in churches and memorials. They've inspired beautiful pieces of music and artwork.

Because God is present with us in every moment, we can inscribe these words over our homes and our daily activities. We are always in the courts of God whether we are wandering a path through a park or sitting near a sunny window or in a hospital room. God dwells in all these places. They are made lovely by God's presence.

This doesn't negate the need for intentional time in Christian community. Christians are called to community for mutual encouragement. Just as our hearts and flesh cry out for the living God, so does the heart of each person we encounter. Christians can be plugged into an electrical outlet of God's power and peace to take God's dwelling place wherever we go, to whomever we meet. When we *live* as though we *dwell* in the courts of God, all of life is worship. We are never alone or without purpose. Wherever we find ourselves, we can praise, serve, and worship God.

Your piece in God's plan
Karen Spiegelberg

Jigsaw puzzles. Chances are you really *like* doing them or you really *don't!* In either scenario, we can appreciate that each piece in a puzzle is completely unique and has its place in the overall picture. And so it is with the body of Christ. The body of Christ is made up of many different members, each a necessary part, each with a diversity of gifts and talents. These members are called Christians.

In 1 Corinthians 12, Paul compares the body of Christ, the church, to a human body—**"The body is not made up of one part but of many. Now if the foot should say, 'Because I am not a hand, I do not belong to the body,' it would not for that reason stop being part of the body. And if the ear should say, 'Because I am not an eye, I do not belong to the body,' it would not for that reason stop being part of the body. But in fact God has placed the parts in the body, every one of them, just as he wanted them to be"** (verses 14-16,18).

We are often tempted to believe that the gifts or abilities we have are not worthwhile or that someone else's are greater. Remember then those words of Paul. It means that the gifts you have been blessed with are suited perfectly for you and for the benefit of the holy Christian church, the whole body of Christ. What a beautiful picture that is!

The broken belong with Jesus
Pastor Mike Novotny

I don't care who you are, where you've been, what you've done, or how often you've done it. Jesus' arms are still wide open to forgive and embrace a sinner like you. How can I be so sure? Because I've read Mary's story.

Mary Magdalene should have had the nickname Scary Mary. Just look at these words: **"Some women** [were with Jesus] **who had been cured of evil spirits and diseases: Mary (called Magdalene) from whom seven demons had come out"** (Luke 8:2). Think about that. If I told you that someone on your block was possessed by *one* demon, would you lock your doors (or start looking for another place to live)? But Mary didn't have one demon. Mary had *seven* demons. A minivan full of fallen angels, spiritual beings who hate God and his people, seven merciless accusers and relentless abusers lived in Mary Magdalene. I don't know what she all did because of those demons, but I do know that Mary was beyond broken.

Until Jesus. Because those seven demons "had come out." Outnumbered one to seven, God's almighty Son commanded, and the evil ones came out of her. Jesus saved Mary. No wonder she followed him all the way to the cross and the tomb.

You can too. You might have your own demons. Some parts of your story might be too dark for a Disney movie. But Jesus won't let that stop him from driving out your sin and calling you his own. Run to him today. His arms are already open.

God's answer to darkness
Pastor David Scharf

How do we answer the darkness of this world? Look around you. There are murders, robberies, child abuse, and the list could go on and on. Does it anger you? It angers God too. In Psalm 90:11 Moses writes: **"If only we knew the power of your anger! Your wrath is as great as the fear that is your due."** If only we knew how angry God was when we clicked that tempting website or hurt that friend or said nothing about another's sin. Just picture it. Take all the praise that this world owes God for his perfect love. His anger over sin is no less. It's terrifying!

Moses goes on to say: **"Have compassion on your servants. Satisfy us in the morning with your unfailing love, that we may sing for joy and be glad all our days"** (verses 13,14). What is God's answer to evil? His answer is Jesus. In Jesus, God became us. He stepped out of eternity into this world of suffering to be near us. He saw our hurt, and he wanted to take it away because he loves us. That is compassion. God judged Jesus guilty on the cross so he could judge us innocent. And as much as it breaks our hearts and God's heart, he lets us wayward people still do wrong things on this earth until he comes again because he wants us to hear about his forgiveness and live. That is God's answer to the darkness.

Look in the mirror
Pastor Clark Schultz

The ancient Egyptians, Romans, and Greeks were quite fond of mirrors and often manufactured mirrors from polished copper and bronze. Glass mirrors were first produced during the third century A.D. and were quite common in Egypt, Gaul, Germany, and Asia. The invention of glassblowing methods during the 14th century led to the discovery of convex mirrors, which increased the popularity of glass mirrors.

Chances are you looked in a mirror today, maybe to see how much last night's sleep made you resemble Shrek. Perhaps it was on lunch break to check that nothing was dangling from your nose or the piece of lettuce had vacated your gums. Mirrors are everywhere, and they come in all shapes and sizes. I'm fond of any mirror that makes me look a few pounds thinner.

In his catechism, the reformer Martin Luther said that God's law can serve as a mirror to show us our sins. We see characters in the Bible who showed their flaws even though they tried to hide them. Yes, even pillars of faith like David needed to have his sinful reflection shown to him by God's prophet Nathan (see 2 Samuel 12:7). So do we.

Friends, we fall short, we need a Savior, and we have one: **"For the Son of Man came to seek and to save the lost"** (Luke 19:10).

Now when you and I look in the mirror, we see children of God.

The golden calf called "have to"
Pastor Mike Novotny

As a goal-setting, calendar-keeping, box-checking man who married a goal-setting, calendar-keeping, box-checking woman, the story of Mary and Martha gets my full attention. In particular, I recently noticed those two dangerous words that Luke records: **"[Martha] had a sister called Mary, who sat at the Lord's feet listening to what he said. But Martha was distracted by all the preparations that** *had to* **be made"** (Luke 10:39,40). *Had to.* Martha couldn't sit and listen like Mary because the preparations *had to* be made.

But did they have to? Did Jesus arrive with a list of demands that had to be done? No. So where did Martha's "had to" come from? Don't miss this, you productive readers! Martha made it up. Martha made her own list, with the best of intentions, but that list got in the way of her love.

I need to hear those words. Don't you? Do you commit yourself to so many things that you "have to" do that you end up rushing instead of resting, being frustrated instead of patient, and getting angry at the people who don't seem motivated by your list of things that "need to" get done? Organized people are wonderfully wired, but just like any personality type, our strengths can lead to sin.

Look at your to-do list; be honest. Do you have to? What would happen if you didn't? Would Jesus be mad? I pray that, in light of the finished work of Jesus, the Holy Spirit gives you wisdom to be a go-getter who doesn't worship the golden calf called "have to."

My joke about Saint Peter
Pastor Mike Novotny

Recently, I came up with a joke about Saint Peter that, in my opinion, is Netflix-special worthy. In fact, my joke is so good that I've seen churches around my community put it up on their official signs and even on the sides of their buildings! Ready for it? My joke is . . . *Saint* Peter!

I know, right? Did you just spew your coffee all over your computer? Did this book get stained due to my supernatural gift of being hilarious? No? Not even close? Well then . . . I guess that makes you like 100% of the other people whom I've shared my joke with.

You know who would have busted up at my two-word one-liner? Anyone who actually knew Peter. His brother Andrew would've loved it. His buddies James and John would've gotten sandy rolling in laughter on the shore of the Sea of Galilee. Because Simon Peter was not a saint. He was a loudmouth—an always-talking, never-stopping, verbal-processing, speak-before-thinking kind of guy. He was a sinner who proved it every time he opened his mouth. (Which was often.)

But here's the funny and beautiful thing about the Christian faith. Jesus turns sinners into saints. Christ is **"our righteousness, holiness and redemption"** (1 Corinthians 1:30). You are righteous and holy and redeemed because of Christ. You are, through faith, a saint!

Tell that to your buddies. I bet they'll think it's funny. But sometimes things that are funny are absolutely true.

Let this mind be in you: Commitment
Jason Nelson

When I got terribly sick recently, my wife's commitment to me was tested to the full. She almost spent as much time in the hospital as I did. She did things for me I couldn't do for myself. When visiting hours were over, she leaned in and kissed me and said, "I just don't want to lose you." The commitment of people to one another is one of God's gifts to humanity.

One of the inspiring stories of commitment in the Bible is the book of Ruth. During the ancient time of the judges, a Jewish lady named Naomi moved from the little town of Bethlehem to the land of Moab with her husband and two sons, who married Moabite girls. After a while her husband died and then her sons. Her family was reduced to herself and her daughters-in-law. In an act of selflessness, Naomi urged her daughters-in-law to get on with their lives because they were young enough to remarry. One tearfully left, but the other, Ruth, pleaded to stay. She said, **"Don't urge me to leave you"** (Ruth 1:16). The two of them returned to Naomi's homeland because they heard the Lord was coming to the aid of his people there. Naomi coached Ruth on how to find favor with a man named Boaz, who was first in line to marry Ruth. After a unique courtship, Boaz honored his commitment and married her. From them the line of Jesus can be traced.

The best way to love
Pastor Mike Novotny

I once attended a wedding with the woman I love and ate dinner with two men who were in love. As we talked, laughed, and broke bread together during the reception, I thought—"These guys are a lot like us. They care for each other, are committed to each other, and deeply love each other."

Love is love. I think my experience is where that saying comes from. Take the gender out of it and their love is not that different from my love. Maybe you have had a similar realization.

But what sometimes gets overlooked in our conversations about sexuality are the terms and conditions of morally accepted love. If you believe that cheating on your partner is wrong, even if your attraction is real, then "love is love" has limits. If you think an eighth-grade girl shouldn't be dating her 48-year-old teacher, then "love is love" has conditions. All of us have a moral standard that makes us judge people's love as right or wrong.

Here's the key question—Who sets the standard? As we try to figure out whose love is okay and whose isn't, who should stay together and who should end their affectionate relationship, whose moral compass will guide our decisions? You? Me? Americans today? Here's a logical and biblical answer—God. Because God is love; he knows the best way to love. Ponder these words today as we start to explore the intersection of sexuality and spirituality—**"Trust in the Lord with all your heart and lean not on your own understanding"** (Proverbs 3:5).

Honor God with your body
Pastor Mike Novotny

Few things are harder than honoring God with your body. Your body is where you feel attraction and desire, long for pleasure and connection, and ache for romance and the joy of sex. Taking all those desires and laying them at the feet of Jesus is not easy.

The early Christians could relate to that struggle because Roman culture was not exactly biblical with their bodies. It was culturally cool for a Roman man to wake up with his wife, take his lunch break with a prostitute, hook up with an underaged boy, sleep with his servants (male and/or female), and then wink at his wife as he crawled back into his marriage bed.

Imagine the challenge, then, for the Ephesians to read Paul's letter: **"But among you there must not be even a hint of sexual immorality. . . . These are improper for God's holy people. . . . Find out what pleases the Lord"** (Ephesians 5:3,10). Doing what's proper and pleasing to God isn't easy, especially when it comes to sexuality. But we Christians find strength to do just that because we know who God is and what God did.

If God loved us enough to make us holy, then he is worthy of our obedience. If God calls us his own, despite the messiness of our past, then he must want what is best for us. While Jesus never promised us an easy road, we humbly try to love God with our bodies, believing that he loved us first.

Our King is worth it!
Pastor Mike Novotny

Twice a year I have the privilege of dialoguing with some local teenagers about my little book *Gay & God*. While I try to be biblical, compassionate, and humble, some of those students end up feeling that the Bible's teaching about homosexuality is unfair. They realize what Jesus is asking them to give up is substantial.

Recently, however, during one of these Q&A sessions, a parable popped into my head. **"The kingdom of heaven is like treasure hidden in a field. When a man found it, he hid it again, and then in his joy went and sold all he had and bought that field"** (Matthew 13:44). If you are stuck on biblical sexuality, ponder these words from our Savior.

According to Jesus, being with the King of heaven is a priceless treasure. When you find it, that is, when you see Jesus with all his unfailing love and unmatchable glory, you will give up anything to be with him. And what will you feel in that moment when you give up everything that used to make you happy? *Joy.*

Submitting your sexual desires to King Jesus feels like a burden . . . until you think less about your desires and more about your King. Jesus and the eternal life he offers you is a billion times better than anything else in the universe. So if you are wrestling with the fairness of biblical sexuality, fix your eyes on Jesus and discover the joy of the gospel. Jesus is worthy, even of this. Our King is worth it!

Wish or hope?

Pastor Daron Lindemann

Christmas, they say, is a season when wishes come true. Yeah right. We only wish that were true! We could make a long list of wishes unfulfilled.

Reconciled relationships remain broken. Careers can be an unfulfilling way just to earn income. Some secretly wish they didn't struggle with gender confusion—but it doesn't disappear.

Christians sometimes wish for things, and that's okay, but we know something better than wishing. We know hope.

When you wish, you wish *for* something, not sure if it might happen.

When you hope, you hope *in* something you already know is true.

"Be strong and take heart, all you who hope in the Lord" (Psalm 31:24).

"Yes my soul, find rest in God; my hope comes from him. Truly he is my rock and my salvation; he is my fortress, I will not be shaken" (Psalm 62:5,6).

"Those who hope in the Lord will renew their strength" (Isaiah 40:31).

"Hope does not put us to shame" (Romans 5:5).

"You are God my Savior, and my hope is in you all day long" (Psalm 25:5).

Meditate on this handful of verses today about hope. Which is most meaningful and draws your soul's attention? Linger there. Think more about why it attracts you. Rejoice in it. Pray it.

Let this mind be in you: Freedom
Jason Nelson

Freedom is one of THE big ideas. It's so big that it shapes the course of history. Jesus said, **"If the Son sets you free, you will be free indeed"** (John 8:36). He bent the arc of freedom away from our private captivities of guilt and shame with the most liberating action known to mankind. Forgiveness. He set us free to serve God and others. That is freedom in his mind, and he invites all who are burdened and heavy-laden to come to him. In the course of American history, many in the tired and huddled masses have set aside personal safety and come to America in order to have this precious gift because it is so closely tied to a better life.

Possessors of freedom need to think long and hard about what they want to do with that freedom. Freedom has real-world dimensions. There is freedom from . . . freedom to . . . freedom for . . . And in our society, our freedom usually overlaps with someone else's.

Rights and freedoms are not the same. I wish our founders would have included a Bill of Freedoms in our Constitution along with a Bill of Rights. The exercise of freedom sets a different tone from the assertion of rights, especially when good people reach an impasse. When it seems that my right to push is competing with your right to pull, one of us needs to exercise our freedom and stand down for the greater good.

Your pilgrimage with God
Andrea Delwiche

As followers of Christ, like the ancient Israelites, our hearts are to be set on the journey of our relationship with Jesus. In biblical times, pilgrimage often required walking long distances. Without radios or cell phones, the journey could be spent in quiet thought, listening, prayer, or reflecting with other travelers. One would certainly have the capacity to consider the journey itself, anticipate arriving at the destination, and on the way home, to reflect upon the trip taken.

"Blessed are those whose strength is in you, whose hearts are set on pilgrimage. As they pass through the Valley of Baca [Valley of Tears], **they make it a place of springs; the autumn rains also cover it with pools** [blessings]**"** (Psalm 84:5,6).

People who set out on a walking journey will have moments of euphoria and times of aching feet and frustration. It's all part of the trip.

Each of us is on a long journey, learning to follow the Lord. We're learning more about his characteristics. We can anticipate where we have yet to go with him. We often pass through valleys of tears—tears of joy, deep sorrow, or wonder. As we follow, streams of living water bubble up from God to bless and refresh us.

Each step of our pilgrimage is taken in the safety of God's world: **"The earth is the LORD's, and everything in it, the world, and all who live in it"** (Psalm 24:1). How is Christ walking with you and urging you on in your pilgrimage with him?

DECEMBER

When Jesus spoke again to the people, he said, "I am the light of the world. Whoever follows me will never walk in darkness, but will have the light of life."

JOHN 8:12

X marks the spot
Pastor Mike Novotny

There are two things that mess with my Christmas joy—the craziness out there and the craziness in here. It can be hard for me to rejoice with the angels and sleep in heavenly peace when my December calendar keeps me racing around. It can be even harder for me to smile when my sinful heart is racing with worries, insecurities, and the embarrassment for some of the things I've said and done.

That's why this Christmas I want to remember that X marks the spot. In Greek, the name Christ looks like this—*Xpistos*—and was often abbreviated with a simple X (thus Xmas). This year I plan to write a big X in my December calendar, a weekly reminder that Christ is in the middle of this busy season. Whether I'm rushing to a holiday party or writing the family Christmas letter, Jesus Christ is in the middle of it.

Even better, I plan to trace that X over my heart, a reminder that Christ will not leave me or forsake me, despite all the reasons I give him to run away. He is forgiving and faithful to his promises. Jesus will be with me always, no matter what, until I see his face at his glorious return.

What might happen this Christmas if you let X mark the spot? Write it in your calendar, save it as the wallpaper of your phone, or trace it over your own heart, remembering Christ's words: **"And surely I am with you always, to the very end of the age"** (Matthew 28:20).

Stay the course!
Karen Spiegelberg

The race was marked out. The middle school girls were on the line waiting for the gun to signal the start. And off they went! My daughter was in the pack and quickly worked her way up to the front. As the 1.5-mile cross country race continued, she managed to keep the lead and fend off nearby competitors. Coming around the last bend, she was exhausted but determined and could taste a sweet victory in sight. But then she veered off course slightly, and it was just enough for the girl riding her heels to win the race.

She was so disappointed, and I didn't blame her. But these are the moments as Christians that are so beautiful in analogy to a favorite Bible passage: **"Let us run with perseverance the race marked out for us, fixing our eyes on Jesus, the pioneer and perfecter of faith"** (Hebrews 12:1,2). It's not always easy to do, is it? The world throws distractions in our faces at every turn, and Satan causes us to doubt. This race that we call the Christian life is a marathon though, not a 1.5-mile race. And despite the trials and troubles and times we veer off course, Jesus is there at the finish line, the victor of our race, arms stretched open and awaiting us. Stay the course, dear brothers and sisters in faith, with Jesus' help.

A much sweeter award awaits you than the one that alluded my daughter! And it's yours for all eternity.

God's mercy seeks you
Pastor Daron Lindemann

I was waiting in line at the store to check out, and the lady ahead of me at the cashier was short by $2.72. I approached her with $3 and said, "I've got you covered." This was a frazzled mom fumbling four kiddos and a handful of coupons. Most people would've helped her. On the way home, I thought, "What if that wasn't a mom in crisis but an irritable, impatient executive, treating the cashier rudely and blaming her for his problem?"

I might not have helped, or at least helped but not as cheerfully.

Imagine you are that irritable executive short on cash and patience and someone approaches you, "I've got you covered." Would that change your attitude?

Jesus teaches us about that kind of mercy, but he does more than that. He teaches the kind of mercy he wants you to show others.

He told a story about a landowner who **"went out early in the morning to hire workers"** (Matthew 20:1). But he needed more. So throughout the day, **"he went out and found still others"** (Matthew 20:6).

God's mercy explores, goes out to find, seeks. God's mercy sees "still others." God's mercy calls you no matter how ashamed you feel or afraid you've become.

God's mercy sees your struggling friend or straying child no matter how far they've gone.

God's mercy finds people who aren't good at finding him. He goes out. He finds. God's mercy has found you.

December 4

Go play in the snow
Jan Gompper

Though I now live in the Sunshine State, I miss the snow. I'd be lying if I said I yearned for the cold, but I especially miss watching that first winter snowfall blanket the ground with what looks like a coating of powdered sugar—clean, spotless, radiant—the grunginess of fall's decay hidden from view.

Have you ever wanted aspects of your life covered like that? I have. Our sins and guilt can cause us to see ourselves as decaying rubble, unworthy of anything but the bonfire Satan has in store for us. But in the midst of our regret, God reminds us, **"'Come now, let us settle the matter,' says the Lord. 'Though your sins are like scarlet, they shall be white as snow'"** (Isaiah 1:18).

Because of what Jesus did for us on the cross, all our grunginess is hidden from God's holiness. And when we put our faith and trust in Christ, God sees us as clean, spotless, radiant.

At times, that's hard for me to imagine. For some, it can be hard to accept. But did you catch the first part of Isaiah's message from God? "Let us settle the matter." God's grace is a once-and-for-all deal. No going back— no reversing his decision.

That doesn't mean our lives won't get grimy again. But we can be confident that we will always remain blanketed with the glistening righteousness of Christ.

Go play in the snow!

Get rid of anger
Pastor Mike Novotny

Have you heard of the church brawl that left 40 people dead? In 1846, two different Christian denominations wanted to hold their Easter service in the Church of the Holy Sepulchre in Jerusalem, built over the spot where Jesus died and rose. Since both couldn't get what they wanted, their anger exploded into a brawl where "holy men" did very unholy things. Priests grabbed crosses off the altars and candlesticks to bludgeon their enemies. Some smuggled guns under their robes and fired them into the angry mob. By the time law enforcement showed up, 40 bodies lay dead in the place where Jesus died.

Yikes. This sad-but-true story reminds us that anger can be an issue even in the church. Despite your faith in Jesus, you might be an angry person who raises your voice often, gets into arguments frequently, or even punches or threatens in your worst moments of rage.

This is no laughing matter. So what should you do? **"Get rid of all bitterness, rage and anger, brawling and slander, along with every form of malice"** (Ephesians 4:31). Don't manage your anger. Get rid of it. Get aggressive in addressing this part of your personality. Confess that sin to your pastor. Ask friends for accountability. Seek professional counseling.

And remember Jesus. His disciples James and John had issues with anger, but he both chose and changed them. His patience with sinners and his grace on the cross had a profound impact on these hotheaded men.

I pray that Jesus' love has the same effect on you.

Christ-like love
Andrea Delwiche

It's easy to look around us and get discouraged. It's useful to consider how things are different when we live in Christ-like love. This duality isn't new. Picture a writer in ancient Israel walking the streets of his city. He goes home and writes a prayer that the Lord speak peace to his followers and revive in them a living faith.

God inspired the psalmist's vision of a better way: **"Surely his salvation is near those who fear him, that his glory may dwell in our land. Love and faithfulness meet together; righteousness and peace kiss each other. Faithfulness springs forth from the earth, and righteousness looks down from heaven"** (85:9-11).

This idyllic scenario is God's vision; he kindles it and provides the sustenance. He's capable of direct intervention, but often he uses his people as his hands and feet. We're commissioned to be bearers of good news and healing, to share the fruit of a living faith.

What is the fruit that we have to offer? In this psalm it's described as love, righteousness, faithfulness, and peace. In the New Testament, we think of love, joy, peace, patience, kindness, goodness, faithfulness, gentleness, and self-control.

Does this fruit of faith characterize how you bring Christ to the place you live or characterize your faith community?

Love is the distinguishing characteristic of Jesus' followers. Christ's unconditional love is the healing we offer. The fruit of Christ-like love is an oasis that we Christians can provide in our corners of the kingdom.

Let this mind be in you: Purpose
Jason Nelson

If you watch the TV show *Shark Tank*, you have seen ambitious entrepreneurs pitch their ideas to the dais of successful investors. The contestants all want money and "shark" expertise to move their ideas forward. The sharks always ask about the predictors of success: revenue trends, profit margins, growth potential. What seems to be most persuasive to the sharks is if the contestants have a compelling idea of what they are trying to do. Do they have a clear mission in mind or just a vague notion? Some contestants struggle to explain what it is they are trying to accomplish. That as much as anything causes the sharks to tap out. But if the idea is novel and the contestants are convincing, they may get multiple offers from the sharks.

Jesus came **"to seek and to save the lost"** (Luke 19:10). He pursued it without wavering. He demonstrated willingness to leave many and go after one lost sheep if necessary, because that is what he came to do.

People who are heavily invested in worthwhile pursuits experience a great deal of fulfillment in their lives. They have a sense of calling and enjoy it most days. People who haven't found that sweet spot are vulnerable to unhappiness and look to unhealthy substitutes for personal satisfaction. Every activity under the sun needs all-in investors. Reflect on your personality, God-given gifts, and talents and find your purpose in his great kingdom.

December 8

A not-so-merry Christmas
Linda Buxa

Merry Christmas!

Except . . . what if this Christmas season isn't so merry? So many people are in a hard chapter of life. Perhaps it's the first Christmas without your spouse. Maybe it's the fifth Christmas that infertility weighs on your heart. Possibly you face the income-versus-expenses struggle or the daily battle against addiction or the pains that come with aging. Maybe you, like many, are just worn down by cumulative hurt, exhaustion, grief, and anxiety.

This pain—your pain—is exactly why Jesus came! It's because God saw this broken world and had compassion on the people he created. He came because he loved you before you were even lovable. He chose to be born because he didn't want you to be separated from him for all eternity. He came because his plan is to make all things new.

That's why Christmas isn't about becoming merry. It's about God becoming human—to live for us, to die for us, to rise for us, to bring us into his family. It's about God with us! It's about hearing Jesus say, **"I have told you these things, so that in me you may have peace. In this world you will have trouble. But take heart! I have overcome the world"** (John 16:33).

So even if your Christmas isn't merry, I pray that because of God-with-us, you are able to have a Peace Christmas, a Take-Heart Christmas, an Overcomer Christmas, a Comfort Christmas, a Strength Christmas.

Anger is ego
Pastor Mike Novotny

The so-pathetic-you-want-to-laugh story of James and John reminds us that most anger is just ego. **"When the disciples James and John saw** [the Samaritans' rejection of Jesus], **they asked, 'Lord, do you want us to call fire down from heaven to destroy them?'"** (Luke 9:54). The brothers wanted to direct a movie called *Sodom the Sequel*, bringing down heavenly fire for a good ol' Samaritan BBQ.

But notice that little word *us*. "Jesus, do you want *us* to call down fire?" James and John made the issue about themselves. Jesus wasn't burning with vengeful anger, but the brothers were, because their egos were offended at the ungrateful Samaritans.

That's a convicting word that we need to hear too. Ninety-nine percent of our anger is our ego. "I'm not getting what I want." "I wanted to drive to work without slowing down or hitting the brakes, but then you got in the way." "I wanted the government, my employer, my church to handle COVID the way I wanted." I. I. I. We love to blame our anger on the circumstances, but maybe the real issue isn't it/him/her/them; maybe the real issue is our ego.

Think of the last time you were angry. What did you want that you weren't getting? Was your anger just your ego in disguise? Be honest, and you'll be one step closer to God's will of getting rid of your anger.

A friend you can count on
Pastor Clark Schultz

Have you ever heard the phrase, "a friend in need is a friend indeed"? I'm not sure what that means, but I know my friends have been there through the good days and the days that seem like one big letdown sandwich.

I've also found in those dark days who my true friends are. They love me with a real concern, not for what I have to offer them.

Jesus took his best friends with him into the Garden of Gethsemane. When he needed them most, they took a nap and later scattered in the other direction. Wow.

As a friend of Jesus, you might say that you'd never do that, but you are lying to yourself. And so am I. We sleep through worship, and I'm not just talking about ZZZZs. We show up physically, but mentally we are elsewhere. We follow Jesus when it's convenient for us and fits into our schedules, but when the going gets tough, we too hightail it in another direction.

We can focus too heavily on the sleeping guys in the Garden with Jesus, but a better focus is on the One who said, **"Rise! Let us go! Here comes my betrayer!"** (Matthew 26:46). He was determined to save us and cover all our sins, to forgive us for those moments we've put ourselves and our stuff before him and others.

That is truly a friend who loves at all times. A friend you can count on. A friend in need has a friend in Jesus indeed.

Christ in the crazy
Pastor Mike Novotny

In my experience, most of us either have a crazy-busy Christmas or a crazy-hard Christmas. If you're blessed with family and friends, a good church, and a good job, then December is crazy busy with all the parties that require (1) a dish to pass, (2) a Christmas sweater, and (3) another night away from home. If you lack such blessings, your December might be crazy hard as you think about (1) the dysfunction of your family, (2) a loved one who isn't around, or (3) the difference between your broken life and the lives of the smiling faces you see on the cards that come in the mail.

Whatever kind of crazy you're facing, here's some good news—Christ is in the crazy. It would have been so much easier for Jesus to stay up in heaven, far away from the dumpster fire called Earth, but he didn't. He made his dwelling among us. Jesus could have picked some more polished people for his closest friends, but instead he did life with Peter, James, John, and Mary, right in the middle of all their mess, their pride and anger and de-mon-possessed pasts. Jesus could have easily escaped his own arrest, but instead he let others drag him into the crazy of the cross, the injustice, and the tomb.

I know Christmas—and life in general—can be crazy. Thank God that's right where Jesus is. **"The Word be-came flesh and made his dwelling among us"** (John 1:14). Among us. That's where Jesus was. That's where Jesus still is.

Jesus didn't compromise
Pastor Clark Schultz

Secular history tells us that Pontius Pilate ruled for ten years. Most governors were only in office a quarter of that time and then were promoted in some way. Why wasn't Pilate promoted? Was it because he loved serving in Judea? Or did his superiors have it in for him? Whatever the case, we can see Pilate was one who did not like confrontation. In his dealings with Jesus and the Jewish mob, he tried to pass the buck.

"I find no basis for a charge against this man" (Luke 23:4). He hoped for sympathy after Jesus' flogging. Next, his ploy to free Barabbas blew up in his face. And then finally when he knew he couldn't win, **"he washed his hands in front of the crowd"** (Matthew 27:24).

Pilate could have said, "Sorry, I'm not going to kill this man." Nope, he caved in to the pressure of the masses. Sound familiar? Compromise is a good thing in marriage and in teamwork. However, compromising our beliefs to fit in or our morals to be loved is a no-win situation. In his painting *Forgiven*, Thomas Blackshear depicts a man who is falling. In his hands are three nails and a hammer to show it wasn't Pilate who put Jesus on that cross; it was us. But what is more comforting is the person who is holding this man up. Jesus, the one who did not compromise but fulfilled the promise to save all people from their sins . . . and that includes you.

Good, better, best vs. bad, worse, worst

Pastor Mike Novotny

We all want to be chosen. Chosen for a team. Chosen for a date. Chosen for a scholarship. Chosen for a promotion. You and I will never outgrow our deep longing for people to choose us.

The problem, however, is that "the chosen" are normally people who are good, better, or the best. You have to be a good player or good-looking or good at relationships. You have to be better than the competition, better than the other students, better than the other dating options online. Sometimes you have to be the best applicant, the best at your position, or the best friend to invite out to dinner. And if you're not, you don't get chosen. Perhaps you've felt the sting of being left out, overlooked, or simply not good enough.

But God isn't like that. The God who chose a loudmouth named Peter, a demon-possessed woman named Mary, and a tax collector like Matthew is obviously operating by different standards. Our gracious God chooses bad people, picks worse people, and elects the worst of people! That means there is hope for all people, including me and you. Praise God for that!

"But God chose the foolish things of the world to shame the wise; God chose the weak things of the world to shame the strong. God chose the lowly things of this world and the despised things—and the things that are not—to nullify the things that are, so that no one may boast before him" (1 Corinthians 1:27-29).

God's church. Your place.
Pastor Daron Lindemann

Who placed your right hand as your right hand and not as your kneecap? God did.

At church, who places people with musical gifts in musical service? And who places those with empathy and caring skills in positions where they can help others? God is at work. God places people like he places a right hand.

At home, I needed a tin snips tool to cut some sheet metal. It was boxed up, so I used a regular scissors. Do you think it cut the metal? Nope. And guess what happened to the scissors? I broke it.

Each tool serves a special purpose, and other tools cannot do what that tool can do. A big wrench seems so strong, but it just can't cut paper as well as a scissors. So the wrench shouldn't think, "If every one of these tools were like me, we'd get things done."

The Bible teaches it this way: **"The eye cannot say to the hand, 'I don't need you!' And the head cannot say to the feet, 'I don't need you!' On the contrary, those parts of the body that seem to be weaker are indispensable, and the parts that we think are less honorable we treat with special honor"** (1 Corinthians 12:21-23).

Would you like more recognition for serving at your church? Probably. Volunteers are often underappreciated. But not by God.

It is God's church, and everybody is honored. That's what God says. Everybody is important. Everybody is needed. Everybody has a place and purpose. What's yours?

Let this mind be in you: Neighbors
Jason Nelson

Jesus knew that everyone loves a good story. He told many in his teaching ministry. There were stories about lost sheep and coins, wayward sons, and a seemingly careless seed scatterer, just to name a few. I think Jesus also knew that everyone loves to repeat a good story. That's why people who haven't read the Bible much are familiar with his stories. Perhaps Jesus' most enduring story is about an underappreciated man from up north who stopped to help an assault victim after others chose not to get involved and just walked by (see Luke 10:25-37).

As world population grows, the density of neighbors is intense, especially in urban areas. Land is expensive and in short supply, so developers build up. People really do live on top of one another. You can listen to your neighbor's music, smell what they're cooking, and overhear their conversations. You might even know what challenges they are facing in life.

Being a good neighbor takes finesse from followers of Jesus. We want to respect people's privacy. We also want to be the arms and face of Jesus when people need help. When we can't or shouldn't avoid our neighbors, we need to assess the situation accurately. "What can I do to help you?" Then we need to be prepared to do it.

In every tragic moment in the human experience, I have seen good neighbors in action. I have benefited from having good neighbors. I want to be a good neighbor.

Joyful love for God
Andrea Delwiche

Sometimes we tend to be more exuberant about our sports teams than we are about God. If God is both the root and apex of everything, wouldn't we rejoice over him the way we do other things? We can take Psalm 87 as an example of praise, even if some of the words are unclear to us.

"He has founded his city on the holy mountain. The Lord loves the gates of Zion more than all the other dwellings of Jacob. Glorious things are said of you, city of God: 'I will record Rahab and Babylon among those who acknowledge me—Philistia too, and Tyre, along with Cush—and will say, "This one was born in Zion."' Indeed, of Zion it will be said, 'This one and that one were born in her, and the Most High himself will establish her.' The Lord will write in the register of the peoples: 'This one was born in Zion.' As they make music they will sing, 'All my fountains are in you'" (verses: 1–7).

This psalm overflows with praise for God, his dwelling place, and his acceptance of all people. At the end, we read a joyous metaphorical outpouring of praise: "All my fountains are in you."

This psalm exudes the refreshment of a cool lake on a hot day. We live in the circle of God's love. He loves all his creation, and praise rises to his ears from every corner of the world.

God's goodness overflows. Holy Spirit, help us learn to take the risk of expressing joyful love for you!

Christmas is more crazy than baby
Pastor Mike Novotny

It took me 41 years of celebrating the birth of Jesus to realize this truth: the Bible's Christmas is more crazy than baby. Read the two accounts of Jesus' birth in the Bible—Matthew 1 and Luke 2—and the baby Jesus is barely mentioned. You won't catch how many pounds or ounces Jesus weighed or how much hair the holy infant had because the gospel writers want you to know about the crazy context of our Savior's birth.

Like Caesar Augustus, the pagan ruler who wanted to count the population so he could tax them and control them. And Joseph of Nazareth, a poor carpenter who would need weeks off of work to travel to Bethlehem for the census. And the B&B of Bethlehem, whose "no occupancy" sign forced Mary to push through the contractions surrounded by animals who didn't go to nursing school. Can you imagine it?! It must have been crazy.

But guess who came in the middle of all that crazy? *The* baby. **"While they were there, the time came for the baby to be born, and she gave birth to her firstborn, a son. She wrapped him in cloths and placed him in a manger, because there was no guest room available for them"** (Luke 2:6,7).

Your life might be crazy right now. Too many miles on the road. A complicated family. But take heart! Our Jesus comes into the middle of the crazy. He did back then. He still does today.

God's mercy
Pastor Clark Schultz

When I think of God's mercy, I think of a particular dog growing up. His name was Buddy, but my father called him Snagglytooth because he had one tooth that hung out. He was a mutt, and his eyes were two different colors. People always asked us where we got that thing.

The story goes that my mother went to pick out a family dog from the humane society. She looked at all the cocker and springer spaniels and was all ready to pick one of those up when she walked past Buddy's cage. Even in the cage, he was not an attractive dog to look at. My mom asked, "What's the story with this mutt?" The worker said he'd been there for weeks and was on doggy death row because nobody wanted him. As the worker said this and as my mom heard the words that he was going to be put to death, Buddy put his paw on the glass of his cage. Needless to say, my mother took pity on him and brought him home to our farm.

The apostle Paul tells us in Titus 3:5, "[God] **saved us, not because of righteous things we had done, but because of his mercy."**

By nature, we are in a cage, chained to our sins and left to ourselves to die. We can do all the good works we want, but they won't save us. Thankfully God in his mercy took pity on us and rescued us.

We are part of his family now!

Will you welcome Jesus?

Pastor Mike Novotny

If Jesus knocked on your front door, would you let him in? The Samaritans didn't. **"[Jesus] sent messengers on ahead, who went into a Samaritan village to get things ready for him; but the people there did not welcome him, because he was heading for Jerusalem"** (Luke 9:52,53). Apparently, when the Samaritans heard that Jesus was heading for Jerusalem, they locked their doors and RSVP'd with a hard no. Why? Because Jesus was "heading for Jerusalem." The Samaritans didn't think they needed Jerusalem; they had their own place for worship on Mt. Gerizim. Thus, when Jesus implied that their religion was wrong and the Jewish religion was right, they wanted nothing to do with him.

This is the tricky thing about Jesus. He wants to talk to you, but part of that talk might be about things you need to change. You might have your own "Mt. Gerizim," a place you go that God doesn't like or a thing you consider spiritually good that God considers spiritually bad. If Jesus wanted to change your mind, change your habits, change your religion, and call you to repentance, would you still welcome him? At the heart of us all is this question—Will I change for Jesus, or will I only accept a Jesus who will change for me?

How will you answer that question today?

What lies beyond the darkness
Pastor David Scharf

Before Moses died, God led him up a mountain that overlooked the Promised Land. God showed Moses what he was giving to his people through Moses' work after all those years marked by pain and sin and death: a land flowing with milk and honey, the very land where the Savior of the world would be born to God's people. Moses' life had meaning.

Sit with Moses on that mountain. Moses prayed in Psalm 90:16,17: **"May your deeds be shown to your servants, your splendor to their children. May the favor of the Lord our God rest on us; establish the work of our hands for us."** Unless judgment day comes first, we will die. I have had the privilege of spending time with people who knew they were dying. We did not talk about how much they loved their nice houses or great vacations. We talked about the joy it gave them to know they would meet their families again in heaven. See what gives your life real meaning. See your children one day telling their children about the way their Savior loves them. See a house of worship that you supported with your prayers and with your offerings filled with people you've never seen and don't know. See the Last Day, when God will call all those souls to the Promised Land we are waiting for. In the middle of a dark world, see *that*; you will see what lies beyond the darkness!

Jesus loves the (very, very) lost
Pastor Mike Novotny

If you ever wonder if Jesus could love you after the ugliness of your past, read this: **"[Jesus] sent messengers on ahead, who went into a Samaritan village to get things ready for him"** (Luke 9:52). If you're not stunned by that verse, you obviously aren't a Jew from the first century.

About 1,000 years before Jesus, things went morally south in Samaria. A sort of civil war divided Israel into two parts, separating Samaria from Jerusalem. For the next 200 years, 20 kings ruled from Samaria's capital, and none of them worshiped the true God, choosing idols instead. Thus God allowed the Assyrians to invade and take Israel into exile. In the process, however, the Assyrians dropped off some of their own idols, meaning Samaria was now a buffet of bad gods. By the time Jesus was born, Jews and Samaritans kept their distance from each other, refusing to associate with those neighboring heretics (John 4:9).

But Jesus was different. He wanted to share the truth with the Samaritans. His love shocked his Jewish friends and the Samaritans he first encountered, a reminder to us that grace, when properly understood, is amazing.

You may have a messy story. Your family may have a dysfunctional past. Your past (or present) may be filled with greed, sexual immorality, or other idols. But Jesus won't let that stop him from reaching out to you with the message of his unconditional love. You might be far from good, but you are not too far gone for God.

What if?

Pastor Daron Lindemann

I'm a certified "what-iffer." What-iffers say things like . . .

"What if our kids make noise in church?" So they don't go to church.

"What if I drive my new car and it gets dinged?" So they don't drive their cars.

"What if I don't meet the deadline?" So they stress out, too paralyzed to get started, and then stress out more because they're behind.

Let me share two healthy responses.

"So what!" What if your new car gets nicked by a piece of gravel thrown from a truck? So what! Almost all cars have little nicks. If it's too bothersome, you can repair it.

"What if God?" Your what-if thoughts will speculate toward the worst-case scenario. God specializes in worst-case scenarios, and he is on your side! If he gave you his own Son, won't he also give you other things you need?

"He who did not spare his own Son, but gave him up for us all—how will he not also, along with him, graciously give us all things?" (Romans 8:32).

So learn to reply to your what-if thoughts by saying, "What if God . . . is on my side . . . answers my prayers . . . has a better plan . . . is strategically putting some pieces together for something even more amazing . . . is never confused . . . provides a way out?"

Anxious thoughts can come, uninvited, and that's not wrong or bad. They're real, but they are not in charge. God is.

Question your "need tos"
Pastor Mike Novotny

If you've ever seen my Instagram page, you may be aware that I am a box-checking addict. Every year, I craft an aggressive list of physical, spiritual, financial, and relational goals, which turn into a master list of boxes that I try to check. Few things bring me joy like checking another box!

If you're wired like me, you might need to hear the tough and tender words Jesus spoke to his organized, driven, box-checking friend named Martha. **"'Martha, Martha,' the Lord answered, 'you are worried and upset about many things, but few things are needed'"** (Luke 10:41,42). While Martha believed that she "needed" to do "many things," Jesus corrected her. She didn't need to. She wanted to, but she didn't need to.

If you find yourself always running, never resting, frequently behind, and constantly saying things like, "I need to/have to/got to," I would encourage you to invite a mature Christian friend to look at your schedule. Be honest about your plans, your pace, and how much caffeine you need to accomplish your "need tos." Don't lie about how little you sleep or how often you get frustrated at people for not working harder.

In love, just like Jesus with Martha, they will remind you that there are few things needed in this life. Goals are great, and to-do lists are terrific tools to get things done, but they are not worth losing the peace that Jesus invites you to experience. Question your "need tos," and remember that in Jesus you have all that you truly need.

Jesus loves YOU
Andrea Delwiche

"He [Jesus] is the image of the invisible God, the firstborn of all creation. For by him all things were created, in heaven and on earth, visible and invisible, whether thrones or dominions or rulers or authorities—all things were created through him and for him. And he is before all things, and in him all things hold together. And he is the head of the body, the church. He is the beginning, the firstborn from the dead, that in everything he might be preeminent. For in him all the fullness of God was pleased to dwell, and through him to reconcile to himself all things" (Colossians 1:15-20 ESV).

How can we begin to grasp the immensity of Jesus' birth and yet be comforted by it personally? Imagine yourself holding a newborn baby. Imagine this infant, heavy in your arms, is Jesus, "the image of the invisible God." That first Christmas, the "firstborn of all creation" was a baby in his mother's arms. This infant is the one in whom "all things hold together."

God loves you in your vulnerability so much that he subjected himself to conform to a vulnerable human body. So today, whether Christmas feels full of warmth or cold and bleak, remember that Jesus, in whom all things hold together, loves you, individually. He is fully present with you just as he was in his mother's arms. God's peace be with you this day, this night.

Happy Easter!
Linda Buxa

I was walking out of church on Easter Sunday when the greeter wished me a "Merry Christmas!" She burst out laughing when she realized her mistake, but in reality it was the perfect reminder. I had just celebrated that Jesus defeated death for me, and I also got to picture the sweet baby whose birth was announced by angels!

The next day I watched a video that shared, "What you hope for shapes what you live for." That woman's Christmas wish on Easter came rushing back, and I immediately thought of Jesus. What he hoped for, an eternity of living with his people, absolutely shaped what he was born for—and what he died for. He *chose* this course of saving action.

Thanks to his decision, we get the best Christmas gift: a certain hope that shapes how we live. **"As God's chosen people, holy and dearly loved, clothe yourselves with compassion, kindness, humility, gentleness and patience. Bear with each other and forgive one another if any of you has a grievance against someone. Forgive as the Lord forgave you. And over all these virtues put on love, which binds them all together in perfect unity"** (Colossians 3:12-14).

Is this the message you were expecting on Christmas? Probably not. But it's the message we share every day. The God of the universe loved you so much that he was willing to be both a baby in a manger and a man on a cross—and that changes your life and your eternity.

Merry Christmas! Happy Easter!

December 26

Broken ribs
Pastor Daron Lindemann

"You're going to break the ribs," he told us. "If you don't hear the snap, crack, and pop—you're not doing it right." The CPR instructor urged our staff to perform chest compressions effectively.

He said that way too often people try to perform CPR but don't push hard enough. "You are the person's heartbeat," he reminded us. "Do you want to save that person's life or be gentle and watch him die? Believe me, if you do it right, he'll be sore but he'll also be alive and will thank you for saving him."

Sometimes, to save a person, you need to hurt him or her.

Do you want God to save you or make life easy for you and your foolish pleasures? Do you want God to give you life the right way or spoil you so that you love the gifts more than the Giver?

"Let me hear joy and gladness; let the bones you have crushed rejoice" (Psalm 51:8).

Believers don't look for joy outside of suffering but in it, through it. With what does this psalmist rejoice? Where does his gladness come from? Is it a lavish banquet or strategic military victory? No. From his crushed bones.

Yes, Christians still experience troubles, but these are not lightning bolts hurled by God to punish us. They are like controlled, targeted electrical power surges or heart compressions when God's love for us must hurt us to save us.

Snap. Zap. Pop. Life from God may hurt. You'll thank him for it.

Certain comfort
Pastor David Scharf

Do you know what the new year holds for you? Are you certain? There's nothing quite so uncomfortable as uncertainty. The uncertainties steal away our peace. Will the value of your house go up? Will your mom's appointment give her a clean bill of health? Will your parents stop fighting? If only we could know what's going to happen, we could finally have some peace.

For all he had been through in his life, King David reminds us in the words of Psalm 139 that if we're looking for peace in the knowledge of what might come, we are asking the wrong questions. The answer that David gives from God's Word is not found in knowing what the future holds for our health or our wealth. The comfort God talks about through David is not even found in *our knowledge* at all. Listen to where David points us for certain comfort in uncertain days: **"You have searched me, Lord, and *you* know me"** (Psalm 139:1).

What does God know? He knows you and me. He knows our doubts and fears. He knows our sin. But he also knows that he has chosen to love us with an everlasting love. He knows that we were worth going to a cross for. He knows that he can make everything that happens in the new year work for our good. He knows that he wants us in heaven with him. Certain comfort is not that we know the future but that God does.

December 28

He knows and forgives
Pastor David Scharf

You wouldn't think there is much comfort in God knowing everything about you. As you think back over the past year, I'm sure you can think of the thoughts and words and actions that you wish no one knew about, maybe even some sins that you actually were able to hide from everyone. Well, almost everyone. God knows everything. He even knows the things you would dare never tell your loved ones, lest they stop loving you.

That's God's omniscience, his perfect knowledge of everything. Is that a terrifying thought? Read Psalm 139:6: **"Such knowledge is too wonderful for me, too lofty for me to attain."** Not too terrifying, not too appalling, but too wonderful. How could the psalmist say that? Because he knew his God. So do you. Your God promises that since Jesus lived a perfect life for you and died on a cross, God has forgiven your sins. God does not love you because you fooled him. God does not love you because you succeeded in hiding your sins from him. God saw even the sins that you would never dare whisper to anyone else, and he loved you and forgave you. Such knowledge is too wonderful, too lofty for you to attain. Is there anyone else who could give you a love like that? Is there anyone else better suited to help you conquer your sins in the year to come than the One who already knows them and forgives them?

Safe in God's hand
Pastor David Scharf

It could not have been easy for King David to write this: **"Where can I flee from your presence? If I go up to the heavens, you are there; if I make my bed in the depths, you are there"** (Psalm 139:7,8). God was there when David stood on his roof and took Bathsheba with his eyes before he took her with his arms. God was there when David had Uriah killed. God had witnessed it all firsthand. As David said, "You are there."

But it's this miracle of God's grace that filled David with such confidence. When he put himself in the darkest depths of danger, God did not leave him. Even when David wanted to be left alone—even when God had every reason to abandon him—God never left him.

Do you know where this next year will find you? You certainly do: **"If I rise on the wings of the dawn, if I settle on the far side of the sea, even there your hand will guide me, your right hand will hold me fast"** (Psalm 139:9,10). No matter where you go in the next year, you will never face a danger alone. Not even your sins can take you to a place where God will not be there. Whether you are in a car accident or at a birthday party or in a wedding or at a hospital, you never have to doubt where you will really be: with your Lord and Savior, held in his loving and protecting hand.

God controls it all
Pastor David Scharf

Have you ever had a dream while you were sleeping that presented you with a situation you were forced to respond to but were powerless to do anything about? You could not move. You were paralyzed. Do you ever feel that way about the future? King David wrote: **"All the days ordained for me were written in your book before one of them came to be. How precious to me are your thoughts, God! How vast is the sum of them! Were I to count them, they would outnumber the grains of sand—when I awake, I am still with you"** (Psalm 139:16–18).

Imagine standing on a beach trying to count the grains of sand. You would fall asleep before you even finished counting the grains clinging to the soles of your shoes! David could find joy in falling asleep thinking about God's plans for him and waking up rejoicing in that truth. David knew that not only did God knit him together in his mother's womb; God was weaving together the days of his life, just as he had planned.

Do you see what David sees? Behind everything that happens next year, you have a God who loves you enough to use everything for your good. There is not a day that will not go according to the plan God has for you. Every day ordained. No wonder David said, "How precious!"

A Christian can hate?

Pastor David Scharf

God knows everything. God is everywhere. God can do anything. But he is more. He is also holy. David wrote: **"Do I not hate those who hate you, Lord? . . . Search me, God, and know my heart; test me and know my anxious thoughts. See if there is any offensive way in me, and lead me in the way everlasting"** (Psalm 139:21,23,24).

It sounds odd, doesn't it? To hear a Christian talking about hating? How could someone who knows the love that God has for them ever talk about hating? When we know that sin destroys souls and that Jesus suffered death to pay for our brokenness, the better question is, "How could we not hate sin?"

No matter who you are, you do not have to wonder what God's will for you is in the year to come. Hate the wrongdoings of your past. Hate the way they have been a rebellion against God and the way they have brought pain to others in your life. Hate your brokenness, and as much as you do that, never forget what God did about it. Never forget that Jesus has already paid the price for those sins. Never forget that Jesus has freed you from them. Never forget that because of Jesus, you can win the battle against them. Never forget that because of Jesus, you can pray to God, absolutely certain that he doesn't see any sin in you anymore. Remember that, and it will be a blessed new year!

DEVOTIONS FOR
SPECIAL DAYS

Never thirsty again
Good Friday
Pastor Clark Schultz

The thirstiest I've ever been was during my freshman year football practices. Our coaches would run us hard, and then the most glorious words were spoken: "Go get water." I remember running to the hose and sticking my whole head and face in the stream.

That, of course, is nothing compared to what our Lord experienced on the cross. One of the worst side effects of being nailed to a cross was raging thirst. Think of the emotional and spiritual struggle that increased his thirst. Judas betrayed him. His disciples deserted him. His countrymen condemned him. His own Father forsook him. Jesus bore the weight of the world's guilt. As the apostle Peter said, **"'He himself bore our sins' in his body on the cross"** (1 Peter 2:24). Jesus did this for us. His reason for doing this—YOU.

You are not a nameless, faceless number to God. The One who knows the number of hairs on your head went to the cross for *you*. He endured the shame, the suffering, the curse, and even the thirst for *you*. And in so doing, he won complete forgiveness and eternal life for you.

In Revelation, John describes the saints in heaven with these words: **"'Never again will they hunger; never again will they thirst. . . . For the Lamb at the center of the throne will be their shepherd; 'he will lead them to springs of living water.' 'And God will wipe away every tear from their eyes'"** (7:16,17). We will enjoy that tear-free, thirst-free place, that place of living water, because the Lamb endured the thirst of crucifixion for us.

New life

Easter Sunday

Andrea Delwiche

In the days preceding his death, Jesus reminded his disciples of a lesson from nature that had application in his own life and the lives of his followers.

"Unless a kernel of wheat falls to the ground and dies, it remains only a single seed. But if it dies, it produces many seeds. Anyone who loves their life will lose it, while anyone who hates their life in this world will keep it for eternal life" (John 12:24,25).

Jesus' followers were contemplating dreams of earthly glory. Jesus pointed them in a different direction. A kernel of wheat is only one seed until it falls to the ground and lies dormant for a season. Then in spring the soil warms; the seed germinates and grows. Later in its growth cycle, it bears fruit. The single kernel produces many kernels, which in turn will die, come back to life, and increase.

Through the giving of his own life, Jesus gave new life to his first-century disciples and to all of us who follow him today. We are in turn asked by God to give up our own lives for others.

Christ's resurrection resonates for us each day—both eternally and in time as we walk each day into the resurrection fields of loving service with Christ, our Savior and Redeemer. We love and serve others because Jesus loved and served us first. What an honor to be Christ-like in this way!

Christ is risen. Praise God! He is risen, and we rise with him. Hallelujah!

Moms, you are valuable to Jesus
Mother's Day
Andrea Delwiche

"Mary . . . sat at the Lord's feet listening to what he said. But Martha was distracted by all the preparations. . . . 'Martha, Martha,' the Lord answered, 'you are worried and upset about many things, but few things are needed—or indeed only one. Mary has chosen what is better, and it will not be taken away from her'" (Luke 10:39-42).

Moms, this is not a devotion to tell you that you are worried over many things. Moms feel incredible pressure to provide for their families. But you are much more than your to-do list and the pressures of post-worthy pictures and idyllic family stories.

You are valuable to Jesus as a human being with a thirsty soul. You are *capable of* and *need to* sit at Jesus' feet and learn from him. Jesus deeply desires to sit and talk with you. He looks at you and says, "Sit with me. Let's talk, and you will learn from me." One sister sat at Jesus' feet, and Jesus *defended her* for doing it.

The time you spend with Jesus will be given back to you. God is so generous in this regard. Your priorities will shift and give you ease.

Only Jesus can fill our deepest longing. Let your mothering flow from that peace, free from self-criticism or criticism from others. You are one of Jesus' most valued followers.

Dads on duty
Father's Day
Linda Buxa

At Southwood High School in Shreveport, Louisiana, 23 students were arrested over the course of three days due to violent fights. About 40 dads decided to step up to be part of the solution. "We're dads. We decided the best people who can take care of our kids are who? Are us," said father Michael LaFitte. Calling themselves Dads on Duty, these men take turns spending time at school, encouraging the students and helping maintain a positive environment. They've turned the school from a fight club into a refuge. "I immediately felt a form of safety," one of the students said. "The school has just been happy—and you can feel it," said another.*

Today is the day in the U.S. that we set aside to honor fathers and recognize the vital role they play in the lives of children. Science shows that children who have a father present have higher rates of performance at school, tend to excel in their careers, have elevated levels of physical and mental health, become better problem-solvers, are more confident and empathetic, and are more economically stable. In addition, their communities are safer, as the Dads on Duty showed.

Children who have a father who believes in Jesus also receive the best positive impact of all: **"Whoever fears the Lord has a secure fortress, and for their children it will be a refuge"** (Proverbs 14:26).

Thanks, dads, for being on duty, for creating a place of both physical and spiritual refuge for children!

* https://www.cbsnews.com/news/dads-louisiana-high-school-student-violence/

Give thanks before . . .

Thanksgiving Day

Pastor Daron Lindemann

Gratitude is good for you.

Research of human brains and behaviors strongly associates gratitude with greater happiness, improved health, better relationships, resilience in adversity, better enjoyment of experiences, and positive expression of emotions.

Participants in one study were asked to write a few sentences each week. One group was instructed to write about things that happened during the week for which they were thankful. Another group wrote down daily irritations. The third group did general journaling. After ten weeks, the first group reported more optimism, exercised more, and had fewer visits to the doctor.

Praise God for this study! But there's more. If you are a Christian, you have another big reason to be healthy and happy. God is good all the time!

Paging through the Bible, you'll see that giving thanks to God can be triggered by events. Healings. Victories. Forgiveness. Heaven. But giving thanks is also triggered purely by God being God.

Try giving thanks just to give thanks—thanks for your God who is good.

"Give thanks to the Lord, for he is good; his love endures forever" (1 Chronicles 16:34). Dear God, thanks for being you.

Can you commit to giving thanks just to give thanks until the end of this year? Give thanks to God, not necessarily related to your experiences but just because he's God. And see what a difference it makes!

About the Writers

Pastor Mike Novotny has served God's people in full-time ministry since 2007 in Madison and, most recently, at The CORE in Appleton, Wisconsin. He also serves as the lead speaker for Time of Grace, where he shares the good news about Jesus through television, print, and online platforms. Mike loves seeing people grasp the depth of God's amazing grace and unstoppable mercy. His wife continues to love him (despite plenty of reasons not to), and his two daughters open his eyes to the love of God for every Christian. When not talking about Jesus or dating his wife/girls, Mike loves playing soccer, running, and reading.

Linda Buxa is a freelance communications professional as well as a regular blogger and contributing writer for Time of Grace Ministry. Linda is the author of *Dig In! Family Devotions to Feed Your Faith, Parenting by Prayer, Made for Friendship,* and *Visible Faith: Living a Fruitful Life in Christ.* She and her husband, Greg, have lived in Alaska, Washington D.C., and California. After retiring from the military, they moved to Wisconsin, where they settled on 11.7 acres and now keep track of 15 chickens, multiple cats, and 1 black Lab. Their 3 children insist on getting older and following their dreams, so Greg and Linda are rapidly approaching the empty-nest stage. The sign in her kitchen sums up their lives: "You call it chaos; we call it family."

Andrea Delwiche lives in Wisconsin with her husband, three kids, dog, cat, and a goldfish pond full of fish. She enjoys reading, knitting, and road-tripping with her family. Although a lifelong believer, she began to come into a deeper understanding of what it means to follow

Christ far into adulthood (always a beginner on that journey!). Andrea has facilitated a Christian discussion group for women at her church for many years.

Pastor Jon Enter served as a pastor in West Palm Beach, Florida, for ten years. He is now a campus pastor and instructor at St. Croix Lutheran Academy in St. Paul, Minnesota. Jon also serves as a regular speaker on Grace Talks video devotions and a contributing writer to the ministry. He once led a tour at his college, and the Lord had him meet his future wife, Debbi. They are now drowning in pink and glitter with their four daughters: Violet, Lydia, Eden, and Maggie.

Pastor Matt Ewart and his wife, Amy, have been blessed with three children who keep life interesting. Matt is currently a pastor in Lakeville, Minnesota, and has previously served as a pastor in Colorado and Arizona.

Jan Gompper spent most of her career teaching theatre at Wisconsin Lutheran College in Milwaukee. She also served six years as a cohost for *Time of Grace* during its start-up years. She has collaborated on two faith-based musicals, numerous Christian songs, and has written and codirected scripts for a Christian video series. She and her husband now reside in the Tampa area, where she continues to practice her acting craft and coach aspiring acting students as opportunities arise. She also assists with Sunday school and other church-related activities.

Katrina Harrmann lives in southwest Michigan with her photographer husband, Nathan, and their three kids. A lifelong Christian, she attended journalism school at the University of Missouri, Columbia, and worked at the

Green Bay Press-Gazette and the *Sheboygan Press* before taking on the full-time job of motherhood. Currently, she writes and lives along the shores of Lake Michigan and enjoys gardening, hiking, camping, doing puzzles, and playing with her chihuahua in her free time.

Ann Jahns and her husband live in Wisconsin as recent empty nesters, having had the joy of raising three boys to young adulthood. She is a marketing coordinator for a Christian church body and a freelance proofreader and copy editor. Ann has been privileged to teach Sunday school and lead Bible studies for women of all ages. One of her passions is supporting women in the "sandwich generation" as they experience the unique joys and challenges of raising children while supporting aging parents.

Pastor Daron Lindemann serves in Pflugerville, Texas. Previously, he served in downtown Milwaukee and in Irmo, South Carolina. Daron has authored articles or series for *Forward in Christ* magazine, *Preach the Word*, and his own weekly Grace MEMO devotions. He lives in Texas with his wife, Cara, and has two adult sons.

Jason Nelson had a career as a teacher, counselor, and leader. He has a bachelor's degree in education, did graduate work in theology, and has a master's degree in counseling psychology. After his career ended in disabling back pain, he wrote the book *Miserable Joy: Chronic Pain in My Christian Life*. He has written and spoken extensively on a variety of topics related to the Christian life. Jason has been a contributing writer for Time of Grace since 2010. He has authored many Grace Moments devotions and several books. Jason lives with his wife, Nancy, in Wisconsin.

Pastor David Scharf served as a pastor in Greenville, Wisconsin, and now serves as a professor of theology at Martin Luther College in Minnesota. He has presented at numerous leadership, outreach, and missionary conferences across the country. He is a contributing writer for Time of Grace and a speaker for Grace Talks video devotions. Dave and his wife have six children.

Pastor Clark Schultz loves Jesus; his wife, Kristin, and their three boys; the Green Bay Packers; Milwaukee Brewers; Wisconsin Badgers; and—of course—Batman. His ministry stops are all in Wisconsin and include a vicar year in Green Bay, tutoring and recruiting for Christian ministry at a high school in Watertown, teacher/coach at a Christian high school in Lake Mills, and a pastor in Cedar Grove. He currently serves as a pastor in West Bend. Pastor Clark's favorite quote is, "Find something you love to do and you will never work a day in your life."

Karen Spiegelberg lives in Wisconsin with her husband, Jim. She has three married daughters, four grandchildren, and has been a foster mom to many. Years ago she was encouraged to start a women's ministry but was unsure of the timing. When her brother died suddenly, it hit her hard—that we can't wait until the time seems right for our ministry; the time is now. And so in 2009, with God's direction, A Word for Women was born. Karen finds great comfort in Psalm 31:14,15: "But I trust in you, O LORD. . . . My times are in your hands." www.awordforwomen.com

Christine Wentzel, a native of Milwaukee, lives in Norfolk, Virginia, with her husband, James, and their fur-child, Piper. After two lost decades as a prodigal, Christine gratefully worships and serves her Salvation

Winner at Resurrection in Chesapeake, Virginia. There she discovered latent talents to put to use for the Lord. In 2009 she began to write and create graphic design for an online Christian women's ministry, A Word for Women, and now also joyfully serves as a coadministrator for this ministry. www.awordforwomen.com

About Time of Grace

Time of Grace is an independent, donor-funded ministry that connects people to God's grace—his love, glory, and power—so they realize the temporary things of life don't satisfy. What brings satisfaction is knowing that because Jesus lived, died, and rose for all of us, we have access to the eternal God—right now and forever.

To discover more, please visit **timeofgrace.org** or call **800.661.3311.**

Help share God's message of grace!

Every gift you give helps Time of Grace reach people around the world with the good news of Jesus. Your generosity and prayer support take the gospel of grace to others through our ministry outreach and help them experience a satisfied life as they see God all around them.

Give today at **timeofgrace.org/give** or by calling **800.661.3311.**

Thank you!

Made in the USA
Middletown, DE
25 November 2022